HOW TO BE A FAILURE AND STILL LIVE WELL

HOW TO BE A FAILURE AND STILL LIVE WELL

A Philosophy

BEVERLEY CLACK

BLOOMSBURY ACADEMIC
LONDON • NEW YORK • OXFORD • NEW DELHI • SYDNEY

BLOOMSBURY ACADEMIC
Bloomsbury Publishing Plc
50 Bedford Square, London, WC1B 3DP, UK
1385 Broadway, New York, NY 10018, USA

BLOOMSBURY, BLOOMSBURY ACADEMIC and the Diana logo are trademarks
of Bloomsbury Publishing Plc

First published in Great Britain 2020

A catalogue record for this book is available from the British Library.

A catalog record for this book is available from the Library of Congress.

ISBN: HB: 978-1-3500-3068-8
PB: 978-1-3500-3069-5
ePDF: 978-1-3500-3067-1
eBook: 978-1-3500-3070-1

Typeset by Newgen KnowledgeWorks Pvt. Ltd., Chennai, India
Printed and bound in Great Britain

To find out more about our authors and books visit www.bloomsbury.com
and sign up for our newsletters.

In loving memory of Pamela Sue Anderson (1955–2017),

friend and collaborator,

and Margaret Waterhouse (1951–2018),

comrade and friend

Both much missed

CONTENTS

Conclusion: Being a failure and living well 205

ACKNOWLEDGEMENTS

No project is just the work of one person, and I am thankful for the support and encouragement of so many people whose conversations and insights helped frame the ideas presented in this book.

I am so grateful to have had Liza Thompson as my editor. Liza's contribution was way more than that of a representative of a publisher. Conversations with her helped clarify my ideas, as well as opening up areas for inclusion that I had not even thought about. Thank you so very much for your guidance and friendship.

The seed of this project first took root at the Britain and Ireland School of Feminist Theology held at Winchester in 2013. Thank you to Lisa Isherwood, Janet Wootton and Lillalou Hughes for their insightful comments. It was at this school that I first met Cathryn McKinney, and our conversations on disappointment and Easter Saturday, as well as loss and friendship, have been vital for shaping the approach of this book.

The Oxford Centre for Methodist and Church History (and its director William Gibson) funded a semester's research leave in 2015 which enabled a ten week trip to University of San Diego, and I am grateful to the members of the Failure Seminar (Lia For, Nancy Kuelbs, Miles Parnegg and Zoë Paris) for their thoughtful contributions which helped shaped the ideas of this book. Thanks, too, to the dean of the College of Arts and Sciences, Noelle Norton, for her support and friendship.

This project could not have been written without the comradeship of Oxford Labour Party, whose members taught me so much about working together for a common cause. Similarly, I give thanks for the fellowship of Cowley Road Methodist Church, and I am especially grateful to Robert Thompson, without whom I would not have met these amazing people, and through whom another chapter has been opened.

Friends, as ever, form a major part of the context for any writing project, and thanks to the following for talking with me about failure and loss in all its many hues: Sally Adams McKone, Luke Brunning, Jill Buckeldee, Jo Campbell, Sarah Claridge, Jane Corrin, Philippa Donald, Gene Flenady, Martin Groves, Penny Hill, Brian Marshall, Tom McKone, Emma McNicol, Michele Paule, Kate Tomas and Denise Wood.

Thanks, too, to my family: Alan Clack, Ann Clack, John Adshead, my brother Brian Clack and Sabrina Kaiser. Much love as ever to Bob, not least for telling me to slow down and let the ideas take their course.

And, finally, thanks to two remarkable women who influenced this project in so many ways, who died during its writing, and to whom this book is dedicated:

Pamela Sue Anderson, who would doubtless find it immensely amusing to have a book about failure dedicated to her. I miss her mischief and wisdom, and I am so grateful for her friendship; and Margaret Waterhouse, comrade and friend, whose lived wisdom I miss every day.

Grief may well be the price we pay for love, but it is a price worth paying for the joy our loving brings.

Excerpts from 'The Sick Wife' from Collected Poems of Jane Kenyon. Copyright © 2005 by The Estate of Jane Kenyon. Reprinted with the permission of The Permissions Company, LLC on behalf of Graywolf Press, Minneapolis, Minnesota, www.graywolfpress.org.

Excerpts from 'AD' from R. S. Thomas, Collected Later Poems 1988–2000 (Bloodaxe Books, 2004). Reproduced with permission of Bloodaxe Books, www.bloodaxebooks.com.

INTRODUCTION

Failure: And How to Live Well

A scene from Elizabeth Kostova's vampire novel, *The Historian*, provides a fitting starting point for an investigation of failure. A young scholar is working late in his university library. He discovers a peculiar book among the items on his desk. Ancient, bound in leather, its spine embossed, its pages are blank except for a picture of a dragon, its wings unfurled, its claws ready to strike. Someone has left this for him: but who, and why? He seeks out his supervisor and asks what he thinks of this 'rather morbid object' (2006: 16). Far from sharing his puzzlement, the professor reaches up to a high corner of his study's shelving and retrieves a similar book. 'I haven't thought about it much in years, actually, or I've tried not to, although I always sort of – feel it, there, over my shoulder' (2006:18). The professor turns his attention to the hidden shelf that held it: 'That top shelf is my row of failures. And things I'd rather not think about' (2006: 19).

Failure is something that seems best left out of sight and out of mind. When we experience it, it can feel like we have been subjected to the assault of a vampire: we have been sucked dry, left to shrivel up, we have become a bare husk of our former self. Our sense of who we are, of why we matter in the world, feels like it has been attacked. How tempting to follow the lead of Kostova's professor and hide it away behind other things that affirm our sense of importance. It is not only our failures that we would consign to that obscure top shelf. Loss is another feature of life which we may be even more inclined to hide from, that we might well prefer to avoid examining. Much as we might like to, however, we cannot hide from the fact that life involves loss. To come to terms with this fact is no easy task, but considering the complex connections between loss and failure enables a greater understanding of why we might fear it, and why, paradoxically, we should embrace both loss and failure in order to experience life in all its fullness.

Let's start by being clear about what defines these twin ideas of failure and loss that are so difficult to contemplate.

Failure is something that no one can avoid. It permeates our experience in one way or another, to one degree or another. We might think of exams we have not passed, or tests that placed us firmly at the bottom of the class. We might think of relationships that have not turned out the way we hoped, ending in separation or divorce, recrimination, even betrayal. We might think of careers that we have not been able to pursue because we messed up an interview, or because we simply did not have the qualities necessary to fulfil our dreams. A whole range of disappointing, frustrating, even devastating experiences can be covered by that one word 'failure'. Common to these experiences is a sense of responsibility: I – or, perhaps, *you* – did not revise well enough; I/you did not work hard enough; I/you did not prepare sufficiently. It can be difficult to admit our failures, and we can go to remarkable lengths to avoid owning up to them. Lying on a CV might be one radical response; pushing responsibility for a failed project onto someone else might be another.

Failure is never, however, something that stands alone. It is also shaped by claims about what it is to be a success. These are context-dependent. To fail at school is different from failing at a marriage. To lose a football or baseball match is different from losing a job. Cultural norms, similarly, determine what it is to fail. So in the medieval period failure was construed through a framework of accepted religious ideas. Social structures were divinely ordained: what mattered was performing correctly the role that had been assigned to you by God. A different set of cultural values determine our understanding of success and failure, and in Chapter One we consider the contemporary shaping of failure. For our times, success and failure are understood through an economic lens, where your life is judged by your wealth and the status of your work. To live well in the twenty-first century is dependent on avoiding failure and striving to be a success.

Failure acts as the shadow for success. Success is far easier to think about than failure. We might well prefer to put a positive spin on our failures. Failure is, we might claim, something necessary for achieving *eventual* success. And so the self-help industry connects all kinds of failure with the inevitable description of the author's sure-fire recipe for turning setbacks into triumphs. 'Why Success Starts with Failure', proclaims the title of a popular book by economist and *Financial Times* columnist Tim Harford. Rather than give up in the face of failure, Harford offers a 'recipe for successful adaptation' that all entrepreneurs should follow. According to Harford, failure should not be construed as something final; instead, it must be utilized to enable future success. Failure is part of the trial-and-error of entrepreneurial business practice. His message is clear: analyse your failures (retrieve them from that neglected top shelf), but do so only that you might learn from these experiences, for in them lie the seeds for your future success.

Harford is not alone in promoting this rather upbeat rendition of failure. Ariana Huffington, founder of the internet news giant the *Huffington Post*, has done more than most to shape the world of news media in the twenty-first century. She, like Harford, is clear as to the importance of failure for becoming a success. In an interview with the *Big Issue* magazine, sold by homeless people in the UK, Huffington revisits her mother's wisdom for a successful life. 'Failure is not the opposite of success', she says; rather 'it's a stepping stone to success'. Her life has been shaped by following this rule. The implication, it would seem, is that the sellers of the *Big Issue* could, likewise, rise to the same giddy heights that she has attained. Other successful entrepreneurs make similar claims. In an interview given in 1994, Steve Jobs, founder of global tech giant Apple, notes that in order to be a successful entrepreneur 'you've got to be willing to fail'.

In practice, the recipe offered for success by business gurus is not as straightforward as they would have their followers believe. Huffington's start in life was not marked by failure: she went to Cambridge University and numbered Bernard Levin among her mentors. Jobs may have been adopted, but he was adopted into a wealthy family. Even if we take seriously their claim that success involves accepting failure, not everyone can be a success, not least because contemporary notions of success and failure are shaped through the lens of competition. To be a success requires that you triumph over others in your field. For there to be winners, there have to be losers.

This narrative of 'winners' and 'losers' finds plentiful examples in the world of politics. Political parties confront each other as rival teams. Elections decide who wins and who loses. Political journalism thrives on the energy this creates: and no wonder. This book was written in the shadow of one of the most startling political failures of recent times. David Cameron, the UK prime minister, took a gamble on winning the 2015 General Election by promising a referendum on Britain's continued membership of the European Union (EU). Seen at the time as the master stroke of a cunning political operator, pundits suggested that the inability of his opponents to offer a similar deal to British voters led to Cameron's unexpected victory at the polls. Contrary to Cameron's hopes, however, the electorate voted in the subsequent 2016 referendum to leave the EU. This decision led to an unprecedented period of economic and political instability with no clear idea, as yet, of where it will end. Cameron's political aspirations almost instantaneously crashed and burned. Three months after the referendum he had not only resigned as Prime Minister and Tory Party leader but had also left politics altogether.

It is tempting to reduce politics to a game: Cameron took a punt on winning, and his gamble, ultimately, failed. Politics is, however, of more importance than an ill-judged bet. The decisions made by politicians extend beyond their own hopes and dreams and have effects on communities and on those not interested in the push and shove of political combat. Neil Kinnock, Labour Party leader from 1983 to 1992, expresses well the relationship between his experience of failure and its social implications. Resigning as leader after his party's unexpected defeat in the 1992 General Election, the emotions felt by him and his wife Glenys (who was later elected as a Member of the European Parliament) ranged from 'disappointment and devastation to a sort of bereavement' (Westlake 2001: 607). For Kinnock, the real sense of loss arose less from the end of his political ambitions and more from the effect his defeat would have on communities unlikely to benefit from five more years of Tory rule: 'It's the outrage of decline and decadence, the economic, industrial, cultural and moral decadence. The effects are on other people, not on me' (Westlake 2001: 607).

In politics, personal and collective failures are not easily separated and nor should they be. It may be easiest to attempt a reading of failure as something individual and personal, but to only consider the personal dimension is to ignore the social realm to which we will return throughout this book. Failure is never something constructed only through the actions of the individual. It is also shaped by the surrounding social and political context. At the same time, no account of failure can ignore the powerful emotions surrounding the individual's experience of it. Indeed, by pursuing these emotions the connection between failure, losing and loss can be most clearly seen. Failure and loss may not be the same, but they interact in important and informative ways. One way of illuminating these connections is through the methods of psychoanalysis, and it is worth noting some reflections from this field that highlight the connection between the experience of losing – so closely related to the experience of failure – and the other theme of this book, loss.

The psychoanalyst Anna Freud considers the feelings that emanate from losing something dear to us. Yes, 'we feel unhappy and miserable', but we also feel 'deprived' in a way which suggests something over and above the actual value of the thing that we have lost. She suggests that if we are to understand what this is, we will need to go beneath the surface, for 'there are further elements involved which originate in deeper layers of the mind' and which require attention if these roots are to be made visible (Anna Freud 1967: 13). Now, Anna Freud's focus is on identifying the emotional connections between losing something as an adult and the forgotten feelings of childhood: particularly the feelings of being 'unloved, rejected, and neglected' (Freud 1967: 18). My focus on the emotions surrounding failure is rather different. With her, I share that belief that something else is going on when we experience the upset of failing or losing; something that strikes at the heart of the self. But what I want to consider is the way in which these feelings open up a dimension that goes beyond the experience of the individual child and which affects us all. And this requires considering the other theme to be explored in this book: loss.

If we are encouraged to take responsibility for our failures, loss indicates the inevitable reality of being mutable beings in a world subject to the laws of entropy. We are born, we grow and develop; yet we also, inevitably, decline, age and die. We lose our capacity, we move from strength to weakness, health to illness, life to death. Our relationships and ourselves are subject to forces far greater than ourselves that mean our lives are always subject to change.

Loss is inevitable, outside our control. Failure suggests the possibility of control. If I work hard and revise hard, I can pass my exams (though much depends on the questions that appear on the paper). I can work at my marriage, thus lessening the possibility of divorce (though much depends on my partner's willingness to do the same, as well as the vagaries of longing and desire). These examples suggest something of the tenuous possibility of being in control of one's own destiny, of being able to shape the extent to which one is successful. Much is uncertain, because we are social beings who never act in isolation. Faced with our lack of control, we might well prefer to emphasize our responsibility, assuming success and failure are things we can control.

The desire for control over that which is uncertain makes the shaping of loss through the lens of failure seemingly easier to cope with. Why did you get cancer? Did you smoke? Were you overweight? What did you *do*? – or more pertinently what *didn't* you do? Yet in the end control runs out when faced with disease, decline and death. There are limits to our actions.

Is there a better way of living that makes a space for loss, that moves it from that hard to reach top shelf, and places it, instead, at the centre of our engagement with life?

This might be a threatening thought. Do we really want to engage with the precariousness of our lives, the fact that health is accompanied by sickness, life by death? What I want to suggest is that, far from diminishing our engagement with life, allowing a space for the reality of loss opens up the possibility of living well. Through paying attention to loss it becomes possible to identify and to value that which really matters in life. This method of attention also effects the way in which we might think about failure. How significant are our failures, *really*? When we chase after success, or are told that the materially successful life is the only vision of the Good Life worth pursuing, it is right to pause and consider whether this is really the case. There are limitations to shaping the meaningful life through the contemporary obsession with success, and the aim of this book is to challenge those who would make it the main indicator of the flourishing life. Failure, I want to argue, may be an even more helpful experience than success if we want to come to live well.

My interest in the relationship between failure and loss stems from personal experience. Feminist scholars have long recognized the connection between the personal and political, for no thinker is completely detached from the things that compel them to write. Audre Lorde linked her experience of breast cancer with a challenge to US health structures and institutions that disadvantaged black women.[1] Michèle Le Doeuff used her experience of sexism in French schooling to illustrate the problems women continue to face in being taken seriously as scholars.[2] Academics from a range of disciplines increasingly pay attention to the lived experiences shaping their ideas. Those who make explicit the place from which they write are often grappling with painful personal experiences. Belden Lane connects his struggles to come to terms with his difficult childhood and his mother's dying to his desert walks and his engagement with the works of the Desert Fathers.[3] Lawrence Hatab describes the sense of relief he felt when he encountered the writings of the nineteenth-century philosopher Friedrich Nietzsche who battled physical and mental illness, and whose struggles provided a salve for Hatab's own sense of alienation.[4] Mark Oakley begins his discussion of the concept of God with a depiction of the slow and painful death of a 24-year-old man, witnessed as a hospital chaplain, that made him question his calling.[5]

In 1999 I miscarried what would have been our first child. I lost a lot of blood, and when I recovered there was a sense of relief that things had not been worse, that I had not died. This experience of the precarious nature, not just of life, but of *my* life, was followed by several years of failed IVF treatments, and attempts at adoption (also unsuccessful). Eventually, we concluded that we would not be parents. It was a sad, upsetting and sometimes desperate time. That is not to say that it was completely devastating. It might even be said to have enriched our relationship, drawing us closer together. It made us acutely aware of the people who mattered most in our lives, and who had been able to accompany us on what was a difficult and painful path.

Yet to say that, to suggest something of the 'good' which came out of that experience, would be to gloss over the pain of running up against the limits of human striving. Here was the experience of loss, pure and simple: the loss of the hope of parenthood, the loss of a particular understanding of myself as someone who always got what she wanted. Here were the limits of working for an end result. The experience of IVF revealed, all too starkly, that, in the words of the Rolling Stones, 'you can't always get what you want'. Here were the limits of human agency and control. Here was the place where we rubbed up against the possibility of death itself, that most real of the Real, as the French psychoanalyst Jacques Lacan puts it.

There was another dimension to this experience of loss, and that was how it morphed into a sense of failure. I felt I had failed in my ability to give birth to a child. More than that: I felt I had failed *as a woman*. The gendering of failure is far from uncommon. As we shall explore in Chapter Two, to fail *as a woman* is to become aware of the transient nature of those things which so often form the bedrock for shaping female identity: motherhood and physical beauty. The experiences of loss and failure are not as discrete as we might wish, and their interconnection is often felt in the feeling of shame. One's life, in such experiences, does not 'measure up' to a socially created and aggressively promoted picture of how one's life *should* be. It does not surprise me that the images I found most difficult to bear during this time were the ones that depicted happy, smiling, nuclear families. It was not just that I felt loss that we did not – would not – have this; there was also a sense of shame that my body could not bring into being this most ordinary of human realities.

The experiences of failure and loss are complex, and we will need to spend time unravelling the connections between them as we proceed. For now, my intention is to highlight the main concern of this book: that if we can bear to stay with the pain of failure and loss it might be possible to arrive at different – arguably better – understandings of one's self and one's world. We might be able to live well, even when we experience failure and loss. We might be able to live well, perhaps, *because* we experience failure and loss. That promise, that hope, is just as well, for the sense of loss never completely leaves the stage. In my experience it becomes more a case of finding a way of holding at the heart of your life those experiences that make you acutely aware of how precious and precarious life is. Indeed, it may be precisely because it is so precarious that it is so precious.[6]

A further experience made the writing of this book a necessity, and it suggests something of the complexity of those feelings of failure. In 2009 I was made a professor. What should have been a moment for satisfaction and celebration quickly deteriorated into a sense of dissatisfaction with my work and my writing. I felt that I was writing because I had to meet the requirements of the 'publish or perish' mentality of the modern university, not because I *wanted* to write. I felt like a fake who was simply going through the motions. I gave up writing one book because I literally had no idea how to write it. I would sit at the computer, stare at the screen and know that I had absolutely nothing to say. To give up on that book felt like another failure. It was not so much that the book was a failure, but that *I* had failed.

This is far from an isolated experience, and the psychoanalyst Stephen Grosz notes how success can be experienced as failure, for 'winning is also losing' (Grosz 2013: 133). This sounds paradoxical, but the story he uses to explore this resonates. One of his clients – an architect – had won a competition that would take him to China. Heading out to celebrate, he lost his wallet. The evening descended into farce, and, far from feeling elated, he ended it feeling depressed. Grosz's reading of this strange turn of events is interesting: with success comes a new life, but not necessarily a *better* life, and in losing his wallet, his client was expressing his fear that among all the money he was now to make as a result of this new venture, he might find that he had lost himself.

The implication of Grosz's story is that it makes sense to pay attention to losing. If I return to my experience, it was the feelings of failure and the dissatisfaction that came with achieving promotion that opened up one of the most important stages of my life. I felt that I wasn't living as I should, that something was lacking. This period of dissatisfaction coincided with the aftermath of the 2008 Global Financial Crisis. In the UK, this crisis was used to instigate a new 'Age of Austerity'. Outraged by the cuts to public services that this entailed, I got involved in politics for the first time, and eventually was elected as a local councillor in 2012. That experience opened up all the joys and frustrations of collective working. But before we see this in terms of a move from perceived failure to political success, we should note the result of the 2015 General Election. My party – Labour – got a good kicking, and while there are some signs of a recovery in our fortunes, the electoral future for the party remains unclear. My relationship with my party has also changed. I am more critical of the path we are treading, and, while still involved in party politics, it does not provide the all-encompassing sense of purpose that it once did.

Through all the experiences of disappointment and disaffection, one text stands out in its ability to help me reorientate myself: Paul Tillich's *Shaking of the Foundations* (1949). Tillich's reputation has been somewhat shaken by his wife Hannah Tillich's frank recollections of their life together.[7] But for this feminist, his work has always opened up the possibility of a deeper understanding of life; and anyway, when you are drowning, you don't resist a lifebelt thrown by someone whose life you don't much approve.

To talk of depth is unfashionable. Consumer capitalism encourages us to be content with the superficial, with the things that money can buy. Clever philosophers encourage us to eschew the depths as part of the old and discredited language of 'the soul'.[8] Scientists reduce human consciousness to chemicals in the brain. Against this backdrop, it might seem that the best way of managing the negative feelings attending to failure and loss is through medication. Common sadness can be eradicated through taking the right combination of drugs.[9]

Tillich's book suggests an alternative. In moments of loss and failure, we are confronted with the truth about existence. Through such experiences we are presented with an opportunity to get closer to the things that really matter. Indeed, Tillich goes further than that by suggesting that without these painful experiences we only scratch the surface of our lives, never moving beyond a superficial understanding of what it means to be human. He puts this powerfully and, I think, poetically:

It is only when the picture that we have of ourselves breaks down completely, only when we find ourselves acting against all the expectations we had derived from that picture, and only when an earthquake shakes and disrupts the surface of our self-knowledge, that we are willing to look into a deeper level of our being. (Tillich [1949] 1962: 62–3)

As a student I had this quote stuck on my bedroom wall. That it has travelled with me for so long says much about the argument to be advanced here. The process of engaging with failure and loss is lifelong; throughout life we are confronted time and again with the question of how to live in more enriching and more fulfilling ways. In what follows, I do not offer a fail-safe method for never experiencing loss or failure ever again. That is impossible. What I do suggest is that there are values and practices that can help us experience more fully our life in this precarious, beautiful and sometimes terrifying world.

Failure and loss have important parts to play in discovering these more fulfilling ways of living. As Tillich puts it, 'There can be no depth without the way to depth' ([1949] 1962: 61). The very disquiet and upset attending to failure and loss makes possible new visions of how we might live well. To experience the depths of which Tillich writes involves challenging some of the dominant views of what makes for the successful life so popular in contemporary Western societies. When we are encouraged to see our lives as isolated units, forged through competition, we are unlikely to have the resources to connect our lives to a bigger whole. When we understand our lives in connection to one another, when we understand the obligation we have to each other, we are able to think differently about that central notion of what it means to succeed, and also about what it means to fail.

Reorientating ourselves through the engagement with failure and loss necessitates something more. If we are to live well we need to challenge the anthropocentrism which encourages us to think, not only that 'I am the centre of the world', but that human beings are, as a species, the beating heart of the cosmos around whom everything else revolves. It is this self-centredness – we might say, self-obsession – that means we fail to live in ways conducive to the planet. It also means we neglect the possibilities open to beings who are able to reflect on their lives in a sometimes beautiful, sometimes tragic, world.

Rather than shrinking from failure or running from loss, it is far better to follow the lead of Kostova's vampire hunters. The way might be difficult and challenging – we might need to go armed with plenty of garlic and holy water – but thinking again about the failures and losses of life makes possible new ways of being. We will never be able to evade the scars left by failure and loss: far from it. But scars show you have lived, and in what follows I want to suggest ways in which we are able to be failures, to live with our losses, and, as a result of such struggles, come to live well.

1

SUCCESS, FAILURE AND THE TWENTY-FIRST-CENTURY GOOD LIFE

For around six years I commuted between Oxford and London. The stretch of motorway just before the turn-off for the notoriously slow M25 was notable for a thought-provoking piece of graffiti on a farmer's fence. Sadly now obliterated under new paint, scribbles and tags, it was written in letters three metres high, readable by all those journeying in the cars, buses and lorries streaming towards the capital city:

'Why do I do this every day?'

Whoever wrote these words might have been a Green activist, a frustrated commuter, a neighbour fed up with the relentless drone of the traffic. Who they were was less important than the question they posed, for it acted as an excellent prompt for asking what it means to live well. Placed as it was, this simple sentence was directed at every individual traveller. The answers we might have given to this question would have been as different as each of us: 'I have no choice, that is where the work is'; 'housing in London is too scarce and too expensive, so I have to make this journey for my job in the capital from the town where I live'; 'I love the excitement of the capital city;' 'this journey shapes my life, I'm not sure what I would do without it.'

Other answers might be given to this question that do not just reflect a set of personal choices, but which, instead, reflect powerful cultural narratives telling us how we *should* live our lives. The graffiti artist set out a question they wanted their readers to ask, and this chapter attempts to answer it by considering, first, the role of work in the life of twenty-first-century individuals, and second, what happens when we allow that question 'why' to challenge how we live and what we consider to be important.

When we ask 'why', we pause in what we are doing: even as, in this instance, we are rushing to the daily grind. We make space for thinking again about the things and activities that we take for granted. That question stuck with me because, at the time, it encouraged me to question my motivations: to think about what I hoped to get from undertaking that daily rush from home to work and back again. But it was never just about *my* life. The sheer weight of traffic on that road at rush hour located me – my hopes and dreams – in a broader context, for millions of us are engaged every day in journeys of this kind.

Why do we do it?

My investigation of failure is shaped by the desire to get beneath the accepted wisdom that made those journeys a necessity. Behind all those journeys is a powerful ideal of what it means to be a responsible citizen, and what it is to live well in the twenty-first century. At its heart is an economically driven image of what it is to be a success and the practices that will be necessary if we are to avoid being failures. That question 'why' has its force because it demands that we consider whether, in practice, the narrative shaping our busyness is enabling a sense of fulfilment. Sure, some might have commuted willingly enough, but I bet most of the people hurrying to work approached their time on the road in the same way I did: as a grim necessity.

The statistics relating to mental health reveal something of the stresses pertaining to contemporary life. Figures released by the UK's Health and Safety Executive in November 2018 showed over half of all work absences were accounted for by stress-related illnesses.[1] The study reported over 15 million working days were lost in 2017/18 due to work-related stress, depression or anxiety. The areas where workers were most likely to be affected in this way were in the public service sectors, such as education, health and social care, and public administration and defence.[2] In the United States, a study conducted by the Centers for Disease Control and Prevention in 2013 claimed that in any given year 18.8 million American adults suffered from a depressive illness: a staggering figure suggesting that nearly 10 per cent of the working population would at some time be afflicted in this way.

As I rushed to work along that road, I not infrequently reflected on how unhappy I was to be making this journey. Why was I doing it? What was the point of it? When would it be over? To the outsider, I had a good job I should have been grateful for. By the external markers for judging a life, I seemed to be successful: I had a decent salary, a nice house, social status. So why did that graffiti artist's question make such an impact on me that I remember it clearly some twenty-five years on?

To get at its importance, we must examine the image of the good life peddled over the last forty years. For the dominant ideology of our times, the meaning of life has become wrapped up with the image of the individual as an economic unit forged by the work they do. Having a good life depends on being a success as an economic unit, and it is here that our investigation of failure begins. Paying attention to the weight work is made to carry in shaping this account of what it means to live well reveals the paucity of this vision. There *are* better ways of living, but they can only emerge if we resist the obsession with cultivating success and instead pay attention to what it means to fail under such a system.

Neoliberalism and the twenty-first-century good life

As a university lecturer, I am well aware of the limits of academic analysis. Our words can seem too abstract, too removed from ordinary life.[3] The terms we use and the theories we employ can obfuscate rather than clarify, confuse rather than make clear: as many of my students would doubtless agree. But critical analysis is helpful for getting us to think differently about the world we inhabit: not least because it can be difficult to look clearly at the world of which we are a part. We struggle to see 'our environment' when we are living in it. Like goldfish, we swim around, not seeing the water or the glass walls of our tank, not paying attention to the way in which these elements shape our every move. We take our surroundings for granted, and it requires conscious effort to see – *really see* – that which we take for granted.[4] It can be all-too-easy to fall back on answers for why we do this or that by saying 'it's just how things are', or 'we have always done things this way'. Critical thinking has the power to move us beyond this kind of position: opening up our world, rather than closing it down; making strange the world we assume to be as natural as the air we breathe. Looked at with new eyes, we can wonder why it is we do the things we do. We can identify the limitations of our worldview, and, as a result, we can start to think again about how we might live.[5]

Helpful for this task are the writings of sociologists and historians of economics who have identified a powerful set of ideals and practices shaping the last forty years of Western society.[6] Described as 'neoliberalism', this worldview builds upon the vision of what it is to be human that lies at the heart of the European Enlightenment of the eighteenth century. For Enlightenment thinkers, the individual was best understood as rational, autonomous, free and capable of choice. In its contemporary reworking, this account of the individual is placed in a specific economic setting. Your destiny is shaped by your ability to make rational choices about your life *in a market place*. Under neoliberalism, the realm of the economic is extended into every area of life, with that Enlightenment vision of the rational, choosing subject shaped accordingly. Now, being defined by your ability to choose is shaped principally through your ability to purchase and consume the material goods deemed necessary for having a good life.

Tracing the story of neoliberalism – and particularly the role given to work – reveals the pressures that have come to shape our lives, as well as illuminating the extent to which being economically successful becomes identical with the vision of what it is to live well. The sociologist David Harvey provides a succinct account of the political and economic practices that define the neoliberal agenda. His description of neoliberalism provides a glimpse into the way our behaviour comes to be moulded through a particular set of economic and governmental practices. We will have cause as we proceed to unpack the abstractions he uses to reflect on how they shape our own experience of life:

> Neoliberalism is in the first instance a theory of political economic practices that proposes human well-being can best be advanced by liberating individual entrepreneurial freedoms and skills within an institutional framework characterised by strong private property rights, free markets, and free trade. (Harvey 2005: 2)

Human well-being – what it is to live well – becomes achievable through adopting a particular set of economic practises. Individuals are liberated when business is freed up, when markets are unfettered by regulation and when trade can move freely between countries. For Harvey and other critics of this economic liberalism, it is necessary to reveal this ideology at work: not least because its proponents suggest that There Is No Alternative to it.[7] While discussion of neoliberalism has become more explicit since the Global Financial Crash of 2008 disrupted this optimistic vision of a world united by trade, there is an amorphous quality to the forms it takes that makes it less easily identifiable than, say, creeds like nationalism or socialism. For one thing, few would self-consciously identify themselves as 'neoliberal'. So here is a diagnosis that stems from the work of its critics to uncover it, and we need to tread carefully if it is to truly help us answer that question of why we do the things we do.

The economic historian Philip Mirowski suggests that part of the problem lies with the sheer success of neoliberalism. Over the past forty years its central ideas – individualism, free trade, private property rights, allowing the market to operate with limited state intervention – have been taken up across the world, albeit in different ways reflecting very different cultural contexts.[8] Neoliberalism is thus 'a movable feast' (Mirowski 2014: 50) rather than an easily identifiable and uniform political theory. Scott Peck, similarly, describes it as a 'Russian doll' (Peck 2010: 43) of ideas, capable of taking on a variety of 'mongrel, shape-shifting forms' (Peck 2010: 276).

Its very success makes neoliberalism difficult to identify. We have come to assume there is no other way to live. And yet as I write this book in 2018, it is impossible to escape the feeling that the consensus identified by Harvey, Mirowski and Peck is no longer quite so certain. Since 2016, a series of political upsets have suggested that many are no longer satisfied with the accepted way of doing things. In the United Kingdom, David Cameron's referendum on continued membership of the European Union resulted in the decision to leave an economic community of which the UK had been a part since the 1970s, but which many felt no longer worked for them. In the United States, the businessman and minor celebrity Donald Trump was elected president. He defeated Hillary Clinton, viewed by many as the continuity candidate, 'the safe pair of hands', with a CV to match: all features that seemed far from attractive to voters wanting change. In Hungary, the re-elected president, Viktor Orban, spoke of his desire to create 'an illiberal democracy' at the heart of the European Union. The certainties of the past forty years no longer seem so certain. Something is shifting, even if no one is quite sure what, or why, or where we will end up.

It is this very uncertainty that suggests we are now in a position to identify and to question the cultural forces we have taken for granted and that have shaped our lives over the past forty years. I grew up in the 1970s, and some of my earliest memories are defined by a similar period of political upheaval. Viewed through a child's eyes, I remember the excitement of power cuts, the rush to retrieve the candles from under the sink, the magical glow that resulted from their flickering illumination. Without the power necessary for a cooked meal, our dinners consisted of things that didn't need cooking or which could be heated up over my dad's old camping stove. Games would be played and stories told by candlelight. As an 8-year-old child, I was dimly aware that behind these out-of-the-ordinary and, frankly, rather exciting activities a struggle was going on between government and an amorphous group known only as 'the miners'. Sometimes I would get irritable when the strikes coincided with my favourite TV programmes, and I recall getting my first political lesson when, in response to my contention that these miners should be *made* to go back to work, my mum replied that I needed to remember that they worked hard, in dangerous conditions, and deserved the pay rise they were seeking.

These vignettes reflect the larger struggles going on as one economic system gave way to another. Not that my 8-year-old self would have understood it if she had been told it, but the events which led to those power cuts were part of a political and economic consensus that was breaking down. After the Second World War, countries in the process of rebuilding had embraced the ideas of the economist John Maynard Keynes. Keynes envisioned the State as something active and enabling, capable of bettering the lives of the people shattered by war through its interventions. In the UK, the adoption of this approach led to the creation of the Welfare State, a National Health Service, free education and a project of nationalization that placed key industries in the hands of the people (or at least their elected representatives).

A series of political crises in the 1970s challenged the effectiveness of Keynesian economics: the OPEC oil embargo, high unemployment, industrial disputes, inflation, fiscal crises and recessions.[9] Politicians struggled to respond to the sheer weight of these interlocking crisis, and so sought new ideas capable of resolving these seemingly intractable problems. Into this political vacuum stepped those influenced by the ideas of the Mont Pelerin Society, a group of economists and philosophers who had clustered around the political philosopher Friedrich von Hayek in the late 1940s. The Society had viewed Keynes' ideas and the structures they spawned with horror, seeing in the interventionist State a threat to individual freedom. Its members spent their time advocating, instead, 'general issues such as liberty and private initiative' (Peck 2010: 47).

Having worked patiently at disseminating their countercultural ideas, those influenced by Hayek and his group saw in the political and economic upheaval of the 1970s their chance, and they seized it.[10] Capturing 'the ears and minds of politicians' (Standing 2011: 1), the governments of Ronald Reagan in the United States (1981–9) and Margaret Thatcher in the United Kingdom (1979–90) set about adopting and implementing their ideas. At the heart of these administrations was the belief that the success of the nation could only be brought about through market competitiveness and freeing up both business and the individual. To achieve this end meant not just that *businesses* needed to be fit for purpose. Thatcherism and Reaganomics required that 'everything should be done to maximise competition and competitiveness, and *to allow the market to permeate all aspects of life*' (Standing 2011: 1; my emphasis).

'To allow the market to permeate all aspects of life.'

If the State was at the centre of Keynesianism, under the new economics of Thatcher and Reagan it was 'the Market' that was now understood as the mechanism which would deliver the good things required by people and nations. Freeing up the Market and business, allowing for greater competition, became crucial to government agendas. 'Deregulation' became the order of the day, with governments cutting the 'red tape' that was believed to hamper the kind of creativity deemed necessary for success. In order to create new business opportunities, there was a concerted effort to extend the arena for business activity. The State was to withdraw not just from areas traditionally associated with trade: it also withdrew, crucially, from areas of social provision in order that new possibilities for the private sector were created.[11]

This was a wide-ranging project, and it required more than simply a restructuring of economics. Here, we arrive at what this meant for individuals, and why much of the upheaval of our own day emanates from personal dissatisfaction with the solutions offered by the new market economics. As its critics point out, it wasn't just new business practices that were required by this economic revolution: it also required a *new kind of individual* in order for societies to flourish under this 'new capitalism'.[12] Just as the economy needed to be made truly global, 'disembedded' from the needs of any one society,[13] so individuals were required who would be able to respond to the demands of a new, global and connected world. As a result, governments increasingly moved their policies away from developing industrial strategies aimed at securing well-paid work for all their citizens, to instigating policies that would ensure 'flexible' labour practices enabling the cheap labour 'required' by business to move freely from nation to nation. Rather than challenge such ideas, parties on the Centre Left accepted the arguments of the new economics, and so governments on the Right *and the Left* adopted the principles of neoliberal market thinking.

The shift from the public to the private sector, from social services to private provision, required a new self who took responsibility for their own actions and who was free to pursue their own goals through commitment to the freedom of the market.[14] The notion of personal responsibility reveals something of the attractions of this new liberal subject. Rather than a producer of goods, I am now framed as a consumer. My ability to buy is framed by my responsibility for shaping my own life. Here we see Harvey's economic principles taking form in the lives of individuals. Take the concern with strengthening private property rights. In the UK, this principle led governments to create a 'home-owning democracy'. Housing that had previously been owned and managed by local councils was sold off to tenants. Anyone who owns their own home will tell you the difference it makes: you feel in charge of this piece of land, you feel free to decorate your home as you deem fit, you can improve your property, you can make it reflect your personality. No wonder early reports of people receiving the keys to the property they now owned show them full of life, exhilarated by this new future. This is the attraction of personal responsibility in one small example. Behind this is another, equally powerful image. Freed up to take charge of my life, I become an important person in my own right. It doesn't matter what I started life with, or where I came from: now I will be judged by what I have made of myself.

All very inspiring, but we do well to note before we get too carried away the role played by the economic. What is it that allows me to be free? In the case of home ownership, having the economic resources to become a homeowner. This emphasis on attaining the material resources to live well extends way beyond the purchase of objects, even if they are as big as a house. If my freedom is expressed through my choice in a market place, I will, of course, need to have the material resources necessary to make those choices. I cannot secure the advantages that come with attending a fee-paying school, or a nice house in a catchment area for a good school, or a university education *unless* I have the money to do so. Health and education become as dependent on material resources as buying a new pair of shoes.

There is nothing particularly new about this: Keynesian economics recognized economic inequality and sought ways of addressing it (to some extent, at least). What the coming of the new liberalism brings in its wake is the shaping of life *explicitly* and *solely* through economic imperatives. To be human is to move away from a set of ideals shaped by *Homo sapiens* ('the wise animal'), towards accepting ideals based on *homo economicus* ('economic man'). It is not seeking knowledge for its own sake, or striving to identify and follow the Good that shapes our humanity. We are now always and everywhere economic units with the freedom to shape our own (economic, social and political) destinies.[15]

Everything is 'financialized'.[16] In other words, nothing can be understood as lying outside the economic: not the individual, not relationships, nothing. All meaning is framed through financial considerations. The role of the Market extends 'to all domains and activities – even where money is not the issue', and this has a particular impact on how human beings are understood. We are now framed 'exhaustively as market actors, *always, only, and everywhere* as *homo oeconomicus*' (Brown 2015: 31). There is nothing outside the financial, and that includes ourselves. We are 'economic men and women'; we are 'homo economicus'. As everything is filtered through the economic, it is easy to see how we lose the sense of this way of living as something constructed out of political decision-making. It comes to be seen as 'natural' and only when we ask that question 'why' are we able to open up the possibility of other ways of living.

Given the importance of the economic for the neoliberal worldview, it should not surprise us that work comes to take on a particular role in shaping the experience of the individual. It is here that the narratives of success and failure take on their force, and here that we get a disturbing answer to the question of why we do this every day.

Success and failure in the life of the neoliberal entrepreneur

What does it mean to *live* as *homo economicus*, to be an economic man or woman? The refiguring of the values shaping human being explains the central role given to work for shaping the neoliberal understanding of the individual. The role work plays in life, the way it is understood, has always been subject to change.[17] The implications of these changes for individuals and communities can be stark. Thomas Hardy provides a fine example of the effect industrialization had on country people in the nineteenth century. In his novel *Tess of the D'Urbervilles*,

Hardy describes Tess and her fellow labourers encountering a threshing machine for the first time. This new innovation is supposed to make the work of harvesting easier and more efficient. This is not, however, experienced as something liberating by Tess and her fellow workers. Rather, this 'red tyrant' (Hardy [1891] 1981: 354) is seen as a fiery, hell-like beast. The effect it will have goes way beyond those first impressions. Its introduction to farming brings mechanized monotony and unemployment, with fewer people now needed to work the land. Its coming also brings something else: redundant labourers will be forced to go to the new cities created by the Industrial Revolution in order to make a living. This move will affect the very patterns of their lives; their historical and familial bonds to the land broken forever. This is dramatic stuff. The shift in how we understand work is arguably more subtle; yet it, too, has reshaped the pattern of life, not least by shaping the notion of the good life through the language of success.

For past generations, the space allotted to work was clearly defined. It was at least possible – if by no means easy, given lengthy working hours – to demarcate a life apart from the labour which the individual traded in the workplace. Even if the working day were long, dull and tiring, there was an end point to its hold over the individual. My father's working life may have been dull and repetitive, but there was time at the end of the working day for him to be involved in fulfilling voluntary youth work with the local Boys' Brigade company.[18] For the world shaped by neoliberalism, there is precious little space for the world outside work. We might welcome the advent of technology which allows us to stay in touch with others. I, for one, love the ease of using a Smart Phone to stay in touch with family and friends through WhatsApp and Facebook. But that same Smart Phone that keeps me connected also ensures that I am always just one click away from my work emails, always on hand for that 'after hours' call, text or email.

For many of us, it is well-nigh impossible to draw a line between where work ends and leisure begins. The image of the businessman taking phone calls on the beach during his holiday is one that no longer relates just to a small group of workaholic entrepreneurs. And it's not just those in what might be called 'the higher professions' – law, teaching, medicine, civil and public service – who experience slippage between work and home. With increasing numbers of people on short-term or zero-hour contracts, the continual process of looking and applying for jobs cuts into so-called leisure time.[19] Even the supposedly 'unemployed' find the time searching for work encroaching beyond the limits of what was once defined as 'the working day'.[20]

Why the extension of work into all aspects of life? Here we see most clearly the effect of the neoliberal reshaping of the individual. Eroding the space between work and home is vital for an economic system which places market values at its centre, and which extends the needs of business to every area of life. The worker is visualized, not as working for a particular company or in a particular institution – the 'job for life' derided and largely destroyed by the practices of global capitalism – but is instead conceived as a mini-business, a 'human resource', with responsibility to monopolize on and market his or her talents, strengths and achievements. No longer a 'worker', a designation which suggests a discrete role that is part of a life, instead, they are framed as '*entrepreneurs of themselves*' (Lemke 2001: 199).

It is the extension of entrepreneurialism to cover every single person that gets us to the heart of the role work plays in the construction of the neoliberal good life. Forget Richard Branson, or Elon Musk, or Arianna Huffington: people who have adopted a particular form of business activity and are thus 'entrepreneurs'. *Everyone,* whatever they do, is expected to adopt this mantel. And note how this entrepreneurial individual is expected to behave: they are to be *responsible* for shaping their own economic, social and political destinies.

'*Why do I do this every day?*'
'*Because I am a responsible citizen who understands the importance of being a productive member of society and thus of travelling for work.*'

When being human is understood in this way, it is not surprising that work becomes the arena – perhaps the only arena – in which we are to find fulfilment.[21] In work, we are expected to 'produce, discover, and explore ourselves' (Rose 1999: 104). Answers to the question 'Why do I do this every day?' shift from practical considerations to idealistic ones:

'Why do I do this every day?'
'I do this to realize my self and my potential.'

As business becomes the principle model for framing human activity, so work becomes the sole place in which the individual is expected to find meaning. But pause a little, and it is clear that the businesses and institutions for whom we work are not that interested in the myriad ways in which each worker might find fulfilment. From the perspective of an owner or a manager, what matters is that the worker is adaptable, innovating, responsible and committed,[22] capable of meeting the ever-changing demands of a global marketplace. The 'fulfilment' you are supposed to find in the workplace is always likely to benefit your employer more than it benefits you. The claim that work *will* fulfil you does not mean that the company or organization for which you work needs to go out of its way to provide for your needs. Indeed, the last few years have seen an increase in business models accepting no responsibility at all for the people they employ, ruthlessly extending the scope of what it means to be 'self-employed'. Uber and Deliveroo are mundane examples of this business model.[23] How different this is from the kind of paternalism that ensured my father, working in the Witney blanket mills, could depend on his employer to provide accommodation for himself and his family, close to his place of work. The advocates of neoliberal business practices might see the end of this concern as a good thing: workers like my father have been freed from the over-bearing control of – and dependence upon – their employer. Today's low-paid workers, grappling with poor and expensive housing, might well disagree.

It is not just paternalism that disappears in the Brave New World of the entrepreneurial individual: so does the sense that you are part of a community. Competition is one of neoliberalism's most important virtues, and it is applied to every area of life.[24] For Von Hayek, this has to be so for competition is 'the only method by which our activities can be adjusted to each other without coercive or arbitrary intervention of authority' (Hayek 1944: 38). In competition, conflict is overcome, and human society resolves its problems. But look at what this means for human relationships: to be free requires that I see you as a competitor. This is so for business activity, for individual endeavour and also for the shaping of government strategies.

Consider the way in which a government might address economic inequalities like homelessness or poverty. Rather than develop policies that would redistribute wealth, governments now focus on creating 'equality of opportunity'.[25] What does this mean? Policies are developed that aim at creating 'a level playing field' on which people can compete with each other. Through this process, it is claimed that the best and the brightest will be revealed, separated out from less capable others. In theory, it is expected that *all* will achieve, for the skills necessary for success are supposed to be things that can – indeed, *should* – be taught. To be a success in this new world of work requires the individual to invest in themselves, cultivating the image of the winner through 'the management of the interpersonal relations upon which winning depends' (Rose 1999: 117). Education becomes reframed as a means of preparing students for the world of work through instilling practices of adaptability.[26]

And yet not all can succeed in this competitive world. Where there are winners, there will be losers. Where there is success, there will be failure. There need be no qualms about the outcomes of these competitions, provided there has been an attempt to create a level playing field. You have been provided with 'opportunities' to succeed: if you fail to do so, that is your problem. And so those who 'lose' are dismissed as 'not bold enough', or 'too weak', or 'too lacking in character' to have succeeded. Society becomes fragmented between those who can respond to the challenges of globalized employment and adaptable skills, and those who cannot.

What does it mean to be a success? Not surprisingly the financialization of everything has a powerful effect on shaping the image of the successful life. Donald Trump's unlikely victory in the 2016 US Presidential contest was in part attributed to his business credentials. His billionaire lifestyle was welcomed by supporters as showing the kind of success needed by the country's next 'CEO'. The language is telling. It is now no longer enough to be a politician committed to public service. Now you should be able to run the country like a successful business. And note how the flashy trappings of Trump's life were read as evidence of his success. Rather than tasteless and decadent, the golden elevator in Trump Tower was held up as evidence of the business acumen the country needed.

Success is defined by what you have, not even by how you got it. Here is the flaw in the claim that hard work will get you what you desire. Trump's supporters weren't concerned that his father gave him a million dollars to help him on his way, or that he tended to walk away from businesses when they encountered difficulties. What mattered was that he presented as a successful individual. Framed financially, material wealth becomes the principle marker for the successful life.

So much for success. If you lack the material elements necessary for showing your success, you can be written off as a failure. This judgement turns on seemingly minor considerations. Here's Margaret Thatcher in 1986 offering a typically trenchant description of what it is to be a failure:

'A man who, beyond the age of 26, finds himself on a bus can count himself as a failure.'[27]

Comments like this suggest the fragility of neoliberal success: it rests principally on the way others see us. The surface trappings of a life – the things we attain or achieve – determine the extent to which others see us as successful individuals. We might wonder whether this is really the best way to judge the meaning of a life. Bret Easton Ellis's novel *American Psycho* (1991) explores this problem rather well, if you can cope with its gory premise. Patrick Bateman, a successful investment banker, is a psychopath and serial killer. While some saw this novel as a satire on the excess of the 1980s, Ellis's aim was to confront his experience of the emptiness of the vision of success on which 1980s glamour depended:

> I was living like Patrick Bateman. I was slipping into a consumerist kind of void that was supposed to give me confidence and make me feel good about myself but just made me feel worse and worse and worse about myself. (Baker 2010)

It is possible to be 'a success', defined through the trappings of wealth and privilege, but to *feel* oneself to be a failure.

How much worse to not have the trappings of success in this system. And here we glimpse the shadow side of responsibility. Success depends upon the extent to which you have (or have not) utilized your talents and skills to the best advantage. Little attention is paid to the social structures that enshrine inequality, and so little attention is paid to considering ways of challenging, resisting and reshaping them. Instead, faith resides in the Market as the neutral arbitrator of value. It will sort the wheat from the chaff. If you are poor or unemployed, it is *your* fault. You are not a victim of economic forces beyond your control, but responsible for your fate.[28] In the best case scenario, training might be offered to help you become the kind of worker required by the contemporary workplace. In the worst case scenario, you might find yourself vulnerable to the casual cruelty Mirowski describes as an aspect of 'Everyday Neoliberalism'. The poor and unemployed are no longer defined as a class but are instead presented as feckless individuals, easy targets for the fury of 'hard-working' others. Rather than protect those rendered vulnerable by market forces or social inequality, this individualized account of poverty enables those relatively better-off to revel in the failings of the poor.

Their failure can even be presented as a form of entertainment. Since the Global Financial Crisis of 2008 heralded in the new 'Age of Austerity', British TV has been saturated with what commentators call 'Poverty Porn'. These Reality TV shows claim to reveal the feckless lifestyles of the 'undeserving poor', and glory in titles such as 'Benefits Street' and 'Benefits Britain'. Even the BBC (the UK's world-renowned public service broadcaster) got caught up in the 'fun', commissioning a show described as akin to *the Hunger Games*, where the unemployed were pitted against the low paid in order to find 'Britain's Hardest Grafter'.[29] It's hard to see what entertainment might be had from such shows, but one effect is the erosion of empathy. To be entertained, you, the viewer, must not see yourself in the plight of these people. For Mirowski, this 'theatre of cruelty' directs attention away from those who benefit from the injustice of a socio-economic system to those who suffer from it. Presented as different from the viewer, the poor may be packaged as the stars of the show, but ultimately the viewer is left with an image of them as to blame for their situation, and therefore they are worthy of 'our' contempt. Poverty no longer elicits sympathy but ridicule: 'In the neoliberal theatre of cruelty, one torments the poor or indigent precisely *because* they are prostrate' (Mirowski 2014: 131).

No wonder if we decide it is better to do anything – travel anywhere – to ensure that we, at least, are 'successes' in the world of work. Here is the effect of work on the sense of self. Those without work are pariahs, in some way to blame for their circumstances.[30] They haven't just failed to find work: they *are* failures. To work is to be virtuous. During the 2015 UK General Election, the Conservative *and* Labour parties produced manifestos committed to helping 'hard-working families'. If we look critically at this much-used phrase, we realize how strange it sounds, given that children in such families are unlikely to be 'hard-working'; indeed, one would hope not. Suggested in the shorthand of this phrase is the claim that 'working hard' is a good thing in and of itself.

There is a long history which rejects this claim. In the Jewish and Christian traditions, work is a curse placed by God on humanity for their disobedience.[31] For Karl Marx, work is inherently painful under the capitalist system: it may frame human life, but its capitalist iteration contributes to a sense of alienation from self and others.[32] Looked at from these very different perspectives, it seems odd to endow work with all our hopes for a meaningful life. The querying of work has been given fresh impetus by the precarious nature of the global economy since 2008 and the historic fall in the value of wages that accompanied it.[33] Work, contrary to the political rhetoric, doesn't pay; or, at least, doesn't pay *properly*. Tellingly, your level of education need not lead to the kind of work it would once have assured.[34] The lack of graduate jobs suggests a student might follow the political mantras, work hard, achieve the grades deemed necessary for a fulfilling professional life, and yet still not achieve that end. A newspaper article from the years after the global crash details the sense of failure emerging from this mismatch between hopes and reality. A young woman describes her sense of disappointment that she has not been able to realize 'the snazzy life' promised by teachers and a consumerist society:

> I imagined being 27 with a Prada handbag, a Sex and the City-type girl-about-town doing really well. I think that level of expectation came from my school, a private girls' school where we were told we could do whatever we wanted … I thought I would be a high-flyer -and married by the time I was 26. I graduated from Durham University with a 2:1 and moved to London, expecting to live the dream. I took the first job I could get as a PA, but I was miserable. I thought that, by 26, I would have this snazzy life. Now I'm 27 and I'll probably be in my forties by the time I have a house. (Radnor 2012: 39)

The advocacy of work as the focus for the meaning of life cannot support the weight of expectations placed on it. Rather than lament that this is so, we might instead think again about what we actually need in order to live well. If Brett Easton Ellis's experience suggests the limits of wealth, this anonymous young woman's lament suggests the problems of making the pursuit of achievement and attainment central to the fulfilling life.[35]

Another feature of contemporary life requires revisiting the entrepreneurial self. The 2008 crash revealed the precarious nature of an economic system where the actions of national governments seemed of little consequence when placed in the context of global capital. Here lies the challenge to neoliberal economics. Free movement of workers – particularly those willing to accept lower wages for their work – might be good for business, but it has also undermined the bargaining power of workers.[36] Precarious employment practices adds another dimension to this. More and more people are trapped in insecure and poorly paid employment in temporary or part-time jobs. These jobs aren't even in the areas traditionally blighted by the scourge of low pay: the service economy, cleaning, nursing. The phenomenon of the university lecturer on a zero-hour contract suggests *all* work is becoming more precarious. The effect of this on mental health is well-documented, with failure to secure well-paid work leading to heightened anxiety and increased fears for the future.[37] Fear of the economic consequences of failing blights the experience of all but the very richest. Hardly surprising that the UK's referendum on continued membership of the European Union became a referendum against the 'uncontrolled' immigration believed to be at the root of poor pay; or that Trump won the support of so many Americans by promising a new age of protectionism for American industry. While not discounting the casual racism of island dwellers or the parochialism of small town America, it is important to recognize the howl of rage from those at the sharp end of economic forces seen as benefiting only the most wealthy.

Work is not doing the job that the past forty years of policymaking and economic practices suggest that it should do in shaping the good life. Social mobility in the United States and the UK has stalled, the gap between rich and poor grows ever wider.[38] And things are set to get much worse, with increased automation threatening around 47 per cent of the jobs currently done by humans.[39] It is hard to see how the rhetoric concerning the fulfilment to be found in work can be sustained. Even if it could be, we might note that only 13 per cent of people worldwide consider their work to be fulfilling: 'Physically degraded, mentally drained and socially exhausted, most workers find themselves under immense amounts of stress in their jobs' (Srnicek and Williams 2016: 126). The nature of twenty-first-century employment reveals the problems of making work – *any* work – the driver that enables a fulfilling life. On the verge of the 'the Second Machine Age', it is time to challenge the role work plays in the contemporary narrative of what it is to live well.[40] The days of the entrepreneurial self seem numbered. What should take its place?

Thinking again about work: Hannah Arendt and the human condition

Pursuing success and avoiding of failure do not seem adequate for establishing a well-lived life. Too much dissatisfaction and anxiety follows in the wake of these ideas to make that goal possible. Is it possible to think differently? Having an active life seems fundamental to human well-being: we might think of the depression accompanying unemployment, or the loneliness that attends to not having a social life. Without work, what would our activities look like? What is the relationship between work and the active human life?

In *The Human Condition*, published in 1958, the political theorist Hannah Arendt turns her attention to the *vita activa*, or 'the active life', which she sees as central to the nature of human beings. Arendt does not take for granted what it means to live an active life. Instead, she explores it through an investigation of three categories: labour, work and action. Arendt's analysis confronts us with the imperative to not take at face value the habitual usage of 'work' for all forms of human activity. She 'makes strange' the idea of work, thereby moving us towards a rather different view of what it means to live well as a human being. It is a view that challenges accounts of what it is to succeed and what it is to fail that emanate from making work the shaping feature of a meaningful life.

Arendt begins with 'Labour', which she relates to the biological processes of the human body. Labouring is that which is unending in the human struggle with the natural world.[41] It describes the human attempt to hold back the processes of nature which threaten the ability of human beings to create.[42] There is an endless quality to labouring. Its very futility explains why the ruling classes have always sought to avoid it: either by using slaves or servants who release them from its burden. Feminist icon Germaine Greer taps into this sense of futility in typically robust form. In a sane world, she says, housework would have been long abolished. The battle with dust is pointless and boring. Better to recognize the 'meaningless repetition of non-productive activity' and see housework as 'a variety of obsessive-compulsive disorder' (Greer 1999: 129).

Perhaps. Arendt sees a close connection between labour and natural processes. The labour Greer dislikes is repetitive precisely because the processes it attempts to contain are themselves endless. As I write, I look out at our garden. The grass is too long, the bushes are taking over. I could – and probably will – head out with the secateurs and the lawn mower later. It will look nice for a bit, and then next month I will have to do exactly the same all over again. No wonder I hate gardening! Now, while Arendt highlights the futility of such labour, she goes on to identify something strange in the construction of the modern world that influences her understanding of her second category, 'Work'. Living in a post-industrial age, consumption has become the organizing principle for life, and this makes even more central 'the endlessness of the labouring process' ([1958] 1998: 125). In-built obsolescence of objects and the vagaries of fashion mean that 'our whole economy has become a waste economy' ([1958] 1998: 134).

An example of what Arendt is getting at. Our kettle blew up a few weeks ago. (OK, it didn't exactly 'blow up', but that phrase makes its failure to work sound more exciting and less obviously tedious.) We examined it, and discovered that the button for opening the lid no longer worked. Cynically we decided that it had probably been designed to eventually break. After all, why would you create a kettle as a company wanting to make money if that kettle lasted for twenty years rather than five? And so my husband set off for John Lewis to buy a new one.

If the relentless repetitiveness of labour suggests the ultimate futility of all human activity, work gives the *illusion* of permanence to human life. Labour, remember, has no beginning or end. (My gardening.) It reveals human beings 'caught in the cyclical movement of the body's life process' (Arendt [1958] 1998: 144). At first glance, 'work' *seems* rather different. Work has a purpose which labouring doesn't seem to share. Labouring reminds us that natural processes are constant. The world of work resists this, offering instead 'the world of machines [as] … a substitute for the real world' (Arendt [1958] 1998: 152). The things we make seem more permanent than the processes of the natural world against which the labourer battles. They exist unless or until we destroy them.[43] (My kettle.) This sense of human control obscures the fact that we *remain* dependent on the world of natural processes. These processes surround us and run through our veins. We are an intimate part of the world of chance and change, even as we construct objects which give us an illusion of power over these natural forces.

To work is to direct your body and mind to achieving an end result. (The people making the components for my shiny new kettle.) Enter what Arendt calls the 'utility principle'. In a world which glorifies work, the most important question concerns *the use* to which any particular thing or practice is to be put. Usefulness (utility) becomes the 'ultimate standard for life and the world of men' ([1958] 1998: 157). Think about our discussion of success and failure: how useful are you?

'Why do I do this every day?'
'Why do I engage in this busyness?'
'I do it to show how useful I am, to show how I am using my talents to achieve an end result.'

My first job was with the Royal Shakespeare Company, as an admin assistant in the Press Office. Every so often, I would find myself with nothing to do, and at such times I took to walking round the building, holding a piece of paper. Try it sometime. People will assume you are busy. How we hate looking as if we aren't.

What happens to those judged *useless* in such a world? Arendt is writing in the aftermath of the horror of the Nazi attempt to destroy entire populations rendered useless by the Third Reich. For our times, anti-work prophets Nick Srnicek and Alex Williams ask what is to happen to 'surplus populations' (2016: 86) in a world of increased automation and high unemployment. Those perceived to lack usefulness are redundant in a world where the value of everything is considered in terms of its use.[44]

In order to resist the shaping power of the utility principle, Arendt draws attention to the thing she wants to cultivate: thoughtfulness. In a world structured by the principle of usefulness, thought emerges as something *utterly useless*. This is not a criticism. It reminds us of the nature of the world: thought is 'as relentless and repetitive as life itself' ([1958] 1998: 171). There is no end to thought, no final resting place for it. It is not directed to one specific outcome. It is never something that reaches an end point. I remember a colleague responding to a workmate's unwillingness to think again about a course of action. 'I've thought about it. I don't need to think again.' My colleague's response to such intransigence had me snorting into my coffee: 'Thought's not like the measles. You don't have it once and then never again.'

It is precisely the relentless, repetitive quality of thought-without-end that brings Arendt to the qualities she places at the heart of the active life: action and speech. These qualities transcend labour and work. They 'insert us into the world'. They are 'not forced upon us by necessity, like labour, and not prompted by utility, like work' ([1958] 1998: 177). They define us in a way that transcends the practices of labouring and working. In the act, we are able to begin, to begin *again*. We are always capable of 'beginning something new' ([1958] 1998: 177). And note that 'action and speech *go on between men*' ([1958] 1998: 182). We have said little about the role of community for neoliberalism, for the economics its proponents espouse has little place for stable communities. Success and failure apply solely to individuals. The global marketplace requires the worker to be 'a global citizen', whose home is in no one place, whose work is not necessarily where she or he lives, who need not work with their neighbours.[45]

Yet for Arendt, the importance of other people shapes the human world. Action is never simply reducible to what an individual does, for 'action is never possible in isolation' ([1958] 1998: 188). Action transcends the world of work. It brings us into contact with others, thereby revealing its *unpredictability*. This is what makes it distinct from work. Work is directed at a particular end. Action is unpredictable and open-ended, *because* it happens *between* individuals.[46] It is located in the social space we create *together*. There is no end for action. It cannot be controlled. It always takes place in relation to others, and its outcomes are dependent on the actions of others.[47]

Arendt's analysis encourages a more complex engagement with the activities frequently lumped together under the one category of 'work'. By highlighting action and speech, Arendt shifts meaningful human activity beyond the world of paid and organized work. We might be able to act in the way Arendt envisages in the workplace; but it is more likely that *real* action, with all the unpredictability that idea implies, will be made manifest beyond the workplace in the myriad ways in which we interact and find with each other meaningful ways of living. We might think of the places where people meet together *outside* work: voluntary organizations, guilds, churches, mosques, temples, local action groups, clubs, political parties. These are places where people come together to shape their world, with an openness to the possibilities of their action. This also suggests the limitations of making economic success the criteria for a meaningful life. If I return to my father's experience, his working life was defined by periods of unemployment which under the neoliberal account would suggest he was a failure. Yet in unpaid youth work, he had a profound influence on the lives of countless young people.

Arendt prompts a critical appraisal of the neoliberal fetishizing of work. Under neoliberalism, *all* work of whatever kind is viewed as offering the means of achieving a meaningful life. Does it *really*? *Who benefits* from the claim that it is through work that you will find fulfilment, that you will become a responsible, capable and independent individual? Who benefits from modelling success through work? Given the lowering of living standards in the years since the financial crisis, it is not the average worker who benefits from their labours.[48]

Even if work *did* pay, Arendt prompts us to ask whether work should be viewed as the primary function of a human being.[49] Sure, some of us will find work more meaningful and life-affirming than others. But even the most worthwhile work cannot ultimately solve the puzzle of what it is to be human. Here, Arendt's reflections take us in a surprising, but vitally important direction:

Common to labouring and working is futility.

Work *appears* to be less futile than labour, but that is only because that which it produces has the *illusion of permanence*. In asking what work is *for*, what it contributes to our sense of ourselves, we arrive at the heart of the matter.

Why do we work?

Our answers to this question may trouble us. According to educationalist Ansgar Allen, the frenetic pace of the contemporary world of work makes it difficult to identify any aim beyond 'the narcotic of constant activity' (Allen 2015: 6). The constant activity of work in a twenty-four-hour, seven-day-a-week world is not just tiring but something which acts as a drug we willingly take. What is being obscured when the meaning of life is located in the activity of work? What is hidden when our energy is directed towards achieving material success?

'Why do I do this everyday?'

Answers to this question can go deeper than the merely prosaic response of 'well, my company is in London'; or 'I need this job to survive'; or 'accommodation is too expensive in the city.'

Why? Why do we do it?

Why do *I* do this? What is it to be *me*, living at this moment, in this time and place, with this set of connections and relationships and activities? Who am *I*? What is it to be a human being? Dante's great poem, *The Divine Comedy*, opens with the suggestion that there is something about middle age that makes us ask this question in an altogether deeper way:

> When halfway through the journey of our life
> > I found that I was in a gloomy wood,
> > because the path which led aright was lost. (Canto 1, lines 1–3[50])

Your life is rushing by as fast as that motorway traffic, and now is the time to take stock. What has become a regular questioning of my working life began in my mid-30s. I enjoyed teaching and writing (sometimes), but the university was being increasingly shaped by a whole host of governmental priorities I didn't share and which I felt acted as a distraction from the very activities that had led me to that career in the first place. Subject to various forms of performance management, engaged in audit activities, the joy surrounding learning and teaching was ebbing away. I never felt I was good enough, always felt I was failing in some imperceptible way. What was the point of this daily journey? What was I doing?

The force of that question can, of course, be felt at any time. *Why* am I in school? *Why* should I study these subjects? *Why* have the things that once made me happy lost their sheen? *Why* don't I ever seem to be able to do anything right?

It's uncomfortable to challenge the things that we do, particularly when we are told they are the means by which we are to carve out a meaningful life. What happens if we look up from the rush of life and think – *really think* – about our lives beyond the daily grind? For the theologian Paul Tillich, asking that question 'why' is exactly what we must do if we are to start out on the path towards a better way of living:

> Look at the student who knows the content of the hundred most important books of world history, and yet whose spiritual life remains as shallow as it ever was, or perhaps becomes even more superficial. And then look at an uneducated worker who performs a mechanical task day by day, but who suddenly asks himself: 'What does it *mean*, that I do this work? What does it mean for my life? What *is* the meaning of my life?' (Tillich [1949] 1962: 62)

To ask such questions puts us on a collision course with the account of the good life offered under neoliberalism. This is not about accepting without a second thought the role work is supposed to play in our life. This is not about coming up with a strategy to become a successful entrepreneur of the self. This is not about fearing that one might fail to achieve the goals one has set or, more likely, *been* set. Tillich's questions are *existential* questions; questions that force us to consider our place in a world far greater than the structures and activities of human beings. These questions demand that we face the reality of our lives as creatures who live for a terrifyingly short space of time. Looked at through the lens of these questions, it is right to consider what achievement could ever stand in such a changing environment.

As Arendt says, even the apparent permanence of the things work creates is illusory. So what *is* the point of work? Can it ever realistically fulfil the role it is given in neoliberal societies as the basis for the well-lived life, or are we better advised to look elsewhere?

Success, failure and life beyond the fetish of work

We have been encouraged to see work as the only way to attain that which is necessary for a good life. Wrapped up in this construction is the belief that work will enable us to become successful individuals who stand out from the rest. Are there other ways of thinking about work that place it in a broader context of the activities and attitudes that might make one's life meaningful? Arendt suggests something of this possibility when she considers art and creativity. Despite attempts to make these things part of the utilitarian working world, reducing them to just alternative ways of 'making a living' (Arendt [1958] 1998: 126–7), these practices continue to have value *over and above* one's ability to make money from them. Here is value not reduced to the profit margin. Here are ways of acting that reveal something of the possibilities open to human beings.

The philosopher and motor mechanic Matthew Crawford resists the claim that what we need to do is become 'more creative'. Instead, he calls for 'the less glamorous virtue of attentiveness' (2010: 82), found through the practice of what he calls 'the useful arts' (2010: 11). Making a pitch for the satisfaction to be found in working as a craftsman, Crawford describes the pleasure of learning a trade and becoming immersed in a practice. These are much-underrated qualities in a world of 'transferrable skills', where flexibility and adaptability are the primary virtues of any employee. By way of contrast, Crawford models a different approach to the working life, drawing upon his experience of the pleasure and fulfilment found in the patient practice of fixing old and broken motorbikes.

If we are not mechanically minded we might feel anxious about this change of direction. Not all of us are capable of this kind of work. Sociologist Richard Sennett makes a helpful intervention by arguing that it is not just in activities like manual craft that 'craftsmanship' is to be found. The aim of the craftsman is 'doing something well *for its own sake*' (Sennett 2006: 104; my emphasis). This commitment can be found in a variety of activities: in 'the effort to write clearly' (what Sennett calls 'mental craftsmanship') (2006: 104); in the 'social craftsmanship' of 'forging a viable marriage' (2006: 104) or friendship. What matters is *the commitment to become better at what you do*. The scope of the activities he suggests is telling. This is not about grounding the meaning of life in paid work. This is about considering a range of activities through whose practice meaningful patterns for the quality of our daily lives emerge.

As we start to think of the things we do in this way, we should not lose sight of Arendt's key point. There *is* an ultimate futility to the things that we do. This is because we are mutable creatures inhabiting a precarious, changing world. Yet, contrary to what we might initially think, this is no bad thing, because being aware of the *limits* of human activity enables us to think more deeply about what gives meaning to our life. There is a different way of orientating ourselves in the world, and it is best approached by resisting the constructions of success and failure considered so far.

Narratives of success depend upon lineal accounts of what makes for the meaningful life. I work at something; I become successful at it; I arrive at a fixed end point where that success is acknowledged and rewarded. What Crawford and Sennett suggest is a different model which sees *the practice* as being more significant than the end point. Meaning emerges as we attend to the practice itself.

Success understood as achievement is always precarious. We will only ever be as successful as our last project. Likewise, even the most successful of us cannot but be aware of the shadow lurking behind success: if we are responsible for our own success, we will also be held accountable for our failure. Pierre Bourdieu's mammoth account of social suffering, *The Weight of the World* (1999), reminds us of the unreality of 'the Self-Made Man' by drawing attention to the global economic and political forces that shape human suffering. The stories of those too-easily written off as failures is told, through their own words and through discussion of the impersonal forces that have shaped their experience. What this reveals is what the proponents of neoliberalism want to deny: *There are things beyond the control of the individual*.

The careful, attentive working that Crawford describes and Sennett develops comes into its own at this point. In the process of fixing – be that in mechanics or medicine (or, if we follow Sennett, in writing or relationships) – we become aware of the world as something that is not always amenable to human willing. What we want does not always happen. Not everything can be fixed, not every relationship saved, not every poem finished. The regular experience of failure acts to reveal something important about our status in the world. Our will is not the most important factor in the world. What *I* want doesn't always happen. Crawford suggests that 'fixing things may be a cure for narcissism' (2010: 81), for it makes this fact clear. Things break down which cannot always be fixed. This reminds us that 'we're not as free and independent as we thought' (2010: 17).

Failure tempers the conceit of mastery. (2010: 81)

The regular failures Crawford's craftsmen and women encounter alert us to the nature of the world. In failure, we confront the fundamental fact of our dependence. We are revealed as dependent on a world bigger than ourselves. We are not principally independent.

And so to live well we need to resist the fantasies peddled by neoliberalism. In making work the arena in which the individual is to *create* themselves, this fundamental dependence is ignored. The entrepreneurial individual, detached from others, is not 'bogged down' in community.[51] The 'global citizen' can move freely, wherever work takes them. At its most optimistic, this image of the individual suggests an open and exciting future. At its worse, it describes the continuing relevance of the philosopher Martin Heidegger's claim that 'homelessness is coming to be the destiny of the world' ([1947] 1983: 243). The rise of nationalism is in part an attempt to challenge this model of the rootless worker; though in practice its xenophobia simply allows for more fear and social division. Yet acknowledging the importance of place for personal identity should give us pause. In constructing an account of the individual that pays little heed to the importance of one's physical locatedness, something significant is ignored about the need people have for stability and relationship. Making the illusion of the independent individual central to the good life ends up enshrining a fundamental disconnection between ourselves and the world.

Despite an increasing sense of the limits of neoliberalism for enabling the flourishing life, alternatives have not been as various as might have been anticipated. The most successful seems to be found in the resurgence of nationalist movements; but, as Srnicek and Williams note, such movements play to 'a nostalgia for a lost past' (2016: 47) which is not likely to be effective in facing the challenges of the future. It is not just, though, that these movements peddle ineffective solutions to contemporary problems. The vision of the world suggested by nationalism depends on a narrowness of perspective, where political action involves shoring up the rights of one's own community rather than seeking to improve the lot of all, regardless of race or nationality. If we are unhappy with an account of the good life based on exclusion, we are faced with the imperative to create alternative models that foster our connection to others and the world. Crawford's discussion of what makes for meaningful work, and Tillich's suggestion that we engage with existential questions, relocates the individual in the structures and processes of a precarious world. In the next chapter these themes are developed by considering how the experiences which reveal most intimately the workings of a precarious world – loss and losing – have become entwined with ideas of failure. Through exploring this connection, it becomes possible to think differently about what it is to fail, and what it means to live well.

2

WOMEN, FAILURE AND THE FEAR OF LOSS

The times when I have most felt that I am a failure have all arisen from the sense that I have failed as a woman. This feeling can be triggered by the asking of a seemingly innocent question:

'Do you have children?'

My heart sinks, I feel sick and I try to come up with an answer that doesn't open up all the pain surrounding this unrealized aspect of my life. At other times, a less innocent version of this question is offered as a statement, usually accompanied by a sense of smug superiority from the person making it, who is, most often, a mother herself:

'I don't think you can be fully a woman until you've had a child.'

It is very difficult to think of a response that doesn't involve swearing or throwing something; though so far I have managed not to do either. I have, after all, been brought up properly and in England. Dinner parties would be much more exciting, I suppose, if I felt able to vent in this way.

Exploring female success and failure does more, you'll be glad to hear, than enable me to grapple with my own, deep-rooted feelings of failure. It also makes possible an engagement with that which is so often caught up with the feelings of failure: loss. These questions about motherhood grip so fiercely at my heart because they remind me of the deepest loss of my life so far: not being able to have a child. In this chapter, I want to suggest that it is by tracking the specifically female forms of success and failure that we encounter the things that human beings (of whatever sex or gender) cannot control.

The pursuit of success considered in the previous chapter acts as a powerful distraction from reflection on what it is to be a human being. Work and its 'relentless activity' makes it possible for us to ignore the forces which make human life precarious and unpredictable. Chuck Palahniuk in his novel *Lullaby* suggests that our society is particularly adept at distraction, peopled as it is by 'sound-oholics' and 'quiet-ophobics' (2003: 15). Noise drives out contemplation; busyness, the space for thinking. Yet the things we would ignore are as important – perhaps *more* important – than the things that are easy to talk about.[1] What happens if we pay attention to the spectre of the failed life; that ghostly presence that hovers at the periphery of our dreams of success? Considering that which is pushed to the margins of life makes it possible to uncover the fears which haunt the desire to be a success.

According to Paul Tillich, all human beings struggle with the anxiety that comes with being finite beings in a world of chance and change. Born into the world, dependent upon it, subject to death, the threat of *non-existence* (of non-being or *not*-being) is ever present.[2] This existential anxiety is felt in our fears of death, our sense of meaninglessness, our feelings of guilt. How do we cope with these feelings of anxiety? Tillich identifies one way of attaining an illusory form of control over the terror that comes with realizing that one day we will no longer exist:

> Anxiety strives to become fear, because fear can be met with courage. ([1952] 1977: 47)

If anxiety is the dull ache in the pit of the stomach, the unease brought about by the shape at the corner of the eye that cannot quite be grasped, fear is something that can be contained, for it can be connected to specific objects that the individual is then in a position to confront. Fear is easier to confront than anxiety, and much easier to manage.

How does this general existential anxiety get transformed into fears that can be confronted and contained? Consideration of the shaping of the idea of Woman reveals the way in which something habitually placed on the margins can be used to manage feelings of anxiety arising from the realization that we cannot always control our destinies. Historically, women's bodies have played a particular role in this attempt to exert control over the uncontrollable. In tracking the specifically female forms of success and failure we come face-to-face with the inescapable realities which are part and parcel of the experience of dependent, finite beings. If we are to live well, we will need to bring these realities out into the light, finding as a result ways of living with them.

Women, success (and failure) and the feminization of work

If I feel a failure as a woman, I might be expected to feel like a success when considering my place in the (supposedly) gender-neutral world of work. I was awarded my PhD in my mid-20s, I was made a professor in my mid-40s and I have a nice collection of books I have written on my bookshelf. (All very pleasing and tangible, blissfully free of the ghosts of bad reviews, rejected articles and books I started but failed to complete.)

If in previous ages I would have been excluded from the work of a philosopher because of my sex, today being a woman in the work place might even be seen as an advantage. Some of the major changes to the nature of work in contemporary Western societies have been construed as particularly beneficial for women. Work has become steadily less industrial, and while numbers working in the traditional (male) manufacturing sectors have declined, the jobs requiring supposedly female skills have steadily increased.

The expansion of the service sector, in particular – which includes hospitality, sales, shops and care work – would seem to put women in an advantageous position, not least because these jobs require skills women are assumed to have in abundance: caring, building relationships, paying attention to the needs of others.[3] Describing this shift in working practices as 'feminization' suggests women will be the ones best placed to take advantage of the new jobs that emerge in a service-driven economy. If anyone seems to be failing in the world of work, presumably it will be men, as the kind of work associated with male physical strength is rapidly disappearing.[4]

Against such a backdrop, we might expect women to be more successful than men. The situation is rather more complex, however, for the work reflecting supposedly female skills continues to be low paid, insecure and of low status. This is even the case in the cosy academic world I inhabit. As the philosopher and feminist activist Michèle Le Doeuff notes in her account of women's entry into the university, 'When a respected activity admits women it loses value' ([1980] 1989: 110). And value means both its status and its pay.[5] There may be more women in paid work, but 'women's work' remains undervalued, even in those areas of life which once excluded but which now admit women.[6] Understanding why the extension of female work might not mean women are more successful requires digging a little deeper into the shape of this changing workplace.

What skills are needed to be a successful worker? As we saw in the previous chapter, what is valued in the contemporary workplace is the ability to shape yourself as a successful entrepreneur of yourself. You must be adaptable, able and willing to acquire the skills needed to be a success. In a 'feminized' work place, it makes sense to assume that the worker – be they female or male – will need to *play out* the skills associated with the feminine if they are to achieve their goals.

The notion that we perform gender is illuminated by the ideas of the critical theorist Judith Butler. For Butler, gender is not something innate, but always a form of performance.[7] Her approach develops Simone de Beauvoir's claim that when we consider what it is to be a 'woman', we find a social construction which reflects society's ideals of what it is to be female.[8] As Beauvoir puts it, 'One is not born, but rather one becomes, a woman' ([1949] 1972: 295). In other words, I might be born with a set of female sex organs – breasts, vagina, womb, ovaries – but these do not by themselves make me 'a woman'. I have to learn to act in accordance with the values my society associates with 'being a woman'. As I grow up, so I attempt to become a (more or less) successful version of what a woman is expected to be.

Butler extends Beauvoir's ideas to cover male as well as female experience. *All* gender identities are forms of performance. This enables a more complex rendition of what it means for the workplace to become 'feminized'. The ideal worker in the post-industrial world is 'one who can claim to possess a flexible or mobile relation to gender performance and hence to have taken up a reflexive stance towards gender' (Adkins 2002: 58). This is less about being able to succeed *because you are a woman*; rather, it is about being flexible in the way you present yourself in the workplace. It is this flexibility that enables you to 'become' a success, not the mere fact that you are female. The *values* traditionally ascribed to femininity are now prized in the workplace, *not* the fact that you are a woman.

The consumerist economics of neoliberalism affects what this means in practice. To be a success in the neoliberal world of work, I must pay attention to 'appearance, image and style at work'; these three qualities are closely aligned to what Lisa Adkins calls 'the aesthetics of the feminine' (Adkins 2002: 61). But this is not about women *per se*: for both women *and men* to be successful, they must perform this aesthetics.[9] In practice, however, it is easier for men to ' "take on" the aesthetics of femininity, perform reversals and gender hybrids' (Adkins 2002: 75). Men may even find it easier to take on the flexible forms of self-presentation required in order to be a success. For women, it may be far more difficult to perform the masculinity required in some work situations. Put simply, men can enact both masculinity *and* femininity, while women can only enact femininity.

An example from the world of politics may help us. During the US Presidential campaign in 2016, any sign of weakness was taken to show that Hillary Clinton was not tough enough to be president. At the same time, her habitual wearing of the 'pantsuit' was seen by her opponents as a form of masculine presentation; and not in a good way. She was somehow less a woman by striving to be more like a man. By way of contrast, Donald Trump for all his weaknesses was seen to look more like a president than she did. It was easier for him to embody the masculinity believed by many to be necessary to become the president of the United States (POTUS) because he was male.

Businesses expected to thrive on 'high testosterone', like the banking sector, raise similar problems for how women are to present themselves in the world of work. Social occasions used to cement connections with business associates are not always welcoming of women. Business women report finding it 'demeaning to try to be one of the boys' (Adkins 2002: 146). Being 'a ladette' doesn't always work: as one woman working in finance comments, 'You can't go out and get ratted as one of the boys in the pub; it just won't work' (Adkins 2002: 154). In contexts where maleness is seen as an advantage, women have to decide whether to be 'more or less female', rather than 'more or less male'.[10] Far from 'levelling the playing field' for women to succeed, the playing out of gender might well be more advantageous for men than it is for women.

A further aspect of women's experience should be considered when exploring what is required to be a success rather than a failure. Here, a vista opens up into the things that haunt the constructions of success as attainment. Here, we get a glimpse of the anxieties accompanying the construction of failure.

What does it mean to be successful as a woman?

As I've suggested, this involves more than pursuing cultural measures of success as defined by the things you attain and achieve in the workplace. What it means to succeed *as a woman* is also shaped by a powerful set of social, historical and political norms where female success is conceived quite differently from that expected of the male.

Let's consider appearance and style, those features which are apparently as important for male success as for female success in a society shaped by consumerism. Appearance remains more important for women in a context where female beauty is more obviously prized. Here are a set of random and common images: the beautiful, young woman used to sell products as diverse as cars, washing powder and perfume; the craggy old businessman (or president) accompanied by the beautiful trophy wife; the habitual description of women – in whatever context – as primarily wives and mothers. When the UK MP Jo Cox was murdered by a right-wing extremist in 2016, her friend and fellow MP Rachel Reeves said in the debate to mark Cox's life that 'Batley and Spen will go on to elect a new MP, but they won't replace a mother'. Reeves is right; but if Cox had been male, would this comment about her status as a parent have been made in quite this way? And here is another vision of what makes for a successful woman: when 71-year-old Manuela Carmena became mayor of Madrid in June 2015, taking up one of the most powerful positions in Spain, the media summed up her warm personality by calling her 'the Hugging Grandma'.

Women are never judged just by what they *have done*; they must also succeed at embodying a particular set of qualities associated with femininity. When Julia Gillard stood to be leader of the Australian Labor Party in 2005, she was photographed at her kitchen table, on which was placed an empty fruit bowl. This innocuous object was endowed with particular significance by her opponents. Gillard did not have children, and so her 'fruit bowl' was empty, a sign of her lack of femininity. She was 'deliberately barren'. To run for high office and not to have children is, for a woman, a sign that something is not right.[11] A similar criticism was directed at Theresa May during the Conservative Party leadership contest in July 2016. Another contender, Andrea Leadsom, drew attention to the fact that Mrs May did not have children. 'She possibly has nieces, nephews, lots of people. But

I have children who are going to have children who will directly be a part of what happens next', Leadsom argued.[12] Not having children lessens, it seems, the ability of a female politician to connect to the future. Rarely are men expected to show their fitness for government as something located in their ability to procreate.

The shadow side of female success modelled as achievement *and* feminine appearance emerges from a survey taken in 2006. When questioned, 90 per cent of American women claimed they felt financially insecure, with nearly half the women surveyed expressing fear that they would become a bag lady, living on the streets, with no home, no security and no support. The language one woman used to describe her fears it revealing: 'The inner bag lady, wrinkle-faced and unkempt, is no joke. She's the worst-case-scenario future' (Standing 2011: 108).

This image of the bag lady provides a telling way into the anxieties masked by the claim that failure is always a result of your own actions. The fears expressed by this woman are not just about failing at work, becoming homeless and without resources: although given the lack of a welfare net to stop such an eventuality, this is far from a baseless set of fears for the majority of Americans. What is significant is *the way* this woman expresses her fears. She fears being 'wrinkle-faced and unkempt'. This metaphor might be read as simply expressing her fears of losing the powers of femininity, so prized in the feminized workplace. Yet her description suggests something more and here we see an opening into Tillich's existential anxiety. The failure this woman fears is connected to the experience of physical loss – ageing and the loss of bodily powers – common, of course, to *all* individuals, not just women. Yet in practice, there is a long history of the female body being used as a container for the anxieties which arise from the experience of being embodied beings subject to change. The body is never 'just' a physical entity: it is always shaped by social mores and values. By exploring success and failure through the concepts routinely played out on the female body, it is possible to discern powerful anxieties regarding loss running beneath cultural narratives of what it is to fail.

Standing out from the world: The masculine roots of 'human' success

As a young student, back in the days when dinosaurs roamed the earth, I remember being shocked as I realized the extent to which women's voices were excluded from the Western philosophical tradition. It wasn't just that there weren't many (any) women philosophers referred to in my classes, it was that the way the world had been shaped reflected male ideas of what was required to live a fulfilling life. Being human was identified with the attributes of reason, choice and autonomy. Far from being 'gender neutral', however, these attributes reflect male experience of the world and have a particular bearing on the framing of success as attainment.

Leonardo Da Vinci's 'Vitruvian Man' provides a fitting illustration for the way in which 'the human' comes to be defined in Western discourse. Placed in a circle, arms and legs outstretched, Da Vinci's image captures the Renaissance ideal of humanity. It is not just any old body that is placed at the centre: Da Vinci employs the male body as a mirror for the movements of the cosmos. All is to be understood through 'Man's' values and activities. While this idealized vision of Man is offered as the exemplar of all that is human, the female body is notable by its absence. Man, not Woman, frames the world. Language, similarly, lends itself to a view of the world where 'the human' can be understood without the female. The male generic – 'he', 'him', 'his', 'man', 'mankind' – is habitually used to denote *all* human beings. 'Woman' is an unnecessary extra, consigned to the margins of experience. If Man is equatable with the Human, Woman is subsumed in Man. The assumption that the male 'includes' the female allows attitudes gleaned from male experience of the world to be taken as emblematic of *all* experience: an habitual assumption not without impact on the way in which success and failure are shaped.

Reflection on male psychosexual development and socialization suggests something of the way in which attainment becomes the marker for the successful life. According to psychoanalytic theory, identity is not a given, but something that has to be achieved.[13] Identity is 'psychosexual', and so bodily experience is significant for the development of mental processes. Early on in the development of this approach, Freud stressed the importance of sexual difference for understanding male and female psychic experience.[14] While we might resist the rigid structure this places on understandings of gender (not least in light of the ideas of Judith Butler we have just considered), the physical differences between male and female and, importantly, the way in which social norms and values have been derived from these differences, cannot be so easily ignored.[15] In psychoanalytic theory, it is the way in which these differences are interpreted that shapes and reflects specific social values and attitudes. In particular, it is the relationship to the mother's body that makes the struggle involved in establishing one's identity different for boy and girl. While the girl sees her identity reflected in her similarities with the maternal body, the establishment of male identity depends upon distinguishing the self from the mother. To be male is to 'stand out from' the mother's body.[16] If we accept this framing of maleness as an achievement rather than a given, it is not so surprising to find the institutions established historically by men reflecting (albeit it unconsciously) the belief that success is to be measured in terms of attainment.

To accept this account of male sexual development is not to suggest that the struggle for female identity is any more straightforward. Freud's account of female sexuality, for all the criticisms directed at it,[17] recognizes the complexity of female psychosexual development. Far from being a static representation of what it is to 'become' a woman, Freud eventually settles on a position that sees a girl moving from identification with her mother, to identification with her father, before finding her ultimate resting place with the mother's identity.[18] Yet the role assigned to the mother assumes a different status for men than for women. In the terms of Freud's argument, the girl will – or at least should[19] – come to locate her identity with that of her mother. For the establishment of male identity, an alternative solution is required. The mother must be escaped if the male is to establish his masculine identity. D. H. Lawrence's portrayal of a son's desperate attempts to escape the cloying clutches of his mother's love in *Sons and Lovers* (1913) offers a dramatic account of what is required by male maturation. A relatively short step is needed to arrive at the view that the female represents that which is to be avoided in order to successfully achieve a male identity.

The existentialist philosopher Jean-Paul Sartre may have rejected psychoanalytic theory out-of-hand, but he accepts the idea of identity as a form of achievement.[20] To become a subject, to 'stand out' from the world, requires resisting the pull of the Other who would turn the developing individual into an object that could be controlled. This 'Other' who would trap the individual in the things of this world is illustrated by a variety of examples Sartre derives from the female body. Body parts associated with sexual desire are turned in Sartre's writing into horrible reminders of the mutability of all flesh. He describes the Other as the full breasts of a woman, flattened out when she lies on her back.[21] An innocuous representation, perhaps: not so the images he derives from female genitalia. Now, the oppressive Other is the 'moist and feminine sucking' that 'draws me as the bottom of a precipice might draw me' (Sartre [1943] 1969: 609). The Other is 'the obscenity of the feminine sex … which "gapes open" ' (Sartre [1943] 1969: 613). I am reminded of the horror movie, *Teeth* (2007), where the 'monster' is a woman whose vagina bites off the penis of the man foolish enough to penetrate her. While not equipping his Other with teeth, Sartre describes this feminine threat as 'a sweet, clinging, dependent threat to male freedom' (Collins and Pierce 1980: 117). This feminine Other threatens to subsume the unwary individual in the things of the natural world which must be overcome in order to attain the status of a transcendent.[22]

Success is the achievement of escaping the physical. Failure is to be trapped in the feminine world of material things.

Sartre is French, and so we might excuse his apparent sexism by accepting that he distinguishes the 'feminine' from the 'female'. However, his language betrays him. The examples he uses are derived from the realities of the *female* body: vagina, breasts, bodily secretions. Such is the problematic nature of this connection between Woman and body in Sartre's existentialism that when Simone de Beauvoir shapes her own philosophy, built on his categories, she takes a largely negative stance to motherhood. To be a mother is to lessen the possibility of claiming one's place as an individual 'standing out' from the world.[23] The conclusion to be derived from such comments seems to be that it is better for women to reject maternity in order that they might become fully creative human individuals. (Perhaps I should cite Simone next time someone tells me I can't be a 'proper' woman if I don't have children.)

Of female success

Beauvoir's solution – while offering me a ready retort – isn't, of course, very helpful. It fits all-too-neatly with a common view of female success: give up those qualities identified with the female, and become, as far as possible, the same as the male. When the successful life is modelled in this way, the experiences associated with the female body become forms of failure to be overcome, not just by manly men, but by women too. There may be good reasons for this radical, if unsatisfactory, solution: not least when we consider the history of philosophical suggestions which would demarcate the scope of female success. A remarkable consensus emerges when male philosophers turn their attention to defining Woman.[24] And their vision suggests a distinct form of female success located in a set of physical attributes which are, in reality, doomed to fail.

In the Western tradition, female success is consistently associated with the things of the body: beauty, sexuality, appearance and reproduction. A powerful expression of this idea is found in the writings of Immanuel Kant, Father of the European Enlightenment, whose ideals sit so closely with the neoliberal construction of selfhood: human beings are rational, free and capable of choice. Kant's account of the complementarity of the sexes, written in 1764, endows each sex with a set of essential qualities. These qualities affect the goals set for men and women. Men are to strive for nobility, depth, reflectiveness, learning, profundity and principled action. Women, by way of contrast, are to be beautiful, charming companions.

Male attributes *require* action: they are to be achieved. Female attributes require the woman to do nothing. As Kant sets about defining 'the fairer sex', he starts with those things with which a woman is born: 'Her figure is generally finer [than man's], her features more delicate and gentler' ([1764] 1960: 76). Emanating from such physical charms are a set of values appropriate to this 'breeding' which, presumably, any woman (given the right social conditions) could acquire:

> Her mien [is] more engaging and more expressive of friendliness, pleasantry, and kindness than in the male sex. (Kant [1764] 1960: 76)

From an early age, she takes delight in dressing up, finding pleasure in 'trivialities' that make her happy.[25] The image that springs to mind is that of the doomed French Queen, Marie Antoinette, who in one year had over 150 dresses made for her. Dresses don't make an intellectual, and we might wonder at the attractions such a vain creature would have for the serious, thoughtful man who Kant thinks should accompany her. Helpfully, he addresses this problem, explaining that Woman exudes 'a secret magic' that inclines Man to look favourably upon her ([1764] 1960: 76). Taking such features as a whole, Kant concludes that Woman is known 'by the mark of the beautiful' ([1764] 1960: 76), while the male sex can 'make a claim on the title of the noble sex' ([1764] 1960: 76). His language is revealing. Women bear the physical mark of 'the beautiful', while men must *work* to be called noble.[26] To be a success as a woman is to be passive; to be a success as a male is to be active. To be successful as a woman requires doing nothing; to be successful as a male requires application.

This affects the expectations placed on the sexes as they confront the difficulties of moral decision making. Woman's moral decisions will reflect the sentimental connections she makes with others, for her moral inclinations result from her 'many sympathetic sensations, goodheartedness and compassion' (Kant [1764] 1960: 77). Male morality will be more robust, shaped by knowing where your duties lie and acting accordingly.[27] There is nothing equal, though, about the values ascribed to male and female, for in practice it is the morality which accords with duty (and which Kant identifies with the male) that expresses the highest form of moral action.[28] If moral action is based on feeling, it is quite possible that there will be circumstances in which you fail to feel sympathy for the other person, and as a result fail to act morally.[29] I can relate to this. Walking through Oxford late at night, I probably feel less inclined to help someone begging than I might be at other times of the day. Feeling isn't always a good way of shaping our moral commitments.

For now, though, the important thing to consider is what all this means for women and how we are supposed to shape our lives. Kant's duty-based morality is arrived at through using the intellect, not through extending your feelings, and this means that men, not women, are those most capable of the serious reflection necessary for arriving at the right moral positions. Here's Kant's conclusion:

> Deep meditation, and a long-sustained reflection are noble but difficult, *and do not well befit a person in whom unconstrained charms should show nothing else than a beautiful nature.* (Kant [1764] 1960: 78; my emphasis)

The differences between the sexes lead to different moralities, but we should be in no doubt as to which morality is preferable:

> The virtue of a woman is a *beautiful virtue*. That of the male sex
> should be a *noble virtue*. Women will avoid the wicked not because
> it is unright, but because it is ugly. (Kant 1764: 81; his emphasis)

Male morality is deep, female morality based on the surface of
appearances. What does it mean to be a female success? It is
not the same as male success. Female success is denoted by the
achievements of the body: desirability, sexuality, appearance and style.
These are the very things that the successful male should avoid, or at
least treat lightly. If 'the principal object is that man should become
more perfect as a man', Kant's goal for woman is different, for she is to
become 'more perfect … as a wife' (Kant [1764] 1960: 95). A woman
who attempts to attain the things that denote male success (intellect
and independently cultivating the life of the mind[30]) runs the risk not just
of failure, but of failure *as a woman*. And Kant has damning words for
the women of his day who have the audacity to attempt such things:

> A woman who has her head full of Greek, like Madame Dacier, or carries
> on fundamental controversies about mechanics, like the Marquise de
> Châtelet, might as well even have a beard. ([1764] 1960: 78)

A woman's ability to embody the beautiful is threatened if she dares
to think: 'Her philosophy is not to reason, but to sense' (Kant [1764]
1960: 79). Female success is defined by the extent to which a woman
aligns herself with the natural forces played out on her body: a
process which suggests something of the luck that attends to being
a successful woman in the terms which Kant sets out. But it also
does more than that. It opens up a kind of failure that is inevitable,
regardless of how beautiful or charming a woman is.

> *A woman's body and the virtues derived from it are subject to the
> ravages of time which ensure that even female success will turn to
> failure.*

Arthur Schopenhauer is more explicit about woman's failure than is Kant, who – rather chivalrously, perhaps – avoids this obvious conclusion. Schopenhauer's jaundiced eye is on motherhood, which, far from being a form of success, he sees as merely revealing the weakness of women. (If he weren't long dead, I might ask him to come with me to the next dinner party.) Where Kant is sentimental, Schopenhauer is ruthless. Here is his description of motherhood:

> She expiates the guilt of life not through activity but through suffering, through the pains of childbirth, caring for the child and subjection to the man. (Schopenhauer [1851] 1970: 80)

Far from being a success, motherhood keeps women as infants.[31] Their very childishness makes them fit only for the repetitive (and boring) task of playing with children. Schopenhauer is convinced that no man worth the name would be capable of bringing up children:

> One has only to watch a girl playing with a child, dancing and singing with it the whole day, and then ask oneself what, with the best will in the world, a man could do in her place. (Schopenhauer [1851] 1970: 81)

Now, we might dismiss these reflections as mere misogyny. The form Schopenhauer's attack takes, however, reveals a disquieting reality. Even when deemed most successful in the realm of 'women's work', female success is ultimately viewed as a form of failure *even by those men who construct it in this way*. And Schopenhauer is highly effective at pointing out the transience of the things deemed necessary for the successful female life. Think what happens to physical beauty and the ability to have children:

> Nature has acted with its usual economy. For just as the female ant loses its wings after mating, since they are then superfluous, indeed harmful to the business of raising the family, so the woman

usually loses her beauty after one or two childbeds, and probably for the same reason. (Schopenhauer [1851] 1970: 81)

Schopenhauer makes explicit what Kant's romantic vision of the female ignores. Female virtues are transient, emerging from processes that render beauty and human relationships fragile and subject to loss.

The peculiarly female form of success, located in physical beauty and the processes of reproduction, is doomed to failure. When the philosopher sets about 'his' quest for that which is eternal, it is not surprising to find him rejecting the female and the attributes associated with her. So Plato shapes the philosopher as one who must resist physical procreation in order to produce 'children of the mind'.[32] The offspring women produce from their bodies are doomed to die. Only ideas – these 'children of the mind' – are truly eternal, truly capable of transcending mutable, fallible human flesh. Hence the person who is truly wise pursues only that which is eternal, and this necessitates putting aside the things which are merely transient.

This might make me, a childless woman, feel better. It doesn't. Rejecting procreation because it leads only to death reflects Plato's broader disregard for the physical world itself.[33] It also acts as a way of belittling the status of women. Despite arguing in the *Republic* Book V that men *and* women are capable of ruling (or at least they would be in his idealized society), a less optimistic destiny is given to Woman in Plato's discussion of love in his *Symposium.* Here, love of women is described as something base. Such a love can only lead to that which is mortal; its ultimate goal is, after all, the production of children who are themselves destined to die. It is a love which cannot lead to the immortal values the philosopher seeks. These values can only be attained through the companionship of another male.[34] Explicitly connected with the world of reproduction, the female body comes to be identified with mutability. Her body becomes a receptacle for forms of failure which are to be avoided. It cannot be allowed to stand as a model for the experiences which accompany *all* human lives, not just women's. The failure of Woman, lived out in her flesh, meets the losses of embodied existence which are common to all experience. Yet rather than accept that loss is a fundamental part of *all* human experience, the female body is connected *exclusively* with the processes of change and, ultimately, decay.

Even the successful female, it transpires, is a failure.

The transience of the qualities viewed as fundamental to female success reflect a deep vein of misogyny within the Western tradition, for, as Schopenhauer's vitriolic words suggest, Woman *herself* is an *ontological* failure: that is to say, she is a failure in her very being. It is not so much that a woman might fail to achieve in the same way as her male counterparts. Nor is it that any particular woman might not be able to embody the values of beauty and fertility ascribed to her by philosophers like Kant. Even if she is 'successful' on the terms they set, she is still doomed to be a failure *because of the specific nature of female success*.

Plato's pupil, Aristotle, makes this clear as he attempts to determine the processes of reproduction. According to his theory, the male is the sole source of life. The female 'merely' provides the passive matter which the male principle shapes.[35] So far, so passive. But Aristotle goes further. Because she lacks this active principle, Woman is 'as it were, a mutilated male'.[36] Her very passivity reveals her failure: and it is a failure grounded in a fundamental lack of agency. When the medieval theologian Thomas Aquinas applies Aristotle to his theology, this failure is given a further (divine) twist. According to Aquinas, woman is a 'misbegotten male' who can only find wholeness through relationship with the man from whom she was made.[37] 'Man' is created in God's image. And before we conclude that he must be using 'Man' in an inclusive way which describes both men *and* women, note how he employs the image of how Woman was made. Just as Eve was made from Adam's rib in the creation story of Genesis 3, so *all* women are created in *Man's* image. Man is closer to God than Woman, for only Man is made in God's image.[38] For Augustine, whose ideas also influenced Aquinas, it is in the mind that the image of God is to be found.[39] Man is defined by godly reason, Woman by her participation in the body of Man.[40] To be Woman is to lack something that only the male can provide.

We might be unimpressed by this sojourn in the world of philosophy. Who cares what a bunch of philosophers from the dim and distant past think? It is not just philosophers who open up this world of female failure. Literary sources also expose the precarious nature of female success. In Tennessee Williams's *A Streetcar Named Desire*, the ageing Southern Belle Blanche Dubois resorts to hiding in dimly lit rooms in order to persuade her lover that she is still young and beautiful. This strategy comes to a brutal end when he turns on the light in order to 'look at you good and plain' (Williams [1947] 1962: 203). If light destroys the illusion of Blanche's beauty, in Emile Zola's *Nana* it is small pox that destroys his heroine's good looks. Zola makes plain just how fragile a thing female beauty is. The novel opens with Nana the theatrical sensation. She has no talent to speak of, cannot sing, nor can she deport herself on stage. But she is so beautiful that she is described as 'Venus rising from the waves' (Zola [1880] 1972: 44), a goddess who captivates her audience. The end of the novel cruelly turns this image on its head. 'What lay on the pillow was a charnel-house, a heap of pus and blood, a shovelful of putrid flesh … Venus was decomposing' ([1880] 1972: 470).

Female success is precarious, and inevitably turns to failure. Woman's very flesh means she can never succeed, because she is too closely connected to the impermanent material of the natural world. When Aristotle and Aquinas claim this failure to be of her very being, they suggest that the male is somehow set apart from the corruption inherent in the physical realm. Human frailty is located in *female* flesh, and so it becomes possible to see the male as standing apart from the facts of mortality and the limitations of being human.[41] Making the male the embodiment of nobility, rationality, freedom and action allows scant regard to be paid to the fact that all human pride and achievement ultimately end up in the grave. By using the female body as a receptacle for the limitations of being physical, the male comes to enact an illusion of control over the limitations of loss and death.

Failure, loss and the ageing female body

And yet ...

There is no escaping the relentless march of Time. Women may age, but so too, of course, do men. A woman's struggle with ageing is, however, never simply a matter of personal concern. Her changing body is greeted with levels of disgust, fear and repulsion rarely directed at the ageing male body. We need only consider the lack of male equivalents for terms like 'crone' or 'hag', 'old bag' or 'battle axe', to realize that the ageing male is not subject to the same criticism as the ageing female.

In the consumerism that drives neoliberal economics, the struggle with ageing takes on a particular shape. To create a market, it makes sense to identify an anxiety in your chosen client group, creating and marketing a product which provides a solution for that anxiety. The cosmetics industry is extremely successful at nurturing women's fears of ageing. In 2015 alone, the US beauty and personal care business had a market value of $80 billion.[42] For a working world that emphasizes the importance of appearance and style, it makes sense for the successful entrepreneur of the self – be they female, or, indeed, male – to pay attention to how they look. Yet as Barbara Walker commented in the mid-1980s, the older man is not subject to the same pressures as the older woman:

Women are socially and professionally handicapped by wrinkles and grey hair in a way that men are not. (Walker 1985: 31)

It is tempting to consign Walker's comments to the dustbin of history: after all, they come from the 1980s. Surely we have moved beyond this kind of crude sexism? In practice, it is far from the case that the working world is less sexist than it was at the time when Walker was writing these words.[43] Indeed, her comments have a particular resonance for those working in that most visual of domains, the world of broadcasting. In 2011, the presenter of the BBC's *Countryfile* programme, Miriam O'Reilly, took her employer to an employment tribunal after she was one of four female presenters – all in their 40s or 50s – dropped from the programme. While her case was upheld on the grounds of age discrimination, the tribunal rejected O'Reilly's claim that she had been the victim of sex discrimination. Yet the numbers of older women broadcasters in the UK would seem to speak for themselves. In a report commissioned by Labour MP Harriet Harman in 2013, 5 per cent of TV presenters were found to be women over the age of 50, while older men were found to outnumber older women by four to one.

This isn't to say that attempts aren't being made to ensure that men feel just as insecure about their appearance in order to expand the market in cosmetic solutions to ageing. A recent advert in the United States had a daughter encouraging her father to use a hair colourant as he prepared for a job interview, so that he might look more youthful, and thus 'more energetic'. While the pressure is on for men, women are far more likely to seek cosmetic solutions to the signs of ageing. A survey by the British Association of Aesthetic Plastic Surgeons found 91 per cent of cosmetic surgery patients in 2007 were women;[44] a figure that remains remarkably static, and which was repeated in the Association's survey of 2015.

Cosmetic solutions hold out the promise of eternal youth: a promise that is gratefully grasped by many. Yet in practice, potions and procedures cannot forever hold back the passage of time. As Jacqueline Zita notes, the failure of these solutions contributes to the experience that to be female is to fail: 'Because these attempted restorations of youth and beauty ultimately fail, it is women in the end who fail, and fall' (Zita 1993: 105). The distinctive form of female success outlined by the philosophers, playwrights and novelists we have considered depends on youth. Physical beauty is equated with it, the ability to reproduce depends on it. And just as cosmetic procedures cannot succeed in holding back the years, so medical solutions offered to women attempting to conceive in later life are also unlikely to succeed.[45]

When female success is defined through looks and motherhood, it is not surprising that ageing should pose a problem for women that goes beyond its construction as a marker of mortality. The introduction to a volume on women and ageing in film from the 1980s still resonates, some thirty years on:

> A woman's greatest social prestige has long been associated with youth, an idealized attractiveness, and reproductive abilities; society offers few comforts or securities to the older woman who, through an inalterable physical process, no longer fits the ideal. (Stoddard 1983: 5)

Representations of the ageing female body reveal more, however, than a simple marginalizing of the older woman. Advertisers routinely exclude older women from their campaigns. The adverts run by Dove Skincare and Marks & Spencers stand out as exceptions that prove the rule, consistently including – and celebrating – women aged 50 and above. More often, the exclusion of women from film and broadcast media is accompanied by disgust if an older woman attempts to conform to the youthful ideal by which all women are judged, and then is found wanting.

The rise of social media has amplified this disgust. In 2014, a 'Twitter storm' accompanied suggestions that the actor Renee Zellweger had had plastic surgery.[46] 'Robert$chultz' (@Bosssexy711) gives a flavour of this with a tweet posted on 17 January 2015: 'Watching Renee Zellweger age is like watching the Titanic hit the iceberg in really slow motion.' In 2016, photos of Zellweger, taken in 'full sunlight', and looking 'like what you would expect a woman in her late 40s to look like'[47], were published, sparking further comments on her 'shocking' appearance. The suggestion that Zellweger avoid bright sunlight implies that all women over 40 should adopt Blanche Dubois's strategy, and dim the lights.[48]

The disgust directed at the ageing woman tells us about more than the number of mean-spirited people inhabiting the Twittersphere. According to psychoanalyst and philosopher Julia Kristeva, disgust accompanies the presence of the abject. The abject is that which is perceived to be a threat to the integrity of the subject. It is that which has to be excluded from the subject, for it 'draws me toward the place where meaning collapses' (Kristeva 1982: 2). It suggests the failure of human attempts to stand out from the physical world, to escape the pull of the finite. Kristeva's examples of the abject include those things which remind us most of our own mutable physicality: blood, the open wound, shit.[49] These things we would rather hide are connected to that which lies behind their offensive qualities: Death, that ever-present reality which has the power to break in and destroy the comfort of both the world of language and human action.[50]

The abject must be excluded if the individual is to preserve a sense of their own integrity. In the ageing female body we get a taste of how this process works. Ageing comes to all of us; it confronts all of us – male and female – with the imminence of death. How to resist? One method: locate ageing and the terror we feel in the bodies of older women. This method is by no means new; it is simply made more explicit by social media and broadcast technologies. To get a sense of the role women play in embodying the abject requires accessing the things ordinarily cast out and excluded from examination. Visual portrayals are particularly helpful for getting at that which is routinely ignored.[51]

Two paintings by the Flemish artist Quentin Massys (1466–1530) suggest something of the old woman cast as abject. In the *Ugly Duchess* (1513), Massys portrays an elderly woman in a low cut dress, more like an ape than a human being. Her skin is wrinkled, her ears and nose extended by age. Her lips curl over toothless gums in a leering smile, while her hair (what we can see of it) is thinning. If we are not revolted enough by this hideous depiction of a coy old woman, Massys repeats this theme in his *Temptation of St Anthony* (*c.* 1520–4; painted with Joachim Patinir). Here, the contrast between the ugliness of the old woman and the beauty of the young woman is made explicit. As a trio of lovely maids tempt the saint with forbidden pleasures of succulent, youthful flesh, a laughing old hag hovers in the background, opening her neckline to reveal one of her breasts which is weathered and wrinkled and sprouting tufts of thick hair.

In making his old women ape the actions and appearance of desirable young women, Massys draws upon a tradition of disgust with women who hide 'their true appearance' through the application of creams and potions.[52] But this is also an image which reveals *all* women, regardless of age, to be connected to the mutable and changeable processes of the natural world. The youthful maiden will one day be the aged crone. This is the terror that lies behind the disgust with the aged female body: *but it is about more than just the female body.* It is about the inevitable passing of Time that affects every single one of us.

In Massys' *Temptation of St Anthony*, the fear of sex leading the saint into sin meets something else in the form of the aged woman. Beneath the paint of the sensual young woman – and beneath that of the dissembling older woman – is a skull. In the bone lying beneath desirable (and not-so-desirable) flesh, we find the source of the anxieties which accompany us through life. Contrary to the myths of immortality with which we like to endow our lives and our accomplishments, we are fragile creatures whose very existence is dependent on the processes of a world defined by change and decay. In the ageing body we come face-to-face with this reality, and with the inevitability of death. In the fear of the old woman, existential anxieties *affecting us all* take on a more manageable shape: they become *her* problem, not ours.

While there are many examples in Western art of the ageing male body, it is seldom treated with the same level of disgust as that visited on the older woman.[53] Representations of elderly males are more often used to elicit sympathy than contempt. In Goya's *Two Old Men Eating* (1820–3), one of the men is so cadaverous as to make one wonder if he is Death Itself, while the other, who appears to have no teeth, is trying to eat. This is a rather pitiful image, and it may make us fear for our own aged future. It does this, however, with pathos and compassion. We, too, will need the care of others. Mariano Fortuny's *Elderly Nude in the Sun* (1871) is rather more upbeat, depicting an old man smiling contentedly as he warms his naked body in the sun; a hopeful view of what the latter part of life might be like.

That the ageing *female* body is treated with disgust, fear and repulsion should give us pause. After all, *all* age and die, regardless of gender, wealth or status. Germaine Greer is onto something when she claims that Western society is 'anophobic', a term she uses to describe the irrational fear of old women.[54] There is something about women and age that stands apart from more general discussions of 'human beings' and ageing. This reflects, I suspect, the regular connection made between women and the natural world.[55] The female body, its changes and cycles, has been routinely connected to the processes of sex and birth in a way in which the male body has not. Historically, women have been valued for their youth and fertility. When they cease to embody these virtues, there is no place for them. If women over the age of 40 have a superpower, it is invisibility (try ordering a drink at a bar).[56] No wonder women fear 'the Coming of Age'.[57]

Loss accompanies ageing, and we should not deny that. For women, menopause can be a difficult and painful time. It marks the end of the possibility of child-bearing, and for those of us who have not had children and who wanted them, this can feel like another failure, perhaps even a bereavement. These complex feelings meet a medical profession that constructs menopause principally as a disease, a dysfunction, a loss of health. It is possible to think differently about it. It can be something that is embraced, rather than feared. With the sadness that comes from recognizing that something is no longer possible can come something else; perhaps not quite the 'positive life transition' that some feminists would suggest,[58] but something that holds out the possibilities of a new stage of life. As a young woman, I found the idea of the end of menstruation deeply disturbing. Hot flushes, mood swings, the end of fertility, the coming of age. All seemed terrifying, and I preferred not to think about their inevitability. Now the menopause is past, the sadness of not having children sits alongside a feeling of liberation. No longer do I have to spend money on tampons and pads. No longer do I have to try to remember when my period is due. The hot flushes I feared, when they came, felt like a burning away of that which was extraneous to my life. They left me with Bev as she *really* is, rather than Bev as she is viewed by others.

Losses of this kind act as provocations for new ways of constructing a meaningful life. Feminist philosopher Pamela Sue Anderson suggests something of this in her work on vulnerability. When we experience loss, 'we glimpse … the potential in vulnerability for transformation' (Anderson 2017: 10). There is pain and there is hope, and these feelings can sit side-by-side. We can think differently.[59] The question is whether we are able to move beyond fear of such changes, and think again about where, precisely, the meaning of our transient lives should be located.

Success, failure and the transience of life

Tracing the gendering of success and failure should not lead to the conclusion that the habitual connection made between women and the physical world renders women's priorities essentially different to those of men.[60] My concern in investigating the use to which women's bodies have been put is to expose the fears surrounding the mutable physical body. Connecting women with the supposed 'failures' of the body reveals more than just the limitations of an account of the meaningful life based around attainment and achievement. More importantly, it reveals how the ordinary losses that come with being mutable human animals have become read as forms of failure. When being subject to loss is constructed as failure, the natural processes of the physical world become problems to evade. Of course, the reality is that these processes *cannot* be avoided: they are the necessary features of a physical universe; they provide the context in which we must live out our lives. Ageing, decay and death are not features of life any of us can avoid; rather they bear witness to the human condition. Instead of framing this reality through the lens of failure, we would be better advised to see these physical processes as providing the necessary limits within which the human task of creating meaning is to be located.

Beauvoir's approach to old age in her later philosophy suggests the problem of denying limits in order to emphasize human striving.[61] Like Sartre, she locates the creation of human individuality in a double movement. To become an individual requires being orientated to the future, *and* committed to meaningful projects. 'The coming of age' challenges the extent to which this approach can ever succeed. For the elderly, the future *is* limited; death is a present reality, rather than an abstract boundary framing the context for choice and decision-making.[62]

> What old age reveals starkly is 'the failure of all success.' (Beauvoir [1970] 1996: 368)

The actor, singer and icon Marlene Dietrich would have understood Beauvoir's conclusion. In her forties, her faltering acting career was invigorated when she recreated herself as a singer, performing for Allied troops. Even as she revels in this new success, she fears it will not last:

> I'm afraid, period. A funny feeling. Fear of failing. Fear of having to give up, of being unable to endure this way of living. And everybody will say, with a smile, 'Of course, of course, that was a silly idea.' I can't confide my fear to anyone. (Wieland 2015: 374)

There is an anxious anticipation of failure that haunts even the most successful, precisely because success is never final in a world of chance and change. Viewed from the perspective of old age, the anxiety that one's achievements will not last seems far from ridiculous.

Now for Beauvoir, recognizing the inevitable end of the achievements on which success depends is not particularly problematic. With Sartre, she accepts all life's projects to be rendered ultimately absurd by death. This rather pessimistic conclusion raises the question of whether there could be an understanding of life that does not arrive at the conclusion that *all* life is meaningless if one's achievements cannot be secured in any lasting way. Is there a different way of understanding the place of loss – and failure – in life?

Beauvoir alludes to just such a possibility in the concluding remarks to her book on old age. Having noted the phenomenon of elderly politicians who cannot accept that their time is over – often with lamentable results – she comments that 'if old age is not to be an absurd parody of our former life' ([1970] 1996: 540), there is but one solution:

> In old age we should wish still to have passions strong enough to prevent us turning in upon ourselves. One's life has value so long as one attributes *value to the life of others, by means of love, friendship, indignation, compassion.* (Beauvoir [1970] 1996: 540–1; my emphasis)

Rather than emphasize the self and its projects, a subtle shift takes place. Now it is about locating one's life alongside others: in love, relationship and political action. Reflection on ageing leads her to an understanding of life where projects still have their place, but where they are located more explicitly in the context of life with others.[63]

Beauvoir's words urge us to think again as to whether the categories of 'success' and 'failure' are the right ways of judging a meaningful life. Rather than 'standing out from the world' through identification with our projects, Beauvoir directs us to that which *grounds* us in the world, drawing attention to the relationships that form our sense of who we are. Far from the world being a problem for our identity, the world which surrounds us becomes the realm in which we discover the things that this world enables; and the four qualities Beauvoir suggests – love, friendship, indignation and compassion – are all linked to our relationships with others. This grounded way of thinking affects the perspective taken on the things that cannot be controlled. Conflating loss with failure might hold out the illusion of control over the things that cannot be controlled: ageing, decay and death. But by making ageing a problem primarily for women, a proper engagement with loss and death is avoided. Excluding the ageing female body makes possible the denial of death, but at a price.

Loss and failure are not the same.

The notion of failure reflects a sense of responsibility for an outcome that could have been avoided. Loss, on the other hand, *cannot* be avoided, regardless of how careful we are, for its experience reflects the very nature of life. If I think of my childlessness, this is not a form of failure, even if, at times, I feel it as such. I am, rather, living with loss. That is painful, at times difficult. But accompanying that feeling of emptiness is something else: something that makes me want to explore more deeply my place in a world which is not subject to human control; where the very processes that make it so beautiful are mysterious, beyond the human, and which therefore hold out a rather different way of thinking about the meaning of life than one which would locate it in a set of goals to be achieved or things to be accumulated.

When women are blamed for failing to consistently embody a desirability based upon physical attributes, we get a glimpse of the way in which failure and loss become intertwined. And this muddling of the two suggests something more. When failure and loss are connected in the bodies of women a strategy is offered for controlling the reality of transient life.

The ageing woman becomes the problem, not age itself.

Tempting as this suggestion might be, it is, of course, impossible to follow through, for the fact is that in the midst of life we are *all* in death. No amount of cosmetic surgery will lessen that reality. No number of nubile young wives can hold that reality at bay forever. If the projection of ageing onto Woman cannot succeed at eradicating death, looking at ageing and death honestly and without fear must become central for thinking again about what it means to live well. When we hide from the ravages of Time, or project its effects onto others in order to escape the fears of our own mortality, we lose the ability to think seriously about what it means to be human in a world of chance and change. We avoid grappling with the existential anxiety which lies beneath the fears that hamper our ability to live well.

If we refuse to run from the things that frighten us, we create the space for thinking differently about the meaning of our lives. Recognizing the reality of transience and dependence makes possible renewed engagement with the question of what it is to be human. Fixating on the striving, independent and resilient individual of neoliberalism does not make for an easy accommodation with such reflections. Paying attention to the experiences of illness and dying opens up better ways of living: as we shall see in the next chapter.

3

DEATH AND SICKNESS, LOSS AND FAILURE

Joan Didion begins her memoir on the sudden death of her husband, John, with three chilling sentences:

> Life changes fast. Life changes in an instant. You sit down to dinner and life as you know it ends. (Didion 2006: 3)

Eating dinner together, he collapses, mid-sentence. Her life is changed in that moment forever. Didion offers a meticulous dissection of her loss, shaped by what she calls her 'year of magical thinking'. This phrase describes her attempts to keep her dead husband in the land of the living. These are not occult or supernatural but painfully ordinary and natural. She refuses requests to give his clothes away, or to allow his body to be used for organ transplants. Her reasoning makes perfect sense: 'How could he come back if they took his organs, how could he come back if he has no shoes?' (2006: 41). It is a distressing read on the most devastating of experiences: the loss of a loved one to the clutches of death.

It is scarcely something new for death to confront us as something overwhelming, something to be feared, something best denied if we are not to succumb to despair. These fears take on a distinctive shape when subjected to contemporary neoliberal ideals. Viewed through a narrative emphasizing progress, achievement and control, death emerges, not as an inevitable part of human experience, but as something revealing the failure of the individual. If we are responsible for our lives, the story goes, so we must be responsible for our deaths.

The shaping of death as a kind of failure reflects, in part, the continued progress of medical science. As longevity increases at a startling rate, it is easy to conclude that death can be evaded forever. This is, like so much of the neoliberal construal of life, an illusion. If we pay close attention to the stories of the sick and the dying, the lost and the losing, they reveal what the entrepreneurial self is not well-positioned to accept: that life is precarious and that there are limits to human achievement. In the presence of sickness and death, the human individual emerges, not as the self-sufficient giant of neoliberal myth, but as a mutable being dependent upon a fragile and vulnerable body.

The problem of death

That death poses problems for the neoliberal construction of the self is not to deny that it has always challenged human grandiosity.[1] We humans are not as special as we might like to think. There is something horrifying about the idea that one day we will not be, that the role we play in life – our thoughts, our connections, our very place in the world – will come to an end. Not surprisingly, human beings have always sought ways to live with this knowledge.

For the Ancient School of Epicurus, the best way of addressing the fear of death was to cultivate practices which denied death its power. Here's an example of the kind of thought exercise Epicurus' ideas prompted in his followers:

> There was a time before we were born when we did not exist;
>> There will be a time, after our death, when we will not be.
>> We don't fear the former state; so why should we fear the latter?[2]

This is a clear and simple mantra to be repeated in order to shape one's attitude to death. Whether it actually works at stilling the troubled mind is a moot point. I fear death, after all, because its presence looms in my *future*; I don't fear the time *before* my birth when I was not because it is something in the past. At the same time, this Epicurean argument feels all-too-cool and detached. There is no engagement with the realities that accompany death and dying. There is no sense, in its neat framing, of the indignities which attend to ageing and decline. When people say they are afraid of dying, that fear often comes down to its *processes* not the mere fact of death itself. What causes anxiety is the fear of losing our capacities; the fear of the loss of our sense of self.

Such fears make Midas Dekkers's attempt to celebrate decay not altogether convincing. In a beautifully presented collection of words and pictures, Dekkers connects the picturesque deterioration of old buildings with the decay to which the human body is subject. Decay adds to life, he claims, it does not diminish it. This rather neat conclusion obscures the horror that the same processes which cover old ruins with ivy will one day turn ourselves and those we love into objects with the potential to disgust.[3] No amount of perkily upbeat text can deny the disturbing quality of the decaying corpse.

The Greek playwright Euripides gets at the horror of decay far more effectively in his depiction of the death of Glauce. The hero Jason has rejected his old love, the sorceress Medea, in order to marry this young and beautiful princess. The furious Medea is bent on revenge and sends Glauce a poisoned coronet and gown. The unfortunate girl puts these on and is consumed by flames which melt her flesh, turning her into 'a ghastly sight' (Euripides 1963: 54). Her father, King Creon, beside himself with despair, runs to help her and is himself caught up in the sticky mess of dissolving flesh that his daughter has become. As his own flesh becomes combined with hers, he is slowly pulled apart, his courtiers watching in horror as father and daughter become a mass of blood and gore.

Creon's attempt to help his daughter provides Euripides' audience with the kind of horrific image common in his plays. But it is more than an example of body horror, for it suggests an aspect of the fear of death rarely picked up by philosophers. For Creon, the loss of his daughter presents the real horror of death; and he gives up his own life in his attempt to save her. Philosophical discussions group around the fate of the self: is there an aspect of personal identity that could survive *my* death? Where is *my* identity located? These are the questions, rather than the loss of the other, that shape the philosophical problem of death.

We will return to the experience of loss at the end of this chapter, for it challenges any account of death concerned only with personal survival. For now, let us consider the forces that come to shape death as a form of failure, for this reveals the deep roots that support its contemporary shaping and make this connection difficult to shake off.

Death has never just been a problem for philosophers: its reality also forms an important backdrop to religious theorizing. Religious 'solutions' to the problem of death take different forms. They might be framed by faith in the all-powerful God of the great monotheistic traditions, whose God is the only hope for the individual faced with death.[4] Alternatively, in Buddhism the aim is to provide the practitioner with methods for enabling the acknowledgement that all is impermanent, a fact borne witness to in the decay of the body.[5] Death is something natural, something which encourages humility. It reveals the disquieting fact that nothing is capable of lasting forever. Rather than kick against this knowledge, the aim is to recognize the reality of human limits, coming to see death as offering peace from the world of striving.

By way of contrast, other religious thinkers have framed death as something profoundly *un*natural. If death is not natural, we should, indeed, fear it. In Early Christian theological debates, attention was paid to the question of whether death was a natural part of God's creation. The torturous process by which the Church reached its conclusion presents a fascinating insight into the refusal to accept human beings as dependent on natural processes. This refusal finds contemporary resonance in the framing of death as a form of failure. For the theologians Pelagius (390–418) and Julian of Eclanum (386–455), death was very much a natural part of life.[6] Pelagius' position was influenced by his reading of Greek scientific and philosophical texts. As a result, his position sits rather comfortably with the cultural assumptions of a scientific age: we might not like it, but science reveals death to be a necessary part of life in a physical universe.

The opposing view was voiced by our old friend Augustine of Hippo (354–430). Augustine rejected the claims of Pelagius and Julian that death was natural, intended by God to be part of his creation from the very beginning. Death, storms Augustine, is an aberration that human beings brought upon themselves.[7] The first humans, Adam and Eve, failed to obey God's command not to eat from the Tree of the Knowledge of Good and Evil and so brought down on their heads – and those of their descendants – the full weight of God's curse. This curse is felt in the necessity to work hard, and in the suffering women go through in order to give birth. Isn't this suffering evidence enough that Nature is *diseased*, Augustine asks? Women suffer 'tortures inflicted by doctors, or the shock and loss of giving birth to an infant stillborn or moribund',[8] and this is because God cursed Eve for her wrongdoing. Had Adam and Eve *not* sinned in Eden, there would be no suffering and no death. As it is, 'the wages of sin is death' (Romans 6.23). Death, then, is something *un*natural, something that has come about as a direct result of human failure; in this case, from the failure to obey God's command.

It might surprise us to learn that Augustine's anti-natural line became the Church's accepted position. Pelagius and Julian – whose ideas may appear far more sensible to our modern eyes – were condemned as heretics. But rather than be surprised at this outcome, we should look a little more closely at how the account of death as 'unnatural' sits with our own twenty-first-century attitudes. Augustine's claims may seem 'antinatural and even preposterous' (Pagels 1988: xxvii); yet they fit rather neatly with the attempt to relate all things to the desires of the individual. If the individual, their needs and wants, their hopes and achievements, is placed centre-stage, it is difficult *not* to see death as anything other than obscene, for it reveals the insignificance of that individual when viewed from the perspective of cosmic forces over which they have little or no control.

Using the story of Adam and Eve to come to a conclusion about the human condition may well strike us as an outdated and ridiculous way of proceeding. Since the Enlightenment, it is the scientific paradigm that has increasingly come to shape our view of the world. Faced with death, science offers two – somewhat conflicting – ways forward. On the one hand, scientific method discloses a world 'in which human beings [are] no different from other animals in facing final oblivion when they died' (Gray 2011: 1). On the other, the techniques of science hold out a rather different possibility. Unlike other animals, there are ways in which human beings might evade – even overcome – death. The self-confident individual shaped by the Enlightenment becomes the individual who *expects* the powers of science to provide a bulwark in the face of death. Thus armed, we come to hope that death can be taken on and defeated.

In practice, however, death cannot so easily be eradicated. Death plays a necessary role in ensuring the life of the planet by removing the old and decaying, thus allowing for the growth of what is new and fresh. *Death is a part of life.* What happens when we find ourselves confronted with limits that no amount of activity can overcome? What happens when, returning to Beauvoir's telling comment from the previous chapter, we are confronted with that which ensures 'the failure of all success'?

The neoliberal shaping of death

The sociologist Anthony Giddens captures something of the challenge of death for the striving individual of neoliberalism. Giddens's work provided the intellectual groundwork for the 'Third Way' political project adopted by the UK's Labour Party in the 1990s. Under the leadership of Tony Blair, this democratic socialist party aligned its policies with neoliberal economics; a move which constituted a radical break from the interventionist economics of the old Left, and which many believed paved the way for Labour's electoral success after eighteen frustrating years in opposition. According to Giddens, death acts as 'a point zero' for human action:

> It is nothing more or less than the moment at which human control over human existence finds an outer limit. (Giddens 1991: 162)

To accept that there are limits to human endeavour, to grapple with the reality of 'being-towards-death',[9] does not sit easily with the relentless optimism of neoliberal aspiration. Acknowledge the skeleton beneath the skin and the claim that social and political policy should be shaped around belief in the responsible individual 'in control' of their destiny seems an odd conclusion to draw. Constructing the meaning of your life around the twin poles of success and failure seems to miss something. Yet the difficulty of moving away from neoliberal ideology stems in part from the way it reflects how *we like to think* about our lives. It 'appeals to our intuitions and instincts, our values and desires, as well as the possibilities inherent in the social world we inhabit' (Harvey 2005: 5). We *like* to think of ourselves as responsible and free.

Despite Giddens's recognition of the limits death provides, it is the idea of control that shapes neoliberal strategies for dealing with mortality. Rather than reflect on the necessary limits of human action, death is framed as something that *should* be amenable to human control. Just as you are responsible for your life, so you are responsible for your death. It is a short step from advocating control to blaming those who are dying for doing something wrong that has brought them to this pass.

How does this transformation happen? How does death go from being an inescapable reality to being something that *you* should be able to control through *your* actions? The contemporary iteration of what it is to be healthy goes someway to help explain this shift. Carl Cederström and Andre Spicer claim that contemporary society is in the grip of 'the wellness syndrome', where maintaining a healthy population has shifted from being an area for public policymakers into being 'a moral demand' (2015: 3) every individual must take on board.

It is not simply that health is a good thing to have in order to enjoy one's life with sufficient energy and vigour. Rather, your health has become a touchstone for assessing your morality.

This vision of health is shaped by the model of the entrepreneurial individual. When identity is shaped by work, the person who is too ill to work becomes a *moral* rather than a social problem. What do you do with the sick, the ill, the unhealthy, the dying? The healthy body is the productive body,[10] and those who, for whatever reason, do not conform to this model – the overweight, smokers, drinkers, the elderly – are placed on the margins or subjected to schemes designed to bring them back into the productive (healthy) mainstream.[11] And note what this means for the understanding of health: ' "To be healthy" means ... to be "employable" ' (Bauman 2000: 77). Those who fail to conform to this demand risk being stigmatized.[12]

A particular idea of the body shapes this approach. Your body is no longer something that is given; now, it is something which you *choose* to shape. Just as you can be a success in shaping this body, so you can be a failure if it does not conform to the expected image. In Chapter Two we saw something of what this meant for being a 'successful woman'. Here, we might think of the treatment meted out to those who are overweight.

Being fat isn't just maligned because of the health problems that can sometimes accompany it. Being fat is treated as a form of personal failure. It is a sign of degeneracy, of lack of control, of your fundamental immorality. I remember someone telling me that they would never employ an overweight person as their body showed them to be 'greedy and lazy'. Such judgements are far from isolated. For countless cooking and dieting shows being overweight is constructed as the result of 'bad choices'. Fat is a sign of irresponsibility.[13] The values by which we live are no longer ideals that transcend the peculiarities of our bodies; now, they are located *in* those bodies. Fat becomes a form of failure.

The desire to blame those deemed 'unhealthy' extends to those suffering from chronic or terminal illness. Reasons are sought to explain a person's brush with mortality. Did you smoke? Drink too much? Fail to exercise? Are you obese? There may be links between lifestyle and some illnesses, but this is by no means always the case. Arthur Frank, a sociologist who is living with cancer, sees in this attempt to assign blame the modern-day equivalent of the attitude expressed by Job's comforters in the Hebrew Scriptures. Job, afflicted by disease and disaster, finds his 'friends' keen to find reasons for his plight that would reveal his responsibility for what is happening to him. Frank suggests a similar desire at work in today's attempts to find reasons for cancer:

> The misfortune of getting cancer frightens people today as much as Job, who represented the complete reversal of fortune, frightened people in biblical times. Like the suddenness of Job's misfortunes, cancer represents how quickly lives can fall apart. We all fear that possibility; we want to be able to believe that we can avoid it, so we, like Job's accusers, blame it on the ill person. (Frank [1991] 2002: 109)

We prefer there to be reasons for an illness like this. We prefer there to be reasons for a sudden death that shakes us to our core. How much more soothing if we can attribute death and dying to the individual's responsibility (or lack of it). Better for cancer to be a marker of the individual's failure than attributable to just plain old bad luck. Better a heart attack to be the result of an overly rich diet than chance. We *want* the sick person to be responsible for their fate, for this is far easier than having to address the possibility that we are *all* prey to forces outside our control.

How difficult it is to accept the limits of our humanity. This is so for the professional physician just as much as it is for those of us who wouldn't know one end of a stethoscope from the other. 'Dying of mortality'[14] is rarely given by doctors as the reason for a person's demise. 'Old age' is no longer viewed by clinicians as a normal part of the life cycle. Instead, it is treated as a disease, that could – or, better, *should* – be capable of cure.[15] Death is reframed as a problem to be solved. Medical training lends itself to this formulation. As surgeon Atul

Gawande notes, doctors are taught to save lives not to accept that there may be times when they will need to 'tend to their demise'. 'I learned a lot of things in medical school', Gawande says, 'but mortality wasn't one of them' (Gawande 2014: 1).

How to come to terms with limits in a culture that has trouble with that very idea? Sharon Kaufman's research on the end of life in American hospitals led her to identify a 'new' problem of death shaped by a confluence of two factors. The first was the aim of medical professionals to prolong life. The second was the desire of families of terminal patients for their loved ones' lives to be extended. This second factor meets with, and entrenches, that first clinical aim. As Kaufman says, 'If you love the person who lies in a hospital bed at the threshold, you want that person's life to be longer' (Kaufman 2005: 18). Who, willingly, would give up the loved one into that undiscovered country from whence no traveller returns? Who would willingly embrace the pain that comes with loss? And make no mistake, the loss of the loved one brings pain. Death is followed by 'the unending absence ... the void', as Joan Didion so powerfully names it (2006: 189).

If doctors are likely to respond to the hopes of families, nurses have a different perspective. Caught up in the day-to-day care of dying patients, nurses are more likely to consider the suffering resulting from well-meant interventions. A nurse with sixteen years experience of intensive care describes the nursing perspective well:

> If it were up to me I would probably change it. I would say, what are the chances of this person living? At what point are we being futile? How many days are we going to pursue this treatment? And if we really did something less elaborate, maybe one out of a hundred would live, but the other ninety-nine would not be tortured. (Kaufman 2005: 42)

How shocking is that final word, 'tortured'. Seeking the continuation of life may not always be the best thing to do. It may add to suffering, rather than diminish it.

The problem Kaufman identifies is complicated further by the neoliberal 'financialization of everything'. It isn't just that institutions approach the dying economically, trying to ensure resources are not wasted or shareholders short-changed; trying to ensure that beds are not 'blocked': though look how this turns the dying into a 'problem' requiring a solution, rather than a person standing at the inevitable end point for all of us.[16] For a system encouraged to think of the Market and money as that which solves all problems, one's financial resources offer the possibility of escaping death entirely. In cryonics, this possibility takes the form of freezing the body immediately after death in the hope that future medical advances will enable the deceased to be returned to life.[17] With cryonic procedures costing anywhere between $80,000 and $200,000, the desire is to extend the advantages of wealth to the most basic fact of our humanity. Not all turn to cryonic procedures: Russian internet millionaire Dmitry Itskov is using part of his fortune to develop technology whereby an individual's mind can be uploaded into a computer.[18]

Before we dismiss such attempts as the actions of eccentric individuals with more money than sense, we should note the role of global corporations in developing this new frontier for scientific research. Internet giant Google has put billions of dollars into its biotech development group, Calico, and its attempt to solve the problem of death.[19] Follow the money and you quickly realize that significant resources are being put to the task of defeating death. This stands to reason. If in life your financial resources dictate the lifestyle you can have and the things you can avoid, why shouldn't you treat death in exactly the same way?

If you are rich enough, even death need not apply.

At the same time, it is possible to identify a rather more subtle shaping of death which reflects neoliberal ideals of the responsible individual. May Sarton's novel, *A Reckoning*, published in 1978, captures the contemporary rendition of what it is to have 'a good death'. Told she has inoperable cancer, Sarton's protagonist Laura describes 'a strange excitement, as though she were more than usually alive, awake, and in command: *I am to have my own death*' ([1978] 1981: 7; my emphasis). Here is a different approach to that of the cryonicist or the computer scientist. It is not about *escaping* death but about *taking charge* of the process of dying.[20] If I have been concerned with creating myself in life, my death, similarly, can become a form of self-expression. This entails more than simply avoiding a hospitalized death, although it is partly about that. Principally it is about finding ways of celebrating individual choice *even in the shadow of death*. Death may bring many things, but it cannot stop you experiencing your own unique way of dying. It is possible to have a 'successful' death.

Taking charge of dying: Studies in the neoliberal way of death

Deaths from cancer provide the most obvious way of thinking about exercising control over the process of your own dying. Not least because such deaths often allow the sufferer and their loved ones time and space to come to terms with the fact that they are dying. That being so, deaths of this kind can be all-too-easily aligned with expectations of death as something which should be taken charge of. This is not without its own pressures on those who are dying; not least because dying in this manner is supposed to allow for the possibility of personal growth.[21] No one is allowed to 'go gentle into that good night'; all are supposed to 'rage against the dying of the light' or, at least, to learn something from it. It becomes difficult to escape the fear of failure even in this arena.

> *Just as I can have a successful death, so I can fail in this last act of my life.*

Two recent autobiographical accounts of dying reflect the extension of neoliberal values – and particularly the ideal of control – to the realm of death. As organized religion plays a less prominent part in contemporary Western societies, the idea that your death is best approached through common rituals and beliefs can seem a rather anachronistic way of dealing with mortality. The individual is encouraged, instead, to look to tales of heroic individuals who have stood up to death, and, if they have not defeated it, have at least found a way of taking charge of their own dying.

The examples which follow show both the extension of the neoliberal ideal of control to the process of dying, as well as its limitations when faced with the final destination of all life. They are particularly interesting as they are written by individuals whose working lives were closely aligned with the Labour Party's 'third way' political project mentioned above. In the memoirs of Philip Gould and Kate Gross, their involvement in this political project takes on a personal dimension as both try to come to terms with the experience of dying.

A key strategic advisor to Tony Blair, Philip Gould was an important figure in the development of the New Labour political project. In 2008, he was diagnosed with cancer of the oesophagus, eventually dying in 2011. His memoir, *When I Die*, was published in 2012 and was something of a media sensation, having three print runs in the first year of its release. In this book, Gould describes his battle with cancer, which, as its subtitle suggests, provided him with a series of 'Lessons from the Death Zone'. Weaving in and out of the account are influential figures from the New Labour project. Blair, not surprisingly, is a key figure, along with his director of communications Alastair Campbell (1997–2003) and former Home Secretary David Blunkett (2001–5).

The opening of Gould's account begins with a visit from Blair, shortly after Gould's diagnosis. Their conversation denotes a shift in their relationship informed by Gould's illness. For the first time they talk about religion, something Blair was famously reticent about doing when in office:[22]

[Blair] believes that these values, and his religious conviction, belong properly to a private realm, not the public world that dominated so much of his life ... But with my cancer we had left the public world and were living completely in the private realm, and his compassion, his religion and his values could in a way be liberated. (2012: 16–17)

Gould accepts that 'all politicians' are forced to divide their public persona from their personal beliefs. In the moment he describes, they are meeting as 'private individuals' (2012: 17), the suggestion being that death belongs to the private and personal realm not to the external world of public politics. We might wonder at the kind of politics which places death on the margins in this way. Would we think differently about the kind of policies and practices best suited to the public realm if we took seriously the possibilities – and, indeed difficulties – that arise from the vulnerability of 'private individuals'? We will return to this question.

Gould spent much of his working life as a political strategist, and so it seems natural for him to approach death through the methods that informed that work:

Everything I thought about the battle with cancer was strategic, as if I was fighting an election campaign. I saw the elimination of the cancer as victory, and the test results as opinion polls. (Gould 2012: 20)

If the elimination of the cancer is 'victory', if the test results highlight whether he is 'winning' the battle, negative results are, conversely, experienced as losing. The question is how to respond to those perceived failures. Gould quickly realizes that to adopt what he calls 'the lizard strategy' – 'hunker down, hide, retreat' (2012: 31) – sent out the wrong signal to his surgeons. It suggested he did not have the strength for the battle ahead, and so he has to adopt a different strategy to show them that he is strong enough to win. He uses the same set of principles that he brought to the political realm to engage with the experience of illness: 'Getting through cancer needs leadership' (2012: 43). Just as when you fight a political campaign, 'you are pretty much on your own' in the battle with cancer (2012: 46).

This comment sounds odd. My experience of running for political office showed me you are never alone when standing for election or when shaping policies. Sure, there might have been the odd evening tramping the streets delivering leaflets or knocking doors on my own, but invariably I was accompanied by colleagues and comrades committed to the same ends. I learnt the power of solidarity through campaigning for political office. Likewise, it is far from obvious that Gould's cancer treatment involves 'being alone'. As his narrative shows, Gould is surrounded by friends and loved ones. He has access to the best health care professionals available. Yet his construction of his illness makes more sense when read through his political commitment to the values of autonomy and choice. He is an individual facing death 'alone'. The greatest challenge he feels he faces emerges when he has dinner with Blair. In response to prompting from the former prime minister, Gould realizes that he needs to find out what 'the purpose' of the cancer is.[23] Far from signalling the end of growth, the cancer is experienced as something which acts as a way of achieving change. Striving for success does not end with the diagnosis of a terminal illness.

Now, there are moments in life, like the one Gould details, when circumstances provide us with a space for pausing and thinking again about the way we are living.[24] Yet whether determining a 'purpose' in such moments is quite the right way of expressing it, I am less sure. To suggest 'purpose' returns us to the centrality of the individual. 'You' are to find a way of learning what this means 'for you'. You are responsible for this outcome, and just as you might succeed in finding this purpose out, so you might also fail. The fear that it might all just be meaningless gets conflated into a fear that *you* might fail in this process of meaning-making.

Interestingly, Gould's story reveals more than the attempt to apply neoliberal principles to the end of life. It also reveals the limitations of this narrative. His journey, it turns out, cannot be reduced to the account of one individual's striving, and his writing reflects this. As his illness progresses, a stronger *communal* narrative emerges. After successful surgery, Gould feels that it is not so much that he is involved in an individual battle, but that he is 'connected to the suffering of others in the world' (2012: 69). His suffering reflects a wider, universal condition. As he realizes he cannot win this battle, his attention shifts towards ways of accepting death. Acceptance accompanies the acknowledgement that what *really* matters is less his individual battle and more his relationships, particularly those with his family (2012: 110). 'I am trying to make sense of the world through emotion, through relationships, through feeling' (2012: 134). He moves from 'being inchoately spiritual to more emphatically religious' (2012: 48). It might be tempting to dismiss this move as the kind of crisis faith that emerges when confronted with one's mortality.[25] But equally it could be seen as an example of the purification which comes with the realization that we are mortal and that our time is limited.

Those things which are really important emerge out of the fog created by the pressures to be a successful individual.

This is not to say that Gould ever gives up the narrative of success entirely. At points where this familiar trope would seem irrelevant he judges his response to the cancer through the language of winning:

I have shown myself that I have the courage to transcend death. Maybe I cannot beat death, but death cannot beat me. (2012: 119)

The worse it becomes, the more he feels he is still left with one last choice:

I can choose – to an extent at least – the kind of death that I want.
I have some freedom, I have some power here. I have the possibility
to shape for myself my own death. (2012: 120)

On his last day of conscious life he is still asking for his laptop.[26] He
dies surrounded by family and friends.

If Gould approaches his death with a studied stoicism, Kate
Gross's account of her own dying expresses an explicit anger. Hers
is an account that reveals the fantasy of the neoliberal self when
forced to confront the reality of death. Gross is the young mother
of twin boys. She has had a glittering career, working for two UK
prime ministers (Tony Blair and Gordon Brown), and at the time
of her diagnosis she is the CEO of a charity working to establish
democracies in Africa. Aged 34, she is diagnosed with colon cancer.
Her memoir, *Late Fragments* (2015), is written with her boys in mind,
and has a subtitle explicitly for them: 'Everything I Want to Tell You
(About This Magnificent Life)'.

Gould pictured cancer as something which confronts the sufferer
with the need to determine its purpose. Gross, rather differently,
acknowledges the limitations of adopting a positive perspective on
this terrible disease. 'Cancer is a pretty terrible kind of gift', she writes.
'It takes and it takes, leaving a trail of destruction in its path' (2015: 4).
She is angry; a response which feels entirely appropriate. Framing
her narrative around the wisdom of the lived-experience she wants
to share with her sons, she notes how 'in a normal world I would
have been granted decades to say all this' (2015: 7). This is where
her narrative hits home. Confronted with death, the unreality of the
language of self-fulfilment is revealed. The neoliberal take on what
is 'normal' is not normal at all. What Gross's experience reveals is
a life which is far more random and uncertain than the predictability
promised if we follow the neoliberal recipe for success. There is no pay
off to be expected from working hard and striving after the glittering
prizes. Gross finds herself in agreement with the boxer Mike Tyson, in
an image that kicks notions of life-planning firmly into touch: 'Everyone

has a plan until they get punched in the face' (2015: 52). Reeling from life's punch, she suggests that the values by which she has structured her life are no longer up to the job:

> I am not used to this uncertain terrain. In every other aspect of my life, diligence and hard work have been rewarded with getting what I want. (Gross 2015: 153)

No amount of hard work will enable her to beat this vicious and invasive cancer. A self-described bureaucrat, the cancer doesn't just destroy her life, it also destroys the familiar world of order and control:

> I am a woman to whom control is everything – see how I am trying to control the world even now, by fixing it in print for perpetuity? But I cannot control *this*, I can't game the outcome, I can't decide how the cancer inside me grows, how quickly, where it attacks next, whether or for how long my drugs do the business, how much pain I am in. (Gross 2015: 152)

Yet the loss of control is not without its compensations, for dying has 'freed me from convention and from ambition' (Gross 2015: 179). This is an important reflection, given the concern behind the neoliberal policies of the Labour government which she served to ingrain aspiration as a key feature for achieving the successful life.[27] Now Gross sees ambition not as something to entrench; if anything, it is something from which she believes she must be freed. In that freedom, new priorities come to the fore. Love for family and for friends becomes the central principle for living. Dying frees you up for 'the business of dealing with what you have, of finding meaning in suffering, and of seeing joy in the everyday' (2015: 148). Meaning grounded in seeking status and achievement does not fulfil its promise when confronted with the Death Zone. Something else is required.

That new focus on love illuminates not just the Death Zone. What is interesting about the different accounts of cancer offered by Gould and Gross is that both arrive at similar conclusions when faced with death. It is in the social world that surrounds and shapes the individual that meaning capable of coping even with the chaos wrought by death can be found. The limitations of the neoliberal individual are made manifest, its self-sufficiency shown to be a mirage. In death, the fact that we are all dependent on the lives of others is starkly revealed. And this is not something to bewail. In the end neither Gould nor Gross mount, as might the cryonicist, 'a rebellion against human existence as it has been given' (O'Connell 2017: 2). Instead, they celebrate dependence on others as evidence that they are loved. Responding to the challenge of death becomes less about 'having one's own death' and more about recognizing the things in life that really matter – family, friends, the natural world. In Gould's case, it requires reengaging with a religious sensibility that had previously been pushed to the margins, and which in the experience of dying becomes capable of offering a far more realistic way of positioning the self in a universe of chance and change than the language and practices of self-actualization.

The limits of the neoliberal account of the self are revealed, not just for individuals like Gould and Gross as they seek to make sense of their own dying. The lived-reality of death also reveals the inequalities promoted by neoliberal doctrine as necessary for the creation of a successful society. Death may be the great leveller which reveals the limits of existence for every one of us; but dying poor is a quite different experience from dying rich. If we return to Philip Gould's narrative, his visits to the top US and UK specialists make him realize the very-real problem of economic inequality. Given his role in shaping policy initiatives which explicitly moved left-wing politics away from addressing economic inequality towards promoting 'equality of opportunity', this is not an insignificant shift. Your income is not without significance for your ability to live well, and Gould comes to realize this through meeting others from a range of backgrounds who are also dying:

I began to understand what cancer meant for those without resources, without help, without insurance, without any kind of reliable medical support. ... Cancer is tough at any time; in poverty, without proper treatment and support, it must be hell on earth. (Gould 2012: 36)

It might strike us as odd that it takes Gould's experience of dying to realize the impact of these fundamental economic inequalities on the ability of individuals to live – and die – well. 'I *began* to understand': as if such inequalities could not be identified from one's ordinary, day-to-day experience. Yet in the everyday world it is possible to be detached from the lives of less-fortunate others, blind to the way in which poverty and limited resources exclude so many from that much vaunted neoliberal bedrock for success: opportunity. In the experience of illness and death, one enters into the kind of social spaces (hospitals) where one rubs up against those who would not otherwise be met. These shared spaces make possible the realization that not all have access to the kind of care resulting from material affluence.

At least Gould recognizes the economic inequality that shapes and separates the experience of those from lower income groups from his own. Government policies designed to get the unemployed or unemployable into work have singularly failed to do even this. People like Gould who have accumulated sufficient resources through well-paid work or inherited wealth are able to rely on these resources to shape their own dying.

Successful dying, like successful living, requires having sufficient material resources.

Those without money are condemned to struggle even as they face up to the inevitability of death. In August 2015, the UK's Department of Work and Pensions was forced to admit that eighty people a month were dying *after* assessments which declared them fit to work.[28] While not all these deaths can be attributed to terminal illness – suicide and accident are also represented in these figures – dying poor is shaped by a lack of support quite different to that experienced by wealthy sufferers. A state primarily interested in producing useful citizens for the workplace is unlikely to deal humanely with the limits mortality places on some of its citizens.

The economic shaping of success and failure also affects the kind of discussions had about the end of life:

> The focus on individual autonomy and on reforms to enhance self-determination … downplays the voices of those without adequate access to medical services and/or without political and media clout. (Kaufman 2005: 26)

Consider the discourse around euthanasia. The dominant shaping of these conversations revolves around ideas of 'choice'. Yet choice is a hollow word if you don't have the economic resources to follow these choices through. Indeed, for those on the margins of society, these arguments are accompanied by anxiety that 'the legalisation of euthanasia could lead to the unwanted deaths of persons deemed "less worthy" by others': a view that gets considerably less airtime than the views of those who 'cry for the right to control the time of one's own dying' (Kaufman 2005: 27). Here we run up against notions of what constitutes 'a useful' life. This is the dark side of neoliberal autonomy. Freedom to choose when you have money looks very different from freedom to choose when you do not.

How, then, do we break 'the destructive illusion of human self-sufficiency' (Lewis 2001: 306) that shapes neoliberal accounts and that lends itself to cruelty when confronted by those with limited financial resources? Rather than start from the position of the responsible entrepreneurial self, what happens if we start from that which suggests the unreality of an account of the individual based exclusively on strength? A different set of values emerge from prioritizing the experience of illness than would be the case if starting with the entrepreneurial individual of neoliberalism. The values derived from paying attention to the sick body acknowledge – indeed, demand – community and connection. At the same time, these values cannot remove entirely the pain that comes with illness and death, loss and losing. There are losses that reveal just how hard it is to be dependent on others and the world, and if we are to find a way of living well we cannot ignore that this is so.

The sick body as *Memento Mori*

Paying attention to death and dying, acknowledging that we too will die, is no easy thing. As we followed the narratives of Gross and Gould, we may have ducked the inevitable conclusion that we, like them, will eventually enter the Death Zone. Their printed words are full of the vibrancy of the still living. To think that they are now dead, and that we, too, will one day be dead, is incredibly hard to keep in mind.

Leo Tolstoy's *The Death of Ivan Ilyich*, written in 1880, offers a classic rendition of just how difficult it is to face up to the fact that one day 'I' will die. Ivan is described as the kind of conventional fellow who has never given the fact of death a second thought. Tolstoy (a man obsessed with the idea of his own dying[29]) describes what happens when a person like Ivan is suddenly confronted with the imminence of his own death. It is impossible for Ivan to grasp, impossible to accept, and Ivan attempts 'to force it out of his mind with other thoughts that were sound and healthy' (Tolstoy [1880] 1981: 94). No wonder this novella stands as a classic account of the fear of dying: how many of us would not readily adopt Ivan's strategy?

There is another aspect to the story that reveals how the practice of denial warps the attempts of the 'living' to engage with the dying. Rather than face the truth that mortality is something we share, an easy way out of the horror of this fact is to fall back on the belief that the dying are somehow responsible for their own fate. Ivan's friends see his illness and subsequent death as an accident that has befallen *him*; an accident they will avoid through showing the requisite care that Ivan lacked. Where he failed, they will succeed. Here is Pyotr

Ivanovich using this strategy to evade the horrible reality that he is as much a prey to death as Ivan:

> 'Why, the same thing could happen to me at anytime now' … But at once, he himself did not know how, he was rescued by the customary reflection that all this had happened to Ivan Ilyich, not to him, that it could not and should not happen to him … With this line of reasoning Pyotr Ivanovich set his mind at rest and began to press for details about Ivan Ilyich's death, as though death were a chance experience that could happen only to Ivan Ilyich, never to himself. (Tolstoy [1880] 1981: 44)

Ivan's friends cannot connect their lives with his experience. This disconnection contributes to Ivan's sense of isolation. No one talks honestly to him about what is happening to him, and he feels increasingly alienated from family and friends.

One hundred and fifty years on, Tolstoy's careful analysis of the psychology surrounding death and dying feels as fresh as the day it was written. If we are to disrupt the sense of death as something outside our experience, we must move beyond the intellectual recognition of human beings as 'beings-towards-death'. Sure, I can accept that death comes to all of us, yet that doesn't mean that I won't struggle with the idea that one day death will come to *me*. Easier to avoid this conclusion and stick with the surface acceptance of mortality. To grapple with the lived-experience of mortality, it might be easier to start with something of which we already have experience: sickness. In the sick body we glimpse a model of what it is to be human which challenges accounts which would focus on responsibility and independence. This approach helps disrupt ideas of death as a form of failure.

What happens when we experience not capability, but incapacity; when we feel weak, not strong; when we are confronted, not with our independence but with our need of others? These are pertinent questions for me, as I have recently been diagnosed with Graves's

Disease, a condition that affects the thyroid and requires life-long medication. I am irritated by this diagnosis, if truth be told. At 53, I don't much like the reminder that I am as much a prey to illness as anyone else. I don't like the idea of being on medication for the rest of my life. I don't like the reminder that I am dependent on a body that is subject to natural forces beyond my control. No amount of thinking changes this, and I will just have to learn to accept a new dependence on little white pills.

The experience of sickness challenges the image we have of ourselves; but it also makes possible a challenge to social values that are unthinkingly adopted. In the experience in sickness, there is something akin to the *memento mori*, the skull placed on the scholar's desk that acted as a reminder of the limits of striving and the end of control. Arthur Frank suggests sickness acts as a reminder of mortality that opens up an important vista for contemplating the nature of our humanity. Far from being an aberration distracting us from health, sickness reveals 'a common condition of humanity' (Frank [1991] 2002: 115). It is common because it affects all of us in one way or another. Its coming reminds us that we are not gods, but that sickness is as much a part of the human condition as health.

What happens when we think of human beings through sickness, rather than health?

At the outset, this disrupts the obsession with striving and achievement. Sickness places vulnerability and weariness centre-stage. This is a disquieting idea, and we might prefer to rush on to the 'healthier' feelings of energy and vigour. Yet if we stick with it, being sick reveals something important about being human which would otherwise be obscured by ideas of capability. Frank uses a phrase that suggests the power of this experience to challenge our thinking, moving us away from the self-sufficient individual and towards a sense of community. In sickness, we discover 'the common bond of suffering that joins bodies in their shared vulnerability' (Frank 1995: xi).

No one can escape sickness. Everyone is ill at sometime or another. What this reveals is the need each has for the other.

The sick (and the dying) are not life's failures. Rather, they show what every life encounters at one time or another: the need for another's care.

Now, we could see this as an unfortunate fact of our existence. But we could also see such experiences as opening up different levels in our commitment to each other. Many a relationship has been taken to the next level of commitment by the simple need to look after a friend or lover. That is the challenge as well as the possibility of sickness.

At the same time, we should be wary of falling into an overly saccharine view of the experience of sickness. Frank is concerned to avoid just this pitfall, and when he tells the stories of the sick, he is hesitant about focusing too much on the tales of individuals 'restored' to good health. These 'restitution narratives' can all-too-easily be co-opted into a social narrative which shapes all experience through the categories of 'winning' or 'losing'. Instead, he directs us to stories that do not lend themselves to such a neat – and pleasing – story arc. In 'chaos' stories, we are confronted with experiences that defy the desire for happy endings. Those living the chaos cannot neatly turn their experiences into words. Here is the story of Nancy, caring for her mother who has Alzheimer's. Her mother cannot tell her own tale, and Nancy's story is one of frustration. Her mother won't leave her alone for a second:

If I'm trying to get dinner ready and I'm already feeling bad, she's in front of the refrigerator. Then she goes to put her hand on the stove and I got the fire on. And then she's in front of the microwave and then she's in front of the silverware drawer. And – and if I send her out she gets mad at me. And then it's awful. That's when I have a really, a really bad time. (Frank 1995: 99)

There is no remedy for Nancy's mother's illness. She will never be restored to health. What Frank sees in Nancy's words is the breaking in of the chaotic. There is a sense in her words of the 'bulwark of remedy, progress and professionalism [cracking] to reveal vulnerability, frailty, and impotence' (Frank 1995: 97). This is what makes chaos stories important. They reveal the limits of language and coherence. They make us uncomfortable, for they suggest a world outside our control; a world that can crush and destroy as easily as it allows for growth and development. How difficult to accept dependence on such a world. How much easier to fall back on narratives of responsibility and irresponsibility, of success and failure. To accept that we are responsible for our life, our health and our death seems far preferable to the alternative, revealed in illness and death. For the religious historian Elaine Pagels, it is this preference that explains the perplexing victory of Augustine's claim that death is unnatural. We are not so different from Augustine, for like him we prefer to 'feel guilty [rather] than helpless' (Pagels 1988: 147). We prefer to believe that we shape our destinies; that there is no limit to our actions.

And yet …

In chaos stories we are confronted with the truth we would rather avoid. All lives are subject to change. All lives are mortal. Neoliberal political discourse may recognize the rule of change, but it does so in a way which avoids reflecting on the experience of the mutable body. For the neoliberal, change is identified with flexibility and adaptation. Nothing is solid or dependable: be that the individual or the traditional ways of shaping human life and experience. This rendition of the changeable individual has little to do with embracing the body's fleshy reality. If we took seriously physicality in all its varied forms, we would have to challenge the organizing ideals of self-sufficiency and control. With that challenge would come a querying of success as the marker for the well-lived life. Such a challenge would also entail looking again at that which is seen as failure, for in such experiences we might well find fertile ground for creating new ways of living.

Limits and loss: The pain of losing

We should not, however, consign the experience of change to a neatly abstract rendition. To do this would be to suggest a fantastical account of life equal to the neoliberal suggestion that control and self-sufficiency are the best ways of approaching our experience. As we head towards my suggestions for ways of embracing failure and loss, it is important that I do not create an illusion of what it is to experience failure and loss. We began this chapter with Joan Didion's description of the shattering experience of losing her life partner:

> '*Life changes fast. Life changes in an instant. You sit down to dinner and life as you know it ends.*'

These words run like a refrain through her memoir, reminding her reader of just how precarious are the things – and the people – that we take for granted.

Struggling to cope with her loss, Didion sought books that described the experience of others trying to live with it and was staggered to find precious little.[30] Given the ubiquity of this experience, how strange are these omissions. Her two books on loss – *The Year of Magical Thinking* and *Blue Nights* – were written in part as a response to this gap. Didion isn't just attempting to come to terms with the sudden death of her husband. His death happened while her daughter, Quintana, was critically ill in hospital; and in *Blue Nights* Quintana's ill health and death are Didion's themes.

These two books explore the different forms loss can take. There is the loss of a life partner, and the loss of a child. The absence of the loved one who has been conversation partner and witness to her life; the death of the child who links her as a parent to the future. She describes the silence of her empty apartment.[31] She details the inability of memory to provide any comfort for her pain. Places that were once well-loved, which offered delightful remembrances, are now subject to what she calls 'the vortex effect' (Didion 2006: 113): they have become gateways to memories of a past that is lost forever. Better to avoid them than to slip into the pain that comes from remembering a time when the lost were still present. Mementoes of past times are now impossible to look at without grief. 'I no longer want reminders of what was, what got broken, what got lost, what got wasted' (Didion 2011: 44), she writes. What to do with all this stuff? Quintana was an only child. What is the point of keeping these relics of a lost past? With no one to come after, there is no one who will want it. As a woman without children, I feel this reflection clutch my heart. All the things my husband and I have accumulated over a life together; all the precious tourist tat of trips together; the photo albums carefully kept as reminders of our life together. Who will want this stuff when we are gone? Didion's words strike home: *No One*.

The real problem of death, the real challenge of the sick body, is not reducible to the problem of personal survival. What emerges from Didion's writing is the difficulty of engaging with the fragility of the bonds that bind us *together*. The poetry of husband and wife Donald Hall and Jane Kenyon gets at this fragility. In *Otherwise*, written by Kenyon, and in *Without*, written by Hall, the two poets address Kenyon's struggle with, and eventual death from, leukaemia.[32] Their poems fit together and expose the real problem of death to lie in the loss of those we love, the people who anchor us by their presence in this world.

Kenyon captures the fear of dying in a set of simple lines from 'The Sick Wife', a poem she edited on her deathbed:

The cars on either side of her
pulled away so briskly
that it made her sick at heart. (Kenyon 1996: 221)

Life is and will be going on without her. For Hall, his grief is shaped by his fear of losing her and its terrible reality. Journeys between Jane's hospital bed and his motel room become spaces for expressing his rage, fear and helplessness: 'I scream/and keep on screaming' (Hall 1998: 18). After her death, he returns again and again to her grave:

Three times today
I drove to your grave …
I imagine you've returned
before me, bags of groceries upright
in the back of the Saab. (Hall 1998: 52)

There is something ordinary about her absence, and it is in the sheer ordinariness – shopping bags in the back of the car – that the fullness of his loss strikes home. The contents of those bags will never find their way to the kitchen if he does not put them there. She who would have carried them is no longer there, *and never will be again*. The poignancy of Hall's graveside cry echoes this sense of loss; it rises up, reaches out and meets the cries of mourners everywhere:

I wish you were that birch
rising from the clump behind you,
and I the gray oak alongside. (Hall 1998: 62)

In shaping different ways of thinking about the meaningful life, the pain of loss must not be evaded. We cannot escape loss. It is woven into the very fabric of the universe. It is the second law of thermodynamics.[33]

Accept loss as a fact, and its packaging as failure falls away.

It is easier to construct it as failure, of course, for precisely the reason found in the writing of Didion, Kenyon and Hall. Here is pain in the raw. Here is the fragility of the bonds that make us human. How much easier to make death the responsibility of the individual who has somehow failed in the task of living. And yet no amount of vitamins diligently taken, exercise pursued, mindful practice or healthy diet will alter the fact that all of us are subject to death and loss.[34]

Didion's reflections and the poems of Hall and Kenyon do more than catalogue disturbing and painful experiences. They offer fragile intimations of how to live with such pain. Hall describes the peonies Jane planted that 'burst out, white as snow squalls … /I carry one magnanimous blossom indoors/and float it in a glass bowl, as you used to do'. How fragile this reminder of her loving tending of the garden and of him. There is hope that he might just be able to live again, but it is as fragile as these delicate blooms:

Your peonies lean their vast heads westward
as if they might topple. Some topple. (Hall 1998: 81)

At the end of *The Year of Magical Thinking*, Didion recalls swimming with her husband into a cave at Portuguese Bend. To enter the cave, to experience its awesome beauty, requires catching the swell. John's words about how to do this come back to her: 'You had to go with the change. He told me that' (2006: 229).

Going with the change is one of the hardest things to do when faced with loss. The world as we know it has been destroyed, and now we are faced with finding new ways of living without the presence of the one we loved. It can feel safer to fall back on failure as the reason for loss. It can feel easier to cling to the fantasies of a control that we might seek to enact even in the shadow of death. In the next chapter I turn our attention to the structures that would make control the answer to the messiness and pain of human existence. In attempting to package life in a safe little bundle, these methods reveal a disquieting reality: that attempts to instigate control over that which cannot be controlled lead ultimately to less fulfilling, poorer engagements with life than those which emerge from a willingness to accept the pain that comes with the forces of chance and change.

4

FACTORING OUT FAILURE, FACTORING OUT HUMANITY: BUREAUCRACY, METRICS AND THE LOSS OF SPONTANEITY

The 'solutions' offered to the pain of loss at the end of the previous chapter might well have left us feeling dissatisfied: the delicacy of flowers which act as intimations of new life; the memory of giving oneself up to the flow of the tide at the bidding of the lost lover. Such small things in the face of the processes that render us vulnerable to decay and death. We might prefer more certain ways of protecting ourselves from the forces of change. We might prefer to think of death as a form of failure, rather than have to accept there are things we cannot control.

It is not just the experience of death and loss that makes us long for an escape from our fragile world. The ordinariness of daily life presents us with similar uncertainty as we try to ensure the right outcome for our actions. We want success to be certain and failure to be kept to a minimum. As I write, I am keenly aware of the pull of this desire. This chapter stands at the half way point of this book. As I embark on it, I'm confronted by my own fears of failure. Am I still holding your attention, dear reader? Have I written it clearly enough? Is my argument making sense? Are you enjoying it? Have I bored you rigid? Have you even gotten this far? These questions plague me.

Compared to the fears of loss and losing encountered in the last chapter, these concerns seem like – well, what they are – small fry. My barrister husband, used to the high stakes world of criminal law, likes to say in response to my fretting, 'well, no one is going to die'. He's right, of course. But I can't escape these fears, can't escape the nagging thought that this book – appropriately, perhaps – might turn out to be a failure. I fear the loss of control that comes with this thought. I fear the words on the page that feel like they are running away from me.

Is it possible to factor out failure? Is it possible to maximise the chances for success?

As I sit drumming my fingers and looking at the screen, the question that runs through my head is whether there might be an easy-to-follow model for this chapter (and for this book) which would ensure a successful outcome. If I followed such a miraculous plan, would I achieve the end of a well-received (preferably best-selling) book?

Much as I might wish for such a solution, I doubt I would use such a model version even if it were offered. I am wary of claims that there are simple methods which can be adopted to ensure successful outcomes. I am warier still of the measures used to determine whether something is, indeed, a literary success. If I sold millions of copies, but felt the book was flawed, fake or just plain bad, would those sales figures alone make it 'a success'?

My own history of failure underscores this sense of disquiet when numbers are used as a measure of success. I had been turned down for promotion. A senior manager met with me to explain why. At one point in our perfectly pleasant conversation I was asked if I knew how many times my work had been cited by others. I looked surprised. I was told that this information was accessible via an 'online tool'. I looked blank. I should have included these figures on my application as they were 'impressive for someone in the arts and humanities area'. On the one hand, perhaps I would have been promoted if I had included these figures. On the other, I felt uneasy that there was no discussion of what had *actually* been written about my work. Those impressive numbers using it could have been doing so in a dismissive way, citing it as an example of poor work in philosophy. For my manager, what had *actually* been said didn't seem to matter much. What was much more important was being able to point to the *number* of times I had been cited. What mattered was being able to fix a figure next to my work which showed its 'value'.

In a world shaped by *homo economicus*, this conclusion shouldn't have surprised me. When everything is financialized, numbers and measuring take on a privileged role. Money talks, and it's easy to move from this belief to the idea that numbers themselves hold a privileged position in every part of life. Why shouldn't philosophical writing be judged accordingly? Think of the benefits! Stick ten philosophers in a room, and you will end up with ten different opinions. Attaining a numerical standard for judgement might well seem preferable to the messiness of human judgement: there is a purity and a simplicity to numbers not easily replicated by human beings.

Increasingly, our lives are shaped through numbers, measuring and metrics. This reflects a history where attention has been paid to ensuring the practices of institutions maximise success while factoring out failure. Tracing something of this history reveals what happens when attempts are made to factor out the unruliness of human fallibility. It also suggests why certainty is not as desirable as we might think. In mapping this terrain, the problems of *homo economicus* for enabling the well-lived life come to the fore. In the attempt to move beyond the fallibility of human judgement, the rich possibilities for a human life diminish, and we may well long for another vision of the human to shape our lives, projects and relationships.

Enacting control: The rise of bureaucracy

In Chapters Two and Three I suggested ways in which the fears of mortality – of ageing and death – are managed through locating them in the bodies of women, the sick and the dying. The things that we fear can be made into forms of failure that can be controlled, or at least relegated to the margins of life. The brilliance of Sigmund Freud, to my mind, is the way he connects these human anxieties to the structures of human civilization. As human beings, we are always trying to control our world: think of me trying to contain my unruly thoughts in words, like pinning still-fluttering butterflies to a page. Freud's focus is on the natural forces that can all-too-easily crush us. Faced with volcanoes, hurricanes and earthquakes, humans feel themselves to be what they are: vulnerable, fragile animals. Freud sees the structures and institutions of civilization emerging from the human attempt to exact control over the terrifying threats to human life presented by the powers of nature.[1] Human society provides a sense of security in the face of this overwhelming nature. Yet the very success of human beings at constructing a bulwark against natural forces gives weight to an illusion. We come to believe that human endeavour can exert complete control over the natural world.[2]

This illusory belief in our ability to control our world is anchored in childhood. As children, we believe our thoughts capable of making the world conform to our desires. We want to secure the presence of the mother who has gone out of the room, and Hey Presto! We find that in response to our thoughts demanding she comes back, she does indeed return to us.[3] The belief in the power of wishing works for a time. The 'good enough' mother responds to our needs,[4] and we can maintain the belief that our wishes have made her act in accordance with our willing. But eventually we have to realise that our thoughts do not have this power over reality and wishing has to be put aside in favour of the maturity that comes from accepting 'the reality-principle'.[5] We give up our belief that our wishes shape our world, coming to terms with the external world, its disappointments and its limitations. Maturity comes with accepting the limits to human action. This is so for the child, but also for the species, and Freud notes, rather sadly perhaps, that 'as for the great necessities of Fate, against which there is no help, they will learn to endure them with resignation' (Freud 1927: 50).

If Freud is sceptical about religious solutions to the problems of living, seeing them as versions of the child's belief in wishes, it is the reality-principle that drives scientific investigation. The scientist directs his attention to understanding the world 'as it really is'. Freud is a scientist, and while he might alert us to the dangers of believing in the success of human attempts at control, he is also optimistic about what science is able to achieve. If we embrace it, its methods will enable a much better world for human beings than one in thrall to the myths and superstitions of religious forms of wishing.[6]

This positive view of the possibilities of science to shape our world is also found, somewhat surprisingly perhaps, in Max Weber's classic account of bureaucracy.[7] We may well recoil from ideas of bureaucracy having anything to do with science or 'the real world', hearing in the very word overtones of Franz Kafka's disturbing visions of what happens when the systems of a bureaucratic state crush the individual. For Weber, however, this form of management merely seeks to extend the powers of reason to the government of human beings. Humans do not always act rationally.[8] They are unpredictable, prone to making mistakes. Human failure makes possible destruction and disaster. This reveals our basic fallibility. Think of the times when 'human error' is found to be responsible for an air, rail or car crash; or when children or vulnerable adults have been put at risk as a result of the bad decisions of social workers; or when someone has not been given the treatment they needed because a doctor wrongly diagnosed their condition. Systems that factor out these kinds of human failures, or at least contain them, should, presumably, be welcomed.

This is the goal to which bureaucratic methods are put. They offer the possibility of more 'scientific management' of institutions, setting parameters within which human failings can be contained and controlled. Through the instigation of these structures, a safer world is expected to emerge. These structures make possible the effective management of resources. Hierarchical structures make clear who is responsible for decision-making, identifying clear chains of command. Decision-making does not depend on the whim of the individual but conforms to a pre-agreed set of rules. Specialization enables workers to focus on a specific set of clearly defined tasks. There is clarity and there is order. The vagaries of human action are controlled by systems and structures which factor out the conditions leading to failure.[9]

Pause for a moment, and this seems an eminently sensible way to proceed, especially if we focus on public services like health or education. We want there to be clarity about who is responsible for what. Taking out the human factor suggests resources will be distributed with the minimum amount of personal involvement. That must be a good thing. After all, when I go to see my doctor, I don't want the treatment she prescribes to me to be dependent on whether she likes me or not. If I lose my job, I don't want the question of whether or not I receive unemployment benefit to depend on whether the person I see at the Job Centre considers me to be the right kind of person for state support. I want a system that judges my need objectively, rather than emotionally, and that responds by making things better.

There is, however, a shadow side to the kind of control that would seek to lessen the ways in which human beings can mess up. 'The System' can become more trusted than the human. The history of bureaucracy makes the consequences of this belief starkly clear. Hannah Arendt details a broader role than merely managing discrete resources for the kind of bureaucratic structures shaping totalitarian states. Writing in the late 1940s, her concern is with the way in which the human was eroded under the Nazi and Soviet regimes. In common to both these political movements was a kind of scientific optimism: a new 'progressive' future was possible that would overcome the failings of past politics. This bold new future was being felt in the birth of the new movement. A kind of mysticism accompanied this belief. Forces 'outside the human' were leading inexorably to the movement's success.[10] The power of Soviet-era posters bears witness to this idea: the faces of the workers, walking arm-in-arm into a New Dawn, are transfigured by the new possibilities for cooperation and flourishing. Nazi propaganda posters reflect a similar aesthetic; albeit with conspicuously more uniforms. The future is coming, do not be afraid, but grasp it as the inevitable climax of historical and cosmic forces.

There is, however, a tension concealed by this sense of inevitability. The Third Reich *will* last for a thousand years; the dictatorship of the proletariat *will* come to fruition. *But*. And it's a big 'but'. These outcomes are not so inevitable that individuals might not be able to jeopardise their success. After all, human beings are unpredictable, prone to failure. If their independence is not to threaten the progress of history to that glorious end point, systems will be required to manage the unruly human. For the believers in progress, unpredictability requires management. Yet as Arendt points out, it is in the unpredictable that human creativity is grounded. There is something startling and unexpected and strange about the ability to bring about something new. Isn't this what is meant by the very word 'creativity'? (If I follow someone else's template for a successful book, it won't be 'new', it won't be something reflecting *my* creativity. It will merely conform to another's idea of what makes for a good book.)

Its very strangeness is what makes creativity frightening for those who would seek control. The future is not predictable if you factor in individual creativity. No wonder totalitarian regimes seek to curb it:

> No ideology which aims at the explanation of all historical events of the past and at mapping out the course of all events of the future can bear the unpredictability which springs from the fact that men

are creative, that they can bring forward something so new that nobody ever foresaw it. (Arendt [1948] 1968: 458)

Her comment explains why such regimes expend so much energy criticizing and banning art that is seen as 'degenerate' or which fails to conform to a specific set of aesthetic standards set by their values.[11] Art suggests freedom, openness and new possibilities. For the Nazi, or the Soviet, the uncertainty of 'the new' stands as an affront to their plans. The individual's potentially devastating creativity must be placed within a system which renders it 'safe'. The personal dimension becomes a problem that must be controlled; the impersonal dimension becomes the method for attaining the movement's success.

The fear of the individual and the multiple possibilities inherent in the personal explain Arendt's conclusion. Here we get an inkling of the way in which the erosion of the personal makes the focus on attaining successful outcomes itself a form of failure. Stripping out the personal, making it a problem in need of a solution, opens up the potential for more dangerous failures than simply the failure to succeed.

The commitment to achieving successful outcomes can itself become a form of failure.

Arendt's reflections are shaped by a concrete and chilling example. In 1961 she went to Jerusalem to report on the trial of the Nazi war criminal, Adolf Eichmann, for the *New Yorker* magazine. Eichmann's job in the Third Reich had been to ensure the efficient transportation of the Nazi's victims to the concentration camps. Fleeing to Argentina at the end of the war, he is tracked down by the Israelis, and captured by Mossad agents in May 1960. Taken to Israel, he is put on trial for his culpability in the murders of millions of people. Eichmann is a figure who confuses Arendt. She tries to get beneath the surface of this grey little man, who is uneasy, in heavily framed spectacles and wearing a badly fitting suit.

As he sits in the dock, chewing the inside of his mouth, she is taken aback by just how ordinary he looks. He is a shabby little administrator, more fitted to working in an office or a library than standing trial for horrific crimes. He could not be further from the dramatic personifications of evil found in the plays of Shakespeare:

> Eichmann was not Iago and not Macbeth, and nothing would have been farther from his mind than to determine with Richard III 'to prove a villain'. (Arendt [1963] 1977: 287)

So what is he, exactly, and what brought him to this place, on trial for his life as a war criminal guilty of genocide?

Eichmann's defence is predictable. He falls back on the 'only obeying orders' defence of so many Nazis confronted with the effects of their actions. Yet he also offers a startling view of himself as a cog within the Nazi state. He does not see himself so much as a man, as 'a mere function' of the state (see [1948] 1968: 215). His actions can only be understood if his critics realise he had acted as someone 'aloof' from 'ordinary' human concerns. He had to do this, he had to resist any personal reflection, for that would have hindered his ability to achieve the goals that had been set him by his superiors. To be successful *as a function*, he had to resist the kind of thoughtfulness that would connect his actions to the sufferings of others. He had to resist the temptation of empathy. Arendt believes he had 'no motives at all', other than 'an extraordinary diligence in looking out for his personal advancement' (Arendt [1963] 1977: 287). Focused on his task and attentive only to ensuring a successful career, she argues that he 'never realised what he was doing' (Arendt [1963] 1977: 287).

This sounds unlikely, and we might well find Arendt's conclusion unconvincing. How could he 'not know what he was doing'? What did he think would happen to the people whose transportation to the camps he had organised? Yet for Arendt, it is the system in which he worked that allowed for this disconnection. The fragmentation of tasks common to any kind of bureaucratic management system concerned with maximizing efficiency allowed Eichmann to cultivate a perspective that never placed his actions in the context of the larger picture. He could well claim that he had 'nothing to do' with the killing of any Jew, or 'the Jews':

> With the killing of the Jews I had nothing to do. I never killed a Jew, or a non-Jew, for that matter – I never killed any human being. I never gave an order to kill either a Jew or a non-Jew; I just did not do it. (Arendt [1963]1977: 22)

Attentive only to his task of arranging transportation, he can ignore the affect of his actions on the lives of the millions rendered 'superfluous' by the Nazi's plans. Dispossession, transportation, captivity and murder can be reduced to neat lists of numbers on pristine sheets of paper; the horror of genocide turned into the sets of figures returned to his superiors.

Judged according to this discrete task, Eichmann might well be annoyed that he did not attain the promotions to which he felt entitled: a theme to which he returned consistently throughout the trial.[12]

Yes, he is dogged by feelings of failure. He feels a failure because he did not achieve his career goals.

Looked at from our perspective, some seventy years after the end of the Second World War, we might well consider him a disturbing example of what 'success' can look like. His actions met their intended target of wiping out the vast majority of European Jews. But how strange – perverse, even – this assessment sounds! To think of Eichmann as a 'success' highlights the problem with making the achievement of a set of prescribed goals the grounds for the successful life and avoiding failing to meet those goals the principle criteria for judging the meaning of a life. Eichmann's success *as a Nazi* ensures that he fails as *a compassionate human being*.

He does not connect his actions to the sufferings of others, and, as a result, fails to act on his obligations to other people as fellow human beings. The system that shapes his actions – a bureaucratic state that fragments action into discrete departments – is not neutral in allowing for this failure. Its promotion of the impersonal in order to achieve that glorious future State obscures his failings by holding out rewards for the successful completion of his tasks. By making the impersonal the hallmark of the correct manner of the employee it actively encourages the kind of thoughtlessness that ensured Eichmann never connected *his* actions to the sufferings of others.

Eichmann is not alone in working within a system that reduced its employees to impersonal functions. Many Eichmanns were required in order to make the terror of Nazism possible; many people worked to ensure the wheels of the Nazi state turned efficiently. Not only were the functionaries of the Nazi state shaped by the belief in the efficacy of the impersonal: the Nazi's victims were also reduced from feeling people, who loved and feared and hoped and dreamed. They were turned into 'problems' whose lives required a 'solution'. No longer names, they became numbers written on Nazi lists; numbers that were tattooed onto their flesh in the factories of death that destroyed them.[13]

Now, we might dismiss Eichmann as an isolated example of a man who was morally weak. Arendt is not convinced, for the Third Reich depended for its efficiency on thousands of Eichmanns. But her concern is with more than merely a description of what happened to the human dimension *under Nazism.* Eichmann should terrify us because the conditions that made him a war criminal have not been eradicated. They are commonplace, and if we think we do not run the risk of failing as he did, we are very much mistaken.

We don't need to look far to find similar forms of detachment allowing for the actions of oppressive regimes in the years after the Second World War. Accounts of Argentina's 'Dirty War' in the 1970s and 1980s include similar arguments about the 'necessity' of eliminating those who stand in the way of the glorious new world being created. We find

Adolfo Scilingo (sometimes described as Argentina's Eichmann) telling of an army chaplain who calmed his qualms about the death flights used by the military junta to drop their drugged opponents to their deaths in the ocean with the following chilling words:

> 'He was telling me that it was a Christian death, because they didn't suffer, because it wasn't traumatic, that they had to be eliminated, that war was war and even the Bible provided for eliminating weeds from the wheat field'. (in Verbitsky 2005: 30)

Arendt's point is more wide-ranging, however, than merely alerting us to the ways in which dictatorships warp human behaviours. New Eichmanns also flourish in the structures of contemporary democracies. He is, she claims, representative of a 'new type of criminal … who commits his crimes under circumstances that make it well-nigh impossible for him to know or to feel that he is doing wrong' (Arendt [1963] 1977: 276). He is not a monster but an extreme example of a more common trend. The thoughtlessness he cultivated in order to be good at his job is a common feature of the bureaucracies found in contemporary institutions.

We might pause here and think of some of the ways in which disconnection from the effects of one's actions occurs in societies which are not dictatorships, not involved in committing genocide. 'Controlled immigration' has become a central theme in the politics of many developed nations over the past ten years. Strategies designed to ensure no immigrants reside in a country illegally can have distressing consequences for individuals caught up in their implementation. In January 2018, Jorge Garcia was deported to Mexico after thirty years in the United States. He had raised a family, worked, paid taxes, had no criminal conviction. He had contributed to the wealth of the nation. Responding to criticism of this decision, a spokesman for US Immigration and Customs Enforcement said they were 'justified' in deporting Garcia: 'All of those in violation of the immigration laws may be subject to immigration arrest, detention and, if found removable by final order, removal from the United States', ran the statement.[14] The law had been followed. The effect on a man who will now not see his wife or children, who will no longer live in the place he calls home, are not considered, and you can imagine the official responsible for Garcia's removal feeling that they had done their job well.

Eichmann's case stands as an example – but by no means the only example – of what happens when the human is rendered secondary to a set of processes believed to secure the right set of outcomes. The personal is rendered impersonal, the human factor something to be overcome. In Eichmann's case, his fear of failure led to worse – unimaginably worse – failures reflecting the belief in impersonal processes which transcend the messiness of human action. It would have been better if he had been a failure in his role than a success. We might wonder whether there are aspects of our working lives in which it would be better to fail than to succeed.

'Economic man' and the internalization of control

Institutional reliance on bureaucratic solutions does not disappear with the end of totalitarianism. Nor does the sense of the human as fallible, something requiring management. Post-war democracies also place their faith in systems designed to achieve a set of prescribed ends. In a neoliberal age, however, control of the fallible human looks significantly different than it does under the practices of the bureaucracies Arendt describes. It looks different even from the world of the monolithic public institutions of the State shaped by Keynes' economics in the post-war period. Public services, as we saw in Chapter One, are no longer delivered only through the State, but, as a result of privatization, are now shaped by the practices of business. Accompanying this shift, the individual – their habits and choices – is given a central position. Attempts at controlling the human look much more complex. Yes, institutions and governments still instigate processes that require following in order for an end result to be achieved. Yes, institutions still require the kind of paperwork designed to manage out risk. But the framing of such processes is different. Rather than being imposed upon the individual from without in order to manage the unruly human dimension, these processes are increasingly *internalised,* shaping the experience of every individual.

When Michel Foucault reflected on the workings of power in the late 1970s,[15] he argued that control is now enacted, less through the imposition of external structures, and more through the way we come to *govern ourselves*. Methods of control are taught *and internalised* in what he calls 'disciplinary societies': schools, hospitals, prisons, factories. These all contribute to the structuring of experience, and so control becomes something that is not simply enacted upon the individual by others. Now it is regulated by the discipline *required of the individual* to inhabit these places. I learn how to behave as a student, a patient, a prisoner or a worker in these institutions. Importantly, the discipline required to be these things is not just something I learn: it is also something I come to *embody*. I shape myself through adopting these practices, and so politics becomes 'biopolitics'.[16]

Foucault's story doesn't entirely explain today's world.[17] The neoliberal commitment to privatization that we tracked in Chapter One requires us to a rethink what 'control' now involves.[18] Schools, hospitals, workplaces obviously still exist, but increasingly their practices suggest 'an alliance between discipline and control' (Davies 2015: 46). Different methods are required to create the self-disciplined citizen required by neoliberal economics. If schools once taught texts that enshrined ideals of nationalism (say, the stirring patriotism of Shakespeare's Henry V), neoliberalism requires the creation of adaptable global citizens: thus the teaching of 'emotional well-being' appears on the school curriculum. These practices aim at training the students' inner life so that they can become self-disciplined and resilient individuals, able to cope with disappointment and unhappiness in such a way that they will become 'productive', 'resilient' and 'adaptable' members of society.[19] The skills necessary for success are now practices to be enshrined in the self.

Talk of 'the self' might seem old-fashioned. If we look at the fragmentation of our lives through the advent of digital media we will need to think a little differently about what it means to be a twenty-first-century individual. Indeed, we might be advised to think of ourselves as 'dividuals' not individuals.[20] We have multiple identifies shaped by different aspects of our increasingly fragmented lives. Alongside – and increasingly shaping – fairly traditional identities (I am a daughter, wife, sister, lecturer, English) are virtual identities shaped by information technology. Facebook, Twitter and Instagram all shape my sense of myself and the way I project that self into the world. Other activities that I might not immediately identify with the framing of my identity but which are increasingly necessary for my involvement in the digital world also shape my experience. Banking, civic presence and shopping are activities increasingly shaped by virtual technologies which allow me 'access to various privileges' (Rose 2000: 325), albeit privileges that depend, ultimately, upon my economic status.

Control is not so much *forced upon* me, as ' "designed in" to the flows of everyday experience' (Rose 2000: 325). If Foucault was concerned with methods of state surveillance, the monitoring that accompanies your presence in the virtual world isn't just accepted but embraced by those of us who want to participate in it. I *choose* this experience, it is not forced upon me. By willingly using a Smart Phone, I am trackable to anyone who cares to find me. By using social media, I make public my views and attitudes. These are open to be used by others to send personalized ads my way. Sometimes this can cause much hilarity. I have lost track of the times Facebook has decided that, as a middle-aged woman, I must be interested in advertisements for cosmetic surgery, extra-marital dating sites or clothes for my grandchildren. If someone told me this kind of control was oppressive, I would probably look confused, or shrug my shoulders. It doesn't *feel* that way. I know if I want to take part in the social realm – which now includes the virtual world as much as the 'real' world – I will have to accept (and ignore) the possibility of some degree of social control.[21]

What I overlook in my rush to embrace the virtual world is the way my identity is being abstracted into data which can be used by government – and business – to monitor *and to shape* my behaviour.[22] This sounds abstract and far removed from me playing around on Facebook when I am bored. Yet those of us who use social media have all become part of a 'quantified community' (Davies 2015: 41) that can be reduced to a set of statistics which then allows us to be 'nudged, mined and probed' (Davies 2015: 54).

Here's an example of this practice in action.

Governments looking to control the 'bad choices' of their citizens have employed 'nudge theory' in order to attempt to alter behaviour in predictable ways.[23] Data is gathered from the target group, and that information used to 'nudge' them into changing their behaviour. Attempts to tackle the health problems associated with obesity increasingly use these methods. Rather than have government ban junk food, simply place fruit at eye level in supermarkets, or let it take the place of chocolate at checkouts. My local supermarket provides baskets of free fruit for children to munch while they are being dragged round the store by their parents. Changing harmful behaviour, so the theory goes, need not involve draconian action but can be achieved through the psychological reinforcement of 'good' decisions. Failure can be factored out and success factored in.

All rather benign. Or is it? Recent years have seen more sinister mining of personal data by companies selling the possibility of political success. My liking pictures of cats on Facebook, or my not-infrequent rants on Twitter, might seem of interest to only me and my more patient friends. As the scandal that enveloped Cambridge Analytica in March 2018 showed, however, my data can be farmed to manipulate my responses: and not just to the products that I might buy. The data analytics firm Cambridge Analytica was accused by an ex-employee, Christopher Wylie, of 'behavioural micro-targeting'. This practice involved harvesting personal information from some

50 million Facebook profiles. This data was then used to create a system that sent personalized political advertisements, based on the user's psychological profile, to millions of US voters during the 2016 Presidential Election.[24] Tailoring news stories on my social media feed to cohere with my desires or anxieties is big business and not only for business. Show me enough stories of political corruption, or the unlawful actions of immigrants, and I might well decide to vote for the candidate who shares my anxieties and offers solutions to these 'problems'. I think I am in control of my decisions. In fact, I am being manipulated by the desires of others. My freedom is eroded as others attempt to maximize their chances of political success.

Measuring, metrics and the desire for perfection

It is tempting to think of the individual as a passive victim in this quantifying of the self. But this is not the case. Control is not something that is simply done to us. *We do it to ourselves*. Why? What do we gain from it? I'm not convinced that it is simply a matter of overlooking the intrusion of such practices in order to gain access to the advantages of the digital world. This is not just a case of going along with something to get something you want. Something else is being offered me when I enter into processes that turn my daily experience into data that can be used by others.

What is the 'other thing' that is held out in the quantifying of the self?

My back is aching as I have sat at my desk for too long. I'm tired from the effort of trying to pin down these word-butterflies. In a moment I will go for a walk to stretch it out. But I won't *just* go for a walk: I will take my iPhone with me to ensure that I know how many of the designated ten thousand steps for the day I achieve. No one forces me to measure myself, but I feel extremely satisfied if I attain this magic number. I feel like it provides evidence that I am living a healthy life. (I'm not sure what this App would make of the decidedly unhealthy

amount of wine I intend to drink later today. But that is another story –
this time involving guilt – from the world of the quantified self.) The
attention I pay to the numbers on my screen suggests something
more than just a desire to count my steps. Through engaging in this
self-quantification, I succumb to the illusion that I am attaining 'self-
knowledge by numbers' (Cederström and Spicer 2015: 103). By setting
myself targets of this kind, I can consider myself to be succeeding or
failing in my quest for a healthier life. They make the shaping of my
life seem somehow safer, more secure. If I dig a little more deeply
into these magic numbers, I am not entirely sure, however, what they
actually reveal about my life or how I am shaping its meaning. Why 'ten
thousand' steps? Why the attention to the number of flights of stairs
I have climbed today? If anything, I wonder if the potential richness of
my life is being reduced when I turn it into a set of readings logged in
my phone.

The desire to measure your world is nothing new. The Early Modern
state was founded through developing systems of measuring and
labelling which were needed in order to exert control over the natural
world and its inhabitants.[25] Managing a state required knowledge of
its citizens: not least, if the government was to raise money from it
in the form of taxation. The most effective way of doing this, from an
administrative point of view, involved some degree of abstraction,[26]
for 'no administrative system is capable of representing any existing
social community except through a heroic and greatly schematised
process of abstraction and simplification' (Scott 1998: 22). The act of
measuring makes the hidden and immaterial 'visible and controllable'
(Burrows 2012: 363). It makes it possible to render people and things
useful.

In our times, numbers shape the self in a way that reflects the
contemporary emphasis on the individual. Numbers have for some
time been used to quantify – and thus to justify – judgements of
success or failure. You only have to think of examination marks to see
the relationship between a numerical grade and the attainment of a
judgement on the individual's capabilities. In the world shaped by *homo*

economicus, this now takes on more force. As the 'financialization of everything' takes root, so numbers inevitably take on a particular role in the attempt to reach judgements about human capacity or value. When economics is the prime way of determining value, mathematics comes to hold 'a general epistemological authority, *regardless of the empirical matter being investigated*' (Davies 2015: 42; my emphasis).

The suggestion is that success (and failure) can be shown through the simplicity of a number, a figure, or a grade.

How this idea takes hold requires us to briefly revisit our discussion of the period that saw the entrenchment of neoliberal values. From the mid-1980s, tools commonly used in accountancy were extended to areas previously untouched by the intrusion of market economics. Determining the value of particular activities required the development of metrics, and by the mid-1990s, the idea that what has value is that which can be measured was entrenched in areas not ordinarily seen through this lens, such as health and education. Metrics are figures derived from accumulated data that act as standards of measurement by which efficiency, performance and progress – of a plan, or a process, or a product – can be assessed.[27] The precision striven for suggests a helpful way of directing scarce resources. It allows for an assessment of the success of any activity that is easy to understand, and that offers the assurance that resources are not being wasted.

But it also does more than that, for it holds out the possibility of reaching secure value judgements about a range of human activities, not all of which are obviously reducible to economic assessment. The fallibility of human judgement is factored out, replaced by something that appears objective rather than subjective, certain rather than flawed. Just as 'The Market' becomes the sole arbiter of value under neoliberalism, so numbers become more trusted than other ways of assessing the value of any human activity. They hold out the prospect that the prejudices of human judgement can be factored out, offering 'a single final criterion' for value: 'A quantitative, economic criterion' (Lock and Martin in Burrows 2012: 356).[28]

Few areas are immune from the application of metrics; probably because few areas are unaffected by the extension of business thinking to every area of life.[29]

Here's an example of how this practice works, drawn from the world I know best: Higher Education in the UK. I became a lecturer because I enjoyed learning new things, cultivating thought and I wanted to convey the excitement with ideas to others. Look at how that desire of my twenty-something self gets distorted through the application of this new kind of economic thinking.

Since the early 1990s, successive governments have used a series of 'Research Assessment Exercises' as a way of determining with precision the right destination for public money for research.[30] These exercises grade the individual researcher's work, the research environment and – increasingly – the impact of the researcher's work on realms outside Higher Education. These factors, taken together, enable an overall star rating – from 1* to 4* – to be assigned to the work of the university's academics working in any particular field. These figures contribute to the ranking of universities in league tables which are intended to help students and stakeholders make informed decisions. Increasingly, attention has been directed at ensuring the security of this grading system. In the Arts and Humanities, this takes the form of a 'heated debate' about whether measurement tools once viewed as only appropriate for the sciences should be applied to research in these areas.[31] The riveting nature of this discussion includes questions about whether the number of times an article is cited and where – common scientific practice – can be extended to quantify the quality of research in Arts and Humanities.[32] (You are forgiven if you found yourself dropping into a stupor as you read this paragraph. Welcome to my world.)

Dull it might be, but in the world of metric judgements, success and failure are closely aligned to achieving the right numerical grade. With success comes money; with failure, possible disaster. A poor

'Research Excellence Framework' (REF) result can be used to close departments which lack financial viability. That sounds like common sense. But let's just consider what bearing this has on the ideals that led me into a university career in the first place. Now subjects succeed or fail, not because they offer ways into the enquiry inherent in being human, but because they have or have not achieved the requisite grade. And look at what happens to the experience of the individual working in this new kind of university. I have lost count of the number of nights I have worried about whether I have enough 'high quality' publications for a REF return. In the run up to one of these exercises, I feel a sense of my own inadequacy, my own inability to be 'the perfect philosopher' who publishes in the right journals. At the same time, my writing is affected by my desire to score well; and not necessarily in a good way. I feel an urge to use more footnotes, to reference more sources showing I know and am engaged in the current debates. I am tempted to frame my argument so only the cleverest few understand it. And who can blame me? My livelihood depends on a good rating, and who wants an unemployed philosopher of religion?

Through mechanisms of this kind, feelings of success and failure become entrenched in the self, distorting our ideas and our view of the world. Guilt arises when you fail to meet the targets set by those managing you: even if they are unrealistic. And just in case you don't feel guilty enough at this point, others will be on hand to ensure that you *should* feel guilty if you haven't performed as it is believed you should.

Systems of 'performance management' can be instigated to ensure targets are met: with distressing results. Professor Stefan Grimm, a biologist at Imperial College London, killed himself in 2014. He had been told he was failing to secure sufficient grant income, and that if things did not improve he would be sacked. He had brought in £135,000 worth of grants, just short of the target set him of £200,000. You'd think this would be good enough. It wasn't. In this one tragedy we see how the purity of numbers and the desire for impersonal judgements are not without a cost for individuals subject to their rule.

The belief in the purity of the number factors out the messiness of the human. In so-doing, it reduces the colour of life to a dull monochrome. It doesn't allow for the false step, the project that doesn't work, the idea that turns out not to have been a very good one in the first place. It stifles creativity, encourages conformity, doesn't allow for work that is out of the ordinary. And as it does this, it holds out the idea that numbers are pure, that the value they determine is independent of human decision-making.

Yet, of course, this is not so.

2+2=4. This does not mean, however, that all numbers are immune from the vagaries of human experience and reflection. Numbers are not always prejudice-free, much as we might like to think they are. Ian Hacking's history of the development of statistics reveals the social construction of that which is counted and how such figures are presented.[33] The determination of *which* categories are to be counted reveals the beliefs of those who construct them.

Hacking offers a disturbing example. The statistical bureau of nineteenth-century Prussia routinely and consistently used the categories of 'Christian' and 'Jew' to order 'biostatistics'.[34] Assumptions of the supposed differences between these groups, shaped by the views of the time, influenced the presentation of the data.[35] Rather than challenge anti-semitism, these categories were all-too-easily adopted to that end. Prejudices and ideology shaped the statistics. Claims for the purity of numbers are never quite what they seem.

What is lost? Factoring in fallibility

What does all this mean for our discussion of failure? Asking the question 'what is lost?' helps us to think about failure in the context of a well-lived life. To ask 'what is lost?' might sound unbearably nostalgic, suggesting that the questioner is hankering after a past that never was, or, at least, is unlikely to have been as they picture it.[36] Yet to ask this question is to consider the possibility that there are other ways of living. At its heart is a challenge to the negative assumptions surrounding the human perpetuated by bureaucratic and metric solutions.[37] What is lost when the messiness of experience is reduced to the purity of a number? What is lost when the human dimension becomes a problem to be solved? What is lost when systems attempt to factor out the possibility of failure?

Here are two responses which hold out the possibility of resistance to the negative accounts of the human on which such purported solutions depend.

Factoring in the personal

Arendt's critique of bureaucratic systems makes plain what is lost when faith in the ordinariness of human action is eroded. 'The System' is supposed to achieve certainty of outcome. Its processes are deemed preferable to the fallibility of human decision-making. What happens to the personal dimension in the wake of this move? Arendt suggests, somewhat surprisingly, that cultivating the impersonal makes possible greater injustice than is the case in societies that do not depend for their governance upon the 'smooth operation' of administrative processes that would detach their actions from wider human life. Her reason for this conclusion is interesting:

> In comparison [to bureaucratic societies], exploitation, oppression, or corruption look like safeguards of human dignity, because exploiter and exploited, oppressor and oppressed, corruptor and corrupted, still live in the same world, share the same goals, fight each other for the possession of the same things; and it is this

tertium comparationis which aloofness destroyed. (Arendt [1948] 1968: 212)

She is not holding up an alternative utopia. Rather, she is suggesting that somewhere in our messy engagements with each other, it is possible to glimpse a common humanity. We look the other person in the face: we *see* the effect of our actions. The problem with bureaucratic desires to factor out the human is that this sense of a shared world is lost. The bureaucrat's aim is to become aloof from the ordinary concerns of other people. Their concern is that correct process is followed to lead to the right result. In the desire to make the system the arbiter of value, humanity itself is diminished. In Arendt's alternative scenario, we might fight each other, oppress each other, exploit each other: but even if/when we behave badly, a shared social world maintains the possibility for other forms of communication. We continue to see each other as human beings not as numbers on a spreadsheet.

These comments suggest how Arendt might respond to critics of her claim that Eichmann is an example of the banality – the ordinariness – of evil. The claim that 'evil' is ordinary was seen by some as an outrageous downplaying of the horrific events of the Holocaust. Bettina Stangneth, in a meticulously researched biography of Eichmann, claims Arendt is misguided, not least when she takes at face value Eichmann's claims that he did not know his actions contributed to the murder of the Jews. Stangneth's study reveals, instead, Eichmann the Committed Nazi: quite different from the opportunistic careerist of Arendt's account. Far from *not* knowing what lay at the end of the railway tracks he managed, Eichmann was, Stangneth says, all-too-well aware of the effects of his actions. More than that, his actions cohered with his own political beliefs.[38]

Stangneth has a point: Arendt underplays Eichmann's political commitments. Yet she does not ignore the fact that at one level he does indeed know about the acts of genocide perpetrated by the Nazi regime. He may not have seen much during his trips to the concentration camps,[39] but what he does see horrifies him. He sees Jews being gassed and says that 'it left behind a certain inner trembling' (Arendt [1963] 1977: 87). He sees their bodies being stripped of everything valuable – including teeth – and says that 'after that time, I could sit for hours beside my driver without exchanging a word with him' (Arendt [1963] 1977: 88).

For Stangneth, detailing these examples is not enough: Arendt still claims Eichmann didn't 'know' the effects of his actions. Does Arendt ignore the different facets of Eichmann's biography and his concern to put forward a defence that gets him off the hook? Arendt's discussion of Eichmann's case has a different focus. She wants to consider what happens to *the ordinariness of human feeling* under bureaucratic systems of government. In doing so, she raises an important question for her readers. What if, when Eichmann feels himself disturbed by these appalling actions, he had acted on his feelings? What if he had understood his feelings, not as a sign of personal weakness to be overcome but as something establishing the *felt connection* between himself and his fellow human beings being killed in the gas chambers? The Nazis recognized the power of empathy to destabilize command and acted to eliminate these felt connections. The Schutzstaffel (SS) officers and soldiers were trained to overcome their ordinary feelings of compassion for the people they were killing.[40] Personal connection had to be factored out if the Nazi's aims were to be met. The institutions of which Eichmann was a part likewise discouraged these very human connections to the sufferings of others.

What if it had been otherwise?[41]

We arrive at the failures that matter. In Eichmann's mind, his failure lay in his inability to achieve the positions he felt he merited. There is something perverse here; but also something important when read in a time that encourages all of us to be successful entrepreneurs of ourselves. In a context that would have us see others as competitors to be overcome in order to be successful ourselves, what lesson does Eichmann teach us?

> *Eichmann's failure was not, contrary to what he thought, the failure to achieve position, wealth and respect. It was his failure to respond to the needs of the other person.*

Prioritizing success does not create the space necessary for considering the failings of relationship that should most concern us as human beings. It may even be that prioritizing successful achievement lends itself to the failure to take seriously the needs of others.

When Elizabeth Minnich offers her revision of Arendt's ideas in her book *The Evil of Banality* (2017), it is this aspect on which she focuses. The problem of Eichmann is the problem of careerism: a problem that is alive and well in our day and age. When being a success in your job is seen as the sole goal to be pursued, it is no wonder if the needs of other people are considered irrelevant. Arendt's ideas continue to challenge, precisely because she demands we critique systems of governance and the values they express which would obscure those very human feelings of connection. We don't live under the horrors of the Nazi state, but we are living with social structures and attitudes that distort human relationship. By extending the economic to all areas of existence, the ordinary messiness of life is framed as something problematic, in need of management. It may not lead to genocide, but it contributes to a diminished account of what it is to be human.

Spontaneity and relationship

A second point should be made, and this requires opening our minds to a different account of human fallibility. What happens if, rather than worry about the lack of predictability inherent in human action, we embrace it? What happens if, rather than me worrying about getting each sentence exactly right, I just go with the flow? I stop worrying about a critical audience and, instead, enjoy the experience of putting my ideas on paper? I can't control this book's reception, so why not just enjoy the experience of writing?

The unpredictable need not be felt as threatening. It could, instead, be seen as vital for the flourishing human life. *Human beings are not predictable*! It is this quality, remember, that Arendt drew our attention to in Chapter One. We are always capable of 'beginning something new'. If we fetishize certainty, if we seek to factor out failure, we lose sight of the fact that 'the new always happens against the overwhelming odds of statistical laws and their probability, which for all practical, everyday purposes amounts to certainty; the new therefore always appears in the guise of a miracle' (Arendt [1958] 1998: 178). You can put in place all the systems in the world, seek ways of factoring out failure, of making success more likely, and still be surprised by events. What a challenge this poses to the quantification and metrification of the neoliberal world.

If we embrace uncertainty, illusions of control slip away. We are left with a view of what it is to be human that recognizes – even relishes – the fact that *we do not know* and *we cannot be certain*.

Things might go wrong, outcomes might not be achieved. But so what?

It might even be exciting to not know what will happen next. We might feel sceptical at this point. We might feel scared of a world where humans are not constrained by systems of control. Here, Arendt is again helpful, for she introduces two concepts vital for well-being in an unpredictable world: promising and forgiveness.

In the promise, we seek to provide some sense of security to the other person.[42] Promises are a serious business because they attempt a degree of certainty in the uncertain realm of human relationships.[43] In the promise, I commit myself to behaving in the way I tell you I am going to behave. The promise makes possible the ground for relationship and helps to ameliorate the fears of the other person.

In holding out the possibility of forgiveness, there is an acceptance that things might go wrong. After all, human beings are prone to deceit, cruelty and betrayal. Yet despite this, there is the prospect of a future should actions be bad or things go wrong.[44] We can start again when it comes to our relationships. This is the hope inherent in forgiveness. Which is not to say that forgiveness is easy to give or to receive. If anything, its very difficulty reminds us of the painful realities of a world where human beings are *not* perfect, but are forged through the pain, as well as the joy, of lived relationship.

Marian Partington's *If You Sit Very Still* is a disturbing, challenging but ultimately uplifting read on the fragility of life. Partington tells the story of her sister Lucy, who went missing. She had gone to catch a bus and was never seen again. Ten long years pass, during which her family make desperate attempts to find her. Eventually, Lucy is identified as a victim of the serial killers Fred and Rosemary West. No 'closure' comes with this knowledge, and Partington spends a further ten years trying to come to terms with her sister's terrible death. She is angry and broken. Eventually, she comes to believe that if she is ever to live well again she needs to find some way of forgiving the Wests for what they had done.[45] This task is far from easy and is not helped by Rosemary West's failure to make any kind of response to Partington's overtures.[46]

Partington's account is a painful acknowledgement of the precarious nature of life. Not everything can be controlled. Not everything can be rendered safe. Bad luck seems to have played its role in Lucy's death: waiting for a bus that failed to turn up, she is thought to have accepted a lift from the Wests that ended in her torture and murder. Partington's memoir makes it clear that some failures matter much more than others. Think of the Wests and their use of women for their sadistic pleasures. These failures are not bound up with achievement or attainment but arise from the failure to treat others as vital, living, feeling individuals like ourselves who demand our care.

Partington does not avoid engaging with the vulnerability of being human in a world like this. Her love for her murdered sister and the gaping void left by her loss screams from every page. Hers is an account of the joy but also the pain to be found in loving another. Yes, love brings joy, pleasure, companionship, intimacy, even new life. Yet to love is also to court the possibility of suffering. Open yourself up to another and you are open not only to the delight of intimate connections. To love is also to be open to the possibility of pain, betrayal and loss.

How to live with the possibility of this pain?

We could seek to manage these unpredictable experiences by never quite letting ourselves connect in ways which make us vulnerable to pain. If we do that, if we never quite give ourselves to another, we run into another kind of risk. We avoid not just pain but also the very experiences that make possible the richness of being human. Even the pain of loving can be transformed into something else. Stories of lost love can become beautiful invocations of the depths of human experience; the magic of language conjuring up feelings from deep inside the self that reach out, beyond the self, to connect with others. Romeo and Juliet, Tess of the D'Urbervilles, Captain Corelli: these tragic stories of love have the power to enrich our experience because of their ability to find the words to shape our own sensibilities. One of my favourite hymns, 'Oh Love That Wilt Not Let Me Go', was written out of George Matheson's devastating experiences of loss. Finding he was going blind, he told his fiancee, who, unable to share this path with him, left him. One of the most moving lines still sends shivers down my spine: 'I lay in dust, life's glory dead, and from the ground there blossoms red, life that shall endless be.'[47] There is the pain of suffering, the hurt of rejection, but there is also, in his words, the tentative hope that this pain might be transformed. His verses speak not only to his plight but offer me a way of grappling with my own pains and struggles. With him, and through his words, I glimpse the possibility that, in time, my losses might become the seed that enables me to find a deeper connection with life. Pain cannot be avoided if we open ourselves to love, and to factor out the pain may eradicate the very human creations emerging from our struggles with it.

Embracing uncertainty

This chapter began with my fears of writing it. I'm not sure that, getting to the end of it, I have achieved what I set out to. Perhaps that is how it should be. It is imperfect. There are paragraphs that have slipped out of my control, words that do not quite capture the meaning I wanted to convey. I am disturbed by the story of Lucy Partington, by the evil that men and women do. I could go back and try again, but is that the best thing to do? Might there even be value in acknowledging that perfect control is not a good thing, that factoring out the possibility of failure is not always desirable?

The Franciscan friar Richard Rohr prompts us to consider this notion: 'The demand for the perfect is the greatest enemy of the good', he writes. How strange this sounds. How can the perfect *not* be something good? His explanation takes us to the heart of the problem with the desire for purity and demands a recalibration of our concerns:

> Perfection is a mathematical or divine concept, goodness is *a beautiful human concept that includes us all.* (Rohr 2011: loc. 332; my emphasis)

What makes for the good life?

The precision of numbers, applied to the social world, cannot capture the nuance and complexity of the human. My words, similarly, have to reach out in their imperfection to meet your experience, your struggles, your hopes, your dreams. Economic assessments seek to contain spontaneity, to ensure certainty. The desire for absolute inerrancy in our conclusions about things and people avoids this basic truth. If we start from the messiness of human relationship, our focus moves from the determination to achieve a particular outcome to consideration of how to live well in our relationships, with all the compromises, missed opportunities, failures and anxieties those relationships inevitably involve.

The desire for the perfect is not flexible enough to accommodate that which is messy and fallible.

James Scott offers a telling example drawn from the (mis) management of forests in the early days of German forestry. Rather than live with the forest in the way a forester would, understanding the intricate web of connections between trees, plants and wildlife, managers sought easier ways of counting trees, now framed as precious resources. Reducing the ecosystem of a forest to a fiscal unit invariably resulted in disaster.[48] Ancient forests were uprooted to be replaced by trees planted in more uniform, more easily countable rows. Insects were viewed only as pests which needed to be removed. The complex web of life that enabled the forest to flourish was ignored. These acts and omissions contributed to ecological disaster and gave birth to a new term: *Waldsterben* or 'forest death'.[49] For forests to flourish *required* their apparent randomness. An ecosystem including features which, to human eyes, seemed useless was absolutely necessary for healthy woodlands. Factoring out the messiness of things in the name of greater control led, inexorably, to catastrophe.

It does not take a great leap of the imagination to see how Scott's example might speak to the attempt to factor out human fallibility. Factoring out failure, factoring out that which is deemed to be useless, seems, on face value, to make sense. Yet the problem is that what can be taken for failure may actually be the randomness required for flourishing. Tidying up the messiness that is part and parcel of human life is not the answer to how to live. Too great an emphasis on ensuring certainty diminishes, rather than opens up, our experience. The desire for certainty, precision and the purity that comes from numbers, when extended to every area of life, obscures the very things that make for human flourishing. Life is random and messy. What we need are ways of working with this fact to create flourishing lives and communities.

It is no easy thing to accept the unpredictability that accompanies human spontaneity. Yet here is the human not as a problem but as something good in itself. We do not need to put our faith in systems and processes, just in our ability to be with each other. This does not mean that we can avoid the struggle that accompanies living together. Bad things will still happen. But what this renewed emphasis on human relationship does is to put in their rightful place the things that should concern us. When all is reduced to the economic, as it is under neoliberalism, the struggle to live well is distorted, reduced to the individual's achievements. What is needed is something else. What is needed is a willingness to accept human fallibility, to see it as part and parcel of life and to work at ensuring the failures that matter – failures in relationship – are not the final word.

How to live well together? How to bring about communities where all – regardless of their income or ability – are able to flourish? If we are to focus on answering these questions, if we are to find better ways of living with failure, we need a model of the human that goes beyond the reductionism of 'economic man'. We need a model that places the personal, the unpredictable and the uncontrollable at the heart of our engagement with life: a task to which we turn in the next chapter.

5
FROM *HOMO ECONOMICUS* TO *HOMO RELIGIOSUS*: REMAKING THE HUMAN

There is a rather lovely passage in monk and mystic Thomas Merton's *Conjectures of a Guilty Bystander* which expresses perfectly the focus of this chapter:

> I was suddenly overwhelmed with the realisation that I loved all these people, that they were mine and I theirs, that we could not be alien to one another even though we were total strangers. It was like waking from a dream of separateness. (Merton 1968: 156)

Investigating the contemporary shaping of success and failure has taken us deep into a landscape where nothing is immune from the reach of economic categories. Everything, every aspect of life, can be framed through financialization: and that includes the human individual. Understood as economic units, there is little sense of the connection we might have with others. In the place of connection, there is fragmentation: we are to act as atomistic units whose purpose is to strive to be a success, and whose successes – and failures – are to be measured in terms of what we attain and achieve. Against this backdrop of self-realization, other people cease to be viewed as friends or neighbours and instead are constructed as competitors in the game of life.[1]

What does it mean to wake from this 'dream of separateness' which has come to define how we are supposed to behave, and through which we are supposed to frame the meaning of our lives?

In March 2010 I gave my inaugural professorial lecture. It was an enjoyable occasion. Lots of people from my past, both academic and personal, turned up. Students, old and new, mixed with colleagues and collaborators. Family and friends rubbed shoulders with professional contacts. There was wine and canapés, chat and laughter.

On 6 May 2010, there was a General Election. The result was a hung parliament, and after five days of political wrangling, a coalition government of Conservatives and Liberal Democrats replaced the Labour government of Gordon Brown.

Linking these two events might sound odd. One is of a personal success, the other of electoral success and failure, the tussle of politics, the cost of electoral defeat. Yet for me, these two events have become inextricably entwined.

My professorial lecture came in the middle of a personal crisis: that question from the motorway graffiti was hounding me again:

'Why do you do this every day?'

Despite the plaudits, I wasn't enjoying the academic life. Becoming a professor encapsulated the problem. I felt guilty most of the time for not producing the kind of work professors were 'supposed' to produce. Articles for prestigious journals, that I thought contained some of my best work, were rejected. And when I say 'rejected', I mean categorically rubbished. A book I'd started to write no longer inspired me. I felt I was failing, and with that feeling of failure came a sense of loss. I'd lost the joy in philosophy that had framed my working life, but more than that I felt I had lost a sense of myself as 'a philosopher'.

All about me, the political landscape was being transformed. In response to the Global Financial Crisis that had started in 2008, the new government was ushering in an era they dubbed 'the New Age of Austerity'. Public services were being blamed for failings that had originated in the worldwide banking system, and cuts were being planned for education, health, social care, policing and criminal justice.

Unable to ignore the news, I was shaken out of my feelings of inadequacy and discontent. My outrage at the unfairness of the Coalition's solution to a crisis that had started in the world of finance got me involved in political activism. I went on demos; I campaigned for local services and with the local Labour and Cooperative Parties. Eventually I became a candidate for the local elections in 2012 and was elected a city councillor. It was an uplifting time. No longer was I an individual working at my own success. Now I was part of a community working to change things.

I had been jolted out of the dream of separateness.

My first meeting as a new councillor with the ruling Labour Group on Oxford City Council was enlightening and remains inspiring. I was nervous, a 'newbie' who wasn't sure what on earth she was doing. The Town Hall is an impressive Victorian building – a testament to nineteenth-century civic pride – and I climbed the impressive Town Hall staircase with a fair degree of trepidation, finally finding the right meeting room. Round a large oval table sat my new colleagues. Drawn from across the city, there was no one profession that defined us, no one level of education or income. We all came with different life experiences. But what struck me forcibly at that first meeting was the way we were gathered *together* to work at holding onto the things our community needed in the face of cuts from central government. There was little room for ego: which wasn't to say that it was entirely absent from that table! But there was a shared commitment to work together to achieve a broader set of political goals.

This sense of solidarity stood in stark contrast to my experience of being an academic. Success and failure were no longer about my individual desires or achievements but about putting in place the policies 'we' had offered to the voters in those elections. What mattered was working at the flourishing of all – and especially that of the people who were now experiencing the rough end of the coalition government's austerity policies.[2]

All this sounds romantic; and of course politics is not always like this. I'm sure if I'd looked beneath the surface I'd have found a host of motivations, not just the altruistic. But the framing of these motivations was not about achieving individual goals. It was about working for something bigger than ourselves. My attitude to my work as a lecturer and researcher changed. My struggles with my sense of failure seemed rather petty and, frankly, self-indulgent. The ward I represented was one in which I'd lived for twenty years, but I was quickly realizing that alongside the wealth and privilege there was poverty and limited life chances, even in as apparently rich a city as Oxford. These were the things that required my attention, irrespective of whether I got a good write-up from other academics.

Time has moved on. I'm no longer a councillor. But those four years in local government changed me fundamentally. I became – and still am – hungry for community, that aspect of our life that goes unspoken and is largely unacknowledged in the framing of neoliberal success and failure. If we take seriously the fact that we are social animals, embedded in community, the way in which we engage with failure and loss changes too. From being experiences that divide the winners from the losers, they become experiences that we share in one way or another. In recognizing our need for each other, we move beyond fragmented accounts of how to live well, and come to alternative ways of thinking about what we need to flourish.

We are able to be failures, and still live well.

And so I want to offer an account of the human that puts community and connection as its heart. I want to suggest ways in which we, with Merton, can break the dream of separateness.

Homo religiosus and the desire for connection

If neoliberalism structures human beings as *homo economicus*, the model I want to advance is *homo religiosus*, or 'religious human being'.[3] This might seem something of a jump from my description of getting involved in the collective working of local politics. As well as seeming innocuous, connecting a vision of what it is to be human with religion might also seem to create more problems than it solves.

We may well be happy to accept claims that we live in a secular age that has largely put aside religious ideas and practices; or which, at the very least, seems to have left religious beliefs to the fundamentalist, the weak-minded, the nostalgic or the terrorist. We may be troubled by the influence of the Religious Right who support political platforms giving voice to racism and misogyny. One of the most disturbing explanations for Donald Trump's victory in 2016 was the support he garnered from Evangelical Christians and Catholics. He could call Mexicans rapists, be taped boasting about his exploits as a sexual predator, but because he said he would end legal abortion, such comments were ignored by many Christians. In developing an account of humans as *homo religiosus*, I must be extremely clear about what I mean when I use it: not least because of the disturbing connection between religious commitments and reactionary forms of politics.[4]

The maverick philosopher Friedrich Nietzsche says there are times when we must do 'philosophy with a hammer'.[5] This description seems to support claims that he is a wild-eyed – possibly mad – outsider we would do well to leave alone. His words fly in the face of more considered philosophical discourse, but it is difficult to find a better image for illustrating my motivation in offering *homo religiosus* as an alternative to *homo economicus*. The categories shaping *homo economicus* are extremely difficult to shake off. Debates on any aspect of life invariably end with questions of economics:

> '*How much will it cost?*' '*How can you measure that?*' '*What financial benefit will accrue?*'

If we are to move beyond reducing all human life to the economic, an alternative image is required that is so shocking that it shakes us free of the belief that only in the economic is the meaning of life to be found. This account of the human must be so strange that it forces us to look up and consider the possibility that it needn't be like this. It must provide us with an image that disrupts our assumptions about life, and that shakes us to the very foundations of our being.[6] How much more shocking could an image be to those of us living in a secular society than one which claims we are 'religious'? Yet the strangest thing about *homo religiosus* is that, if we shelve assumptions about what it means to 'be religious', an approach emerges that reflects – much more accurately than *homo economicus* can – the conditions which shape human individuality and which show the importance of relationship for the human animal.

Let us begin by unpacking the etymology of *homo religiosus*. This exercise challenges preconceptions about what religion involves. To be religious does not necessitate belief in unscientific accounts of the world or ourselves; neither does it require us to be conservative; nor need it support hatred and bigotry towards those not sharing our beliefs or way of life. Rather, the ideas which construct 'the religious' open up the importance of relationship between ourselves, others and the world.

How does it do this? The Latin 'homo', meaning 'Man', relates to the word 'humus' or 'earth'. This word suggests that humans are earthly beings; that we are, literally, 'beings born from the earth'. The promotion of the independent, resilient individual of neoliberal myth looks rather odd when placed alongside this idea. The entrepreneurial self is defined by its willingness to 'stand out' from the world. The world is viewed as something separate; a resource that can be plundered.[7] Yet the overtones of 'homo' suggest that humans are, first and foremost, of this earth, that it is our home, and that it makes no sense to define ourselves as fundamentally separate from the physical processes that have brought us into being. Rather than strive to distinguish ourselves from the world, there is in the first part of this formulation an acknowledgement that we are fundamentally dependent. We are 'earthly beings'.

These earthly beings are then described as 'religious'.[8] There is a much-disputed, but evocative, definition that links the world 'religion' to the Latin *religare*, meaning, literally, 'to bind'.[9] What we have in religion, if we follow this through, is the attempt to bind oneself or to connect oneself – to bind oneself *again* – to the world and to others. Under this reading, religious practice (its rites, beliefs and ideas) attempts to *reconnect* human beings to the world beyond themselves. We are dependent on the world out of which we have been created; but there is also the suggestion here that we are not entirely at home in this world. We need to connect *again.* For Augustine, the desire for connection comes out of this feeling of disconnection: 'Thou [God] hast formed us for Thyself, and our hearts are restless till they find rest in Thee.'[10]

Augustine is, of course, a Christian theologian, and so he frames this feeling of disconnection through his own faith position. Let us explore this sense of restlessness a little more closely, for there is something here that transcends any one faith position. Born out of earthly processes, the experience of consciousness makes us capable of reflecting on life in a mutable world. Here is the rich possibility inherent in our humanity: we can reflect on our world.[11] Yet, as Augustine's words suggest, this ability is accompanied by anxiety arising from awareness of our fragility in the face of natural forces threatening our very existence. We need to discover ways of being 'at home' in a perilous world. Even Freud, hostile as he is to religion, shares with Augustine this sense that human beings must find ways of being at home in the world. Ritualistic behaviours become for Freud part of the more general human attempt to make the world *feel* more homely.[12] Now, unlike Augustine, Freud also aligns religious behaviours with superstition. Rituals like prayer can be reduced to the same status as touching wood, or crossing your fingers. Prayer, like superstitious actions, is an illusory attempt at making the world feel safe.[13] What makes Freud's intervention interesting, however, is that he does not confine the desire to reach out to this threatening world as something only the formally religious do.

Here is an anecdote from Freud's *Psychopathology of Everyday Life*:[14]

One of Freud's daughters had recovered from a life-threatening illness. As he walked through his study he 'yielded to a sudden impulse and hurled one of my slippers from my foot at the wall, causing a beautiful little marble Venus to fall down from its bracket'. Finding himself strangely unmoved by this 'attack of destructive fury', he sees it as serving to 'express a feeling of gratitude to fate and allowed me to perform a "*sacrificial* act" – rather as if I had made a vow to sacrifice something or other as a thank-offering if she recovered her health!' (1901 [1907]: 169). The presence of the exclamation mark suggests he is somewhat embarrassed by this action. Yet it also reflects something of the understandable (and entirely human) desire to *reach out* to something in order to express thanks for his daughter's recovery.

Freud makes the desire to control the basic human motivation behind an action of this kind. Can we make the world conform to our wishes? I want to offer an alternative interpretation. In superstitious actions there is the (sometimes desperate) desire to reach out beyond the self, to connect with that which lies outside ourselves and our control. And this desire for connection does more than just point up human weakness. It tells us something about the things human beings need if they are to flourish. Let us return for a moment to the neoliberal understanding of the individual as fundamentally self-reliant and independent. What this image fails to engage with is what figures as different as Augustine and Freud point out: human individuality cannot be reduced to an atomistic vision of the self as radically separate from earth and others. There is a need for something more. There is a need for connection with the other, be that 'other' understood as other people or the world itself.

Look again at how Freud responds to the healing of his daughter. His sense of gratitude for her recovery cannot be met simply by sending a card or a gift to her doctors. His feelings of relief go beyond such obvious ways of giving thanks. His desire reaches beyond himself to the very world itself. His desire is to communicate with 'fate': an image that he uses throughout his theorizing in a number of different ways.[15] What he seems to be getting at here – even as he rejects it – is a force which transcends the ordinary world of human relationships. He might later laugh at his desire for this connection, but in this moment – in this action – there is a reminder of the fragility of life. Dependent on natural processes that limit human power, we, with Freud, might well long for something outside ourselves to which we can appeal.

Homo religiosus acts, then, to remind us that humans are beings in need of connection. We are 'zoon politikon', 'political animals', shaped by the desire for connection.[16] Why does this matter? Well, if we frame human being through the need for connection, failure and loss come to look rather different than when they are shaped through economic ideals. Placed in the context of human relationship, these features emerge, not as aberrations that might be avoided but as experiences which are central to life in this world.

Loss and the relational animal

I am arguing, then, that there is something about human beings and their socialization that is better reflected by *homo religiosus* than by *homo economicus*. If we are to live well, to come to terms with failure and loss, we need to recognize the importance of community and connection for human individuals.

Consideration of the processes that lead to the creation of the individual reveals something of the depth of our dependence on others and the earth. It also reveals just how central failure and loss are to these processes. Let us turn to psychoanalytic theory for a way into the investigation of these processes. While some might not enjoy the drama of its story of human development, I think it provides a compelling narrative of the role loss plays in psychosexual development. It is important to note that psychoanalytic theory is far from a static body of work. Freud's theories might be read as principally concerned with exploring what motivates and shapes the behaviour of the individual. His focus on the drives and the psychic structure of the mind lend themselves neatly to such a reading.[17] Yet his postulation of the Oedipus complex[18] also suggests the significance of relationship for the child's psychic development. In describing the three agencies of the mind – Id (unconscious), Ego (conscious self) and Superego (aligned with conscience) – Freud argues that the Superego emerges out of the child's internalization of its relationships with its parents and with wider society. Later 'object relations' theorists pick up on this theme, focusing specifically on the way in which the relationship with the first love object (the mother), along with the other figures in the child's world, form its character and shape its engagement with the world.[19]

What is important about this move from describing agencies of the mind to thinking about the relationships between the child and its first love objects? For our purposes, it reveals a human individual created through and by relationship. A particular role is played by loss in the experience and construction of these relationships.

Far from being an aberration which could be avoided, the experience of loss is deeply embedded in the forces that make us.

We might even go further: loss is essential for establishing identity. Julia Kristeva's work consistently explores this connection. While her psychoanalytic framework is shaped by Jacques Lacan's claims that language provides the way into the world of the unconscious,[20] her emphasis on the role of the mother in the creation of individuality also reflects her reading of Melanie Klein's groundbreaking work on the child's relationship with its mother.[21]

What interests Kristeva is the *tragic* dimension of the mother–child relationship. In order for the child to grow and to become capable of relationship, it must lose the original closeness of its symbiotic connection to its mother. Where there was once a duality – mother and child – space needs to be made in order to accommodate 'the third' who makes possible language. In her essay 'Stabat Mater' she explores what is entailed for this break to be made. The title of this piece is derived from the Latin description of Mary as 'the sorrowing mother who was standing' at the foot of Christ's cross and suggests something of the use to which she will put religious story. The text itself oscillates between reflections on her own experience of mothering and a more obviously academic discussion of the Virgin Mary.[22] The use of both narratives makes space for her to reflect on the pain of mother and child as separation the one from the other takes place:

> One does not give birth *in* pain, one gives birth *to* pain. (Kristeva [1977] 2002: 120; my emphasis)

Separation is experienced not just in the event of birthing, but throughout the experience of mothering, for 'a mother is a continuous separation' ([1977] 2002: 130).

Artistic representations reveal something of Kristeva's 'continuous separation' of mothering. On Berlin's Unter den Linden stands the city's War Memorial. A nineteenth-century temple-like structure, complete with Grecian-style pillars, an enlargement of Käthe Kollwitz's statue *Mother with Her Dead Son*, sculpted in 1937, was placed in it in 1993 to commemorate 'victims of war and tyranny'.[23] Also known as the

Pieta, this designation reflects a connection between motherhood, the Virgin Mary and loss, which is similar to that made by Kristeva. It is a melancholy memorial for the countless mothers and sons caught up in the bloody conflicts of the twentieth century. For Kollwitz, her sculpture is a deeply personal representation of grief. A mother cradles a dead child, and this image expresses her pain at the death of her son Peter during the Great War. She writes poignantly of the cost of his loss:

> I sometimes think, it was then that I gave up my strength. At that moment I became old.
> Began the walk to the grave. That was the break. The stoop to such a level, that I could never again stand straight.[24]

The image of Mary the Mother of Jesus resonates down the ages as a way of representing this anguish for a lost child. It is Mary again who offers a way into the grief and pain of loss in Colm Tóibín's short novel, *The Testament of Mary*. Written in the first person, Tóibín's Mary is struggling to contain her fury at the torture and execution of her son. She is angry with those responsible but even more so with the disciples who are busily creating a myth of her son's life. Some solace is found, not in the Father-God of the Jewish tradition, nor in the God that Jesus' followers are writing up. Instead, it is Artemis, the Mother Goddess, 'bountiful with her arms outstretched and her many breasts waiting to nurture those who come towards her' (2013: 103), whose temple eases Mary's feelings of brokenness and death.

Kollwitz and Tóibín offer dramatic representations of the loss of a child. What Kristeva suggests is that even ordinary mothering is caught up with loss. It has to be, for the child's coming to maturity *requires* a break with the mother. Language, which enables the child to reach out to the other in order to experience new forms of love and relationship, depends on losing this first relationship. In *Black Sun*, her investigation of depression and melancholia, Kristeva makes the pain underlying this move plain:

> The child king becomes irredeemably sad before uttering his first words; this is because he has been irrevocably, desperately separated from the mother, a loss that causes him to try to find her again, along with other objects of love, first in the imagination, then in words. (Kristeva 1989: 6)

This is an important reflection. The loss of the mother enables language; but it also leaves the child sad and seeking after the mother's shadow in others, in its dreams and also in language. Desire is shaped by that original longing to return to the Eden of closeness experienced with the mother. This leaves us in a tragic situation, for this longing is for that which can never be attained.[25]

That loss is necessary for the process of human individuation returns us to *homo religiosus.* Kristeva's account alludes to both the making and – crucially – the unmaking of connection.

It is that original unmaking of the relationship with the mother that makes possible the making of new relationships.

For Kristeva, the act of splitting takes on particular significance for understanding the attraction of religion, which in her writings is exemplified by Christianity. Reflecting on Hans Holbein's painting of the Dead Christ, Kristeva sees in the separation of Christ from God a representation of the 'splittings' of 'birth, weaning, separation, frustration, castration', which are the very 'processes [which] necessarily structure our individuation'. What makes Christian forms powerful is that they 'brought to consciousness the essential dramas that are internal to the becoming of each and every subject' (Kristeva 1989: 132). Loss sits beneath the surface of our experience and is made explicit in religious stories. The narrative of the dying and rising Christ reflects the making, unmaking and remaking of relationship, which is a necessary part of human experience.

What begins with the separation from the mother and the need to make connection with others is not something restricted to the time of childhood. In therapy, a common focus is on the need to free up experience when a person is stuck in destructive or outmoded patterns of behaviour.[26] Freud describes such stultifying experiences as 'the compulsion to repeat', and if we have ever witnessed someone caught up in the repetitive cycling of the same kind of destructive relationship, we will doubtless understand what he means. In such behaviour Freud identifies the presence of 'the death drive', and it can certainly feel as if you are watching or experiencing something deathly in destructive repetitive behaviour.[27] These repetitious, destructive actions 'hinder the processes of transformation' (Green 2011: 68). The work of therapy is to open up the possibility of new ways of engaging with one's world. In this work, there is recognition that if we are to flourish we will need to make *and* – crucially – *unmake* our experience of the world. We need to be prepared to give up on things, to find ways of feeling more comfortable with the losses that come in life's wake.

This is not easy. Once again we encounter the way in which loss can become merged with failure, for to give something up can feel like failure. When a relationship ends, it can be difficult to accept that something once precious is now over. Frida Kahlo's paintings are celebrated, not least for her ability to capture the myriad forms that brokenness can take. She details the torment of being unable to bring a child to birth, the struggle with the pain of a back broken in an accident, and the agony of the end of her relationship with the artist Diego Rivera. It is that heartbreak which provides visceral insight into the end of love. In one of her most famous paintings, 'The Two Fridas' sit side-by-side, staring out at the viewer. One is dressed in the white lace of a colonial lady; blood from an open vein, held shut – rather precariously – by a pair of surgical scissors, is dripping onto her skirt. The other Frida, dressed in Mexican clothing, represents the 'more natural' side of Frida that Rivera was supposed to have loved. This Frida holds the hand of the more conventional wife. Here is an image that speaks of felt failure, for it is as wife that Rivera has rejected her. This image also acts as a reminder of lost love and her desperate desire for her no-longer husband. Kahlo's fans, ruminating on Rivera's frequent betrayals, may well want the artist to move on, to resist feeling pain at the hands of a lover unworthy of her loyalty. In suggesting that this is somehow an easy thing to do, we ignore how difficult it is, in practice, to make similar breaks in our own lives. Even when we know it is for the best, we do not always want to give up on something. Kristeva, rather more wisely, traces this hesitance back to the ambivalence greeting the child's loss of the mother: we both want and we don't want her. Taken into the pains and upsets of adulthood, we might well be confronted with the same desire for change, for a new life, and yet still desperately cling to the security of the old one. Things are rarely as clear-cut as we want them to be.

Establishing relationship and identity requires us to become comfortable with loss. If we follow Kristeva's psychoanalytic reflections, loss cannot be reduced to something bad that we should hope to avoid. There is pain; but there is also, in embracing that pain, the possibility of new life: 'There is losing and there is the transformative effect of loss' (Butler 2004a: 18). Loss (and failure too) do not leave us untouched. This is what makes both such difficult and distressing experiences. But here, in their disruptive energy, is the potential of both. If we are to live well, we must find ways not of excluding, but of embracing, loss and failure.[28]

Making good relationship

That relationship is a continual process of making, unmaking and remaking suggests there is nothing certain about its outcome. Just because I am suggesting we need to acknowledge the way in which we are made by relationship does not mean that the relationships we enter into will always be good or will always enable the flourishing life. That would be naive in the extreme. The promise of *homo religiosus* is that by making central the role of connection in shaping us as individuals we can also acknowledge the need to think seriously about the conditions necessary for creating good relationships. Community is not something separate from the formation of human individuals. We are animals who must bind ourselves – must bind ourselves *again* – to others and to the world. What are we to do about the failures of relationship and the experiences of loss that denote the context for mutable human life? If we accept the ever-real presence of failure and loss, what will it mean to live well?

In the previous chapter we considered what is lost when attempts are made to remove the personal dimension from human decision-making and judgement. Here, my aim is to enshrine the personal in our engagements with each other. What happens if we recognize in each other the fleshy beings who hope, love, fear, desire, make mistakes, grieve, suffer and die? The totality of the human person is central to my vision of a flourishing society. There is a degree of risk involved in this move. After all, we know that human beings do not always act well in their engagements with each other. Emphasizing relationship moves us beyond *homo economicus*, but it also entails consideration of what is required for the kind of relationships that make possible the flourishing life.

The art of conversation and the shaping of community

In Kristeva's account of individual development, language emerges from the break with the mother, the loss which enables relationship. In language we connect with 'the third' – the father, the other person, or society more generally – who is outside the maternal bond. Through language we seek to create connections with others and the world. Here is the basis for an account of human connection which makes conversation vital for the creation of individuality. In conversation we attempt to make, and remake, relationship.

Language need not imply the use of words. There are other ways in which we converse: through the body, through facial expression, through touch. 'To touch is to signify relation', as the feminist theologian, Carter Heyward puts it (1982: 152).

Here are just a few examples of a range of conversations, which in their variety suggest the diverse activities which create the social world. I walk along a busy street and swap smiles with a woman that I pass. I go for a walk in Christchurch Meadow and exchange greetings with the man who is invariably sat on the same bench everyday, and who feeds the ducks on the river. The pattern of our conversation follows a familiar pattern: how we are doing, the weather, the ducks, the way the Meadow looks. All very ordinary, but I miss him if he is not there. A conversation with a fellow church member who I don't know very well, but who has become valued for her wise approach to life. A phone chat with an old friend which runs the range of topics and reflects the fact that we have known each other for the past forty years. These conversations bind me to the world. They create a bond between myself and others.

Connections of this kind are more than incidental. They enable creative engagements with the world. In these engagements is the capacity to shape the political world, for politics is nothing grander than the actions of 'the social animal'. Small scale and personal enactments, of the kind just described, have the potential to encourage the individual to think differently.

Consider my friend in Christchurch Meadow. He is one of Oxford's many homeless. Alongside his bag of bread for the ducks, he also carries cans of beer. He is there from morning till night. I might dismiss him as 'a transient', 'a vagrant', 'a failure' who clearly can't hold down a job. But through talking with him, through sharing the minutiae of the day, I have come to a different relationship with him. He is, I realize, as much a part of the social fabric of Oxford as I am with my nice salary, my expensive house, my friends and my family.

Making conversation opens us up to others. This involves conversing, mind, not *talking*. In talking, I don't necessarily accept the parity of the other person; I could just be engaging in an egotistical monologue. It is only when I treat the other person with mutual regard and reciprocity that talking becomes a conversation.

Something else happens in this process. The possibility of retreating into the impersonal recedes. I meet the other person as they are, in all their fleshy otherness. I acknowledge their presence in the moment we share.

What happens to politics if conversation of this kind is placed at its heart?[29] As a local politician, it's true that I spent considerable time talking to constituents on the doorstep, hearing their concerns and trying to do something about them. In practice, I am not entirely convinced that this was about enshrining that sense of a broader conversation. Since the 1990s, politics has been shaped by 'the focus group'. A key group of voters is identified whose support makes the difference between winning and losing. Policy is then crafted to appeal to them. To a large extent, this method continues to shape the themes driving our politics. The problem with this ends-driven approach is that the conversations to be valued are narrow and exclusive. There is an agenda driving them which has little to do with allowing for an open-ended discussion of a range of themes. Might we be more ambitious, creating a public space that takes seriously the art of conversation itself?

When we converse, we create a space with others where we listen and contribute. There is a fluidity to the ebb and flow of language, as well as to the kinds of response we might make to what the other person says. A good conversation is not lineal or directed towards one predetermined end. It meanders. If it were given a visual representation it might look like a murmuration of birds, rising up, falling down, moving backwards and forwards. A shifting kaleidoscope of thoughts, words, impressions and feelings. A free-forming conversation like this can only happen when those engaged in it are all deemed worthy of respect.

In the realm of conflicting ideologies and party politics, accommodating this openness is difficult. The other person can too-easily be shaped as an opponent with whom we engage in 'the battle of ideas'. I'm not keen on this military analogy. It's too bound up with ideas of winning and losing; too reminiscent of framing everything through that corrosive lens of success and failure. Linked to the desire to achieve certainty of outcome, it is difficult to see how the political realm might be constituted through recognition of a plurality of concerns.[30] If we started with the things that unite us, perhaps we would be less likely to vilify the people whose ideas we don't much like, or who seem so different from us. As we have seen, mortality reminds us that we are vulnerable beings, dependent on others and the world. If we were able to meet each other, to talk with each other, perhaps we would come to think of ourselves less as competitors and more as companions who together are shaping the social world.

The potter Grayson Perry's vases 'The Matching Pair' suggest what might come out of this kind of shared political conversation. These two vases look remarkably similar. They are of similar colours, they show similar figures. They were created out of the artist's conversations with two groups who, in the context of Brexit Britain, could not seem further apart: a group who had voted to Remain in the EU, and a group who had voted to Leave. Perry asked them what they loved about Britain, 'to send in their ideas for what should be included, what represented the whole thing to them, even what colour they should be, and they've come out surprisingly similar', he said. This is 'a good result, for we all have much more in common than that which separates us'.[31]

We might raise our eyebrows at the naivety of the artist. Ideological differences surely matter, as the horrific events of the twentieth century and the continuing human rights abuses in Syria and Myanmar show us today. But perhaps Perry has a point about how our political conversations could be modelled. Less a series of requests and demands, a conversational politics would be modelled on the practices of friendship. We don't want our friends to be precisely the same as us. We recognize our equality while allowing space for our differences.[32] Allowing a respectful starting point for our political discussions would enable an attitude where we are willing and able to challenge each other's views in a way which does not seek to rubbish them, but to learn from them. We might even change our views, and it could be that our conversation partners change theirs too. Out of that process of learning from each other comes the possibility of something that becomes *our* belief or *our* action: something that we have created *together*.[33]

For a flourishing public realm, shared spaces are required to enable people with different views and life experiences to meet together for real conversation about their lives and their communities.[34] To take seriously this idea requires the political will to value local forms of government and to enshrine political engagement as a key feature of life. There would need to be time outside the working week put aside for everyone to engage in this kind of civic conversation. We should not underestimate how radical this shift would be in shaping public life. Not all have access to the spaces currently shaping our social and political landscape. Not all have access to the realms of power and policymaking. For too many, power is something inflicted upon them, not something which arises from the life in which they participate.

Something else is lost when our politics takes the form of an exclusive conversation. Nowhere is this more plain than in the political shaping of ideas of failure: a shaping that excludes some, even as it makes unhealthy demands on those deemed to be successful. Social anthropologist Gillian Evans provides a telling example of this lacuna in her investigation of policy initiatives designed to challenge the 'educational failure' of white working class children. Evans had come to live on a Bermondsey Council Estate. Middle class, her partner's life as a musician and the fact that she had 'failed to translate my university education into a well-paid career' (2006: xiii) required somewhere 'cheap' to live: hence the Estate. She became fascinated by her new neighbours, and this provides the impetus for her research. She is not an insider. Her outsider perspective could mean that she becomes just another 'poverty tripper' who doesn't really have to engage with the lived experiences of others. In practice, it is this neither-in-nor-out positioning that gives her study its sense of movement. The children and their families challenge her, just as she is an oddity to them. She does not, importantly, adopt a 'view from above'. She is part of this community, even if her background is different. And her research takes on this personal dimension. She does not reduce her research to a neat set of statistics that might conform to the metrics culture we investigated in the previous chapter. Instead, she gets the children and their families to tell their stories. Her research offers a series of vignettes of life on the estate: she is not just the recorder of these events, she is also a participant. What emerges from her research is an Evans changed through her engagement with her neighbours, and you can't help wondering if this change is also felt by the people she interviewed.

This personal approach is not without impact for the development of public policy. Evans challenges the kind of political conversations that would impose one set of values on the experience of every citizen. She is fascinated by the lack of fit between policy interventions designed to make the children 'more successful' in educational terms and the children's own values. The attempt to impose the neoliberal value of 'aspiration' met – quite rightly, in Evans's view – with a determined resistance on the part of the children and their parents. They saw behind this language of how to be a success an assumption that the only 'proper life' (2006: 32) was one in which this value was acted out. They resisted this, because they recognized the paucity of the model of success being offered them. To avoid failure, they were supposed to give up on the community that formed the context for their living. They were supposed to be grateful for the opportunity to escape through becoming 'a success'.

The tight knit community from which the children came was not necessarily a place from which they wanted to 'escape' by becoming good neoliberal 'global citizens', educated to work in a variety of places. Struggling with economic uncertainty, they felt the strength that came from strong social bonds. They felt pride in their community's 'resilience in the face of adversity' (2006: xvi). They did not associate the estate with a failed community; on the contrary, they were proud of where they lived.[35] They felt the importance of the sense of connection I identify with *homo religiosus*. Tony Blair might have claimed that 'we're all middle class now' (Evans 2006: xiii), but for Evans this crude soundbite denied the economic and social differences of British people. The children she met were doomed to fail when measured against Blair's criteria, not because they were stupid or indolent but because they were forced to adopt the 'intrinsic middle class bias in the education system' (2006: 13). The model of success being held out to them ran contrary to everything they held to be important. They were supposed to welcome becoming mobile, flexible and adaptable individuals. Instead, they wanted to maintain their connection to the place where they lived.

Modelling human being as *homo economicus* does not allow for this positive recognition of community. Here is its major flaw. Womanists[36] make similar criticisms when highlighting the inadequacy of the kind of 'white' feminism that speaks only to the concerns of middle class, professional women. It is all very well considering the problems of sexism that stop individual women achieving their goals, but that kind of individualism does not capture the importance of community. Black women are better placed to understand this importance, given the role collective struggle has played in combatting white racism. As Keri Day points out, this means that 'the quest for selfhood is not the quest for atomic individualism. The cultivation of authentic selfhood is the pursuit of healthy individuality that finds its ultimate meaning in love of Divine, self, *and neighbour*' (Day 2016: 71; my emphasis). There is a decided lack of romanticism in the writing of womanists on community. It is not a straightforward good, but always something felt as ambiguous. Communities can ignore sexism, forcing women to take on particular, culturally-determined and submissive roles,[37] even as they provide the context for the joint struggles necessary for challenging unjust economic and social conditions.[38] But to assume that the individual, alone, can overcome injustice is misguided, and whatever else may be the case, womanist thinkers make a powerful argument for taking seriously the significance of community for shaping identity.

If policymakers conversed with – and took seriously – the values shaping a diverse range of communities, it might be possible to move beyond the monolithic construction of the striving, acquiring individual as the only model for living well. It's not just that this vision does not appeal to all. It's also that those dismissed as 'failures' may well have much to teach about the conditions that make possible the flourishing life. Something important is opened up when we seek to establish meaningful conversations with those with whom we share the social world. This is, of course, a challenging thing to do. We may hear much that we don't like, approve of, or will want to actively resist. If we are to create a political space open to all, to reach out beyond the confines of our own attitudes to have genuine conversations capable of change, then we will need to develop an openness – a generosity even – towards those we meet, the theme of the next section.

Generosity and the cultivation of relationship

The practice of generosity looks different depending on whether it is framed by the attributes of *homo economicus* or *homo religiosus*. The model of economic man ensures that generosity is financialized, located in the realm of philanthropic giving. As Margaret Thatcher famously put it in her interpretation of the biblical story of the Good Samaritan: 'Nobody would remember the Good Samaritan if he had only good intentions. He had money as well.' Microsoft founder Bill Gates's and business magnate Warren Buffet's charitable giving reflects Thatcher's view. Here are two billionaires using their wealth to address a variety of global ills. Doubtless in a world where resources are spread unequally, it is better to follow their lead and be philanthropic rather than miserly; yet to identify generosity exclusively with philanthropy is far from unproblematic.[39] This construction places the power to shape the world in the hands of a few rich individuals, while undercutting the kind of systematic governmental initiatives that could address poverty more effectively. It also enshrines the importance of being an economic success. The creation of wealth becomes a necessary factor in one's ability to enter – and shape – the political world.

Philanthropy might be an indicator of a person's economic success, but it can be seen – somewhat surprisingly, perhaps – as a form of failure. Nietzsche's critique of pity suggests precisely this reading, at the same time as it opens up the possibility of an alternative account in tune with the values of *homo religiosus*. For the one pitying the other, 'the thirst for pity is … a thirst for self-enjoyment, and that at the expense of one's fellow men' (Nietzsche [1878–80] 1996: 39; HAH (Human, All Too Human) I §50). Far from enabling a sense of solidarity with the one who is suffering, pity depends upon condescension. Think of the difference between receiving charity dependent on the goodwill of another and receiving something from the State to which one is entitled.[40] In the act of pity, Nietzsche spies the movement from the one above to the one perceived as below. This reveals, he says 'the pleasure of gratification in the exercise of power' (1996: 56; HAH I §103). In pity, an attempt is made to create distance between the generous individual and the one who is suffering: 'We remove from ourselves the suffering we ourselves feel by performing an act of pity' (1996: 56; HAH I §103).[41] From our perspective, Nietzsche's critique reminds us of the encounter with loss considered in Chapter Three. His critique suggests that, rather than grapple with loss as something we *all* experience, in philanthropic action it gets located only in the experience of the sufferer. It is *their* problem that we seek to address, rather than something that has the potential to unite us.

For the one on the receiving end of the pity Nietzsche describes, the effect is to be rendered invisible. To be pitied is to experience contempt for one's humanity:

> Pity is felt as a sign of contempt because one has clearly ceased to be an object of *fear* as soon as one is pitied. One has sunk below *the level of equilibrium.* (1996: 322; HAH: WS §50; my emphasis)

We might resist Nietzsche's assumption that a relationship of equals depends upon the possibility of violently asserting your rights. But there is an aspect of his claim that brings us to the heart of the matter. What happens to *parity of relationship* between the one who needs help and the one who offers it? If pity becomes the basis for generosity, what happens to the possibility of the mutual regard I've identified as necessary for the kind of conversations that might shape an open political space? To equate generosity with philanthropy is to accept the unequal starting point between the one who gives and the one who receives. Instead of *seeing* the one in need, instead of hearing their story and recognizing in it our shared struggles, the bestower of pity overrides that story and 'gaily sets about quack-doctoring at the health and reputation of its patient' (Nietzsche 1996: 229; HAH2: §68). Pity becomes a means of asserting inequality rather than *assuming* equality of humanity. It frames the other person as a failure, while reinforcing the sense of one's own success.

An alternative way of shaping generosity emerges if we start with the shared experience of being vulnerable human beings standing in the face of death. It might surprise us to find support for this idea in the writings of Arthur Schopenhauer, last encountered in Chapter Two making some outrageously misogynistic comments. Nietzsche's erstwhile mentor, Schopenhauer bases morality in the emotions, specifically in experiencing another's suffering *as your own*. In compassion for the other person there is the *felt recognition* of a common humanity.[42]

> *Here is an ethic of generosity based in the values of homo religiosus. We are connected; we need each other.*

Nietzsche dismisses Schopenhauer's notion of compassion as yet another variety of the pity he so devastatingly critiques.[43] He ignores the connection Schopenhauer makes between the two parties. In Schopenhauer's account of compassion,[44] 'the other's misery assumes the same status as my own by moving me to relieve it' (Cartwright 1988: 561). Faced with the one who is suffering, 'I feel his woe just as I ordinarily feel only my own' (Schopenhauer [1839]

1995: 143). I identify myself with the other person.[45] I look in the other's face and realize 'an intuitive and immediate truth' (Mannion 2003: 19): the other's suffering matters as much as my own.[46]

This conclusion might surprise us. After all, racism and sexism would seem to rely on a surface summation of the worth of the other person derived from that first glance: I don't see the reality of the person in all their idiosyncratic fullness; I see instead someone who is 'black' or 'a woman'. Yet Schopenhauer suggests that it is not the face that elicits these prejudicial responses, but later ideological overlays. In the first look in the other person's face he sees something much more ordinary; something, in fact, that underpins our day-to-day relationships. This is the 'everyday phenomenon of compassion', of 'participation … in the suffering of another' (Schopenhauer [1839] 1995: 144). I acknowledge the other person as requiring my attention as I look them in the face, and this fellow-feeling acts as a call to action. If they are suffering, that suffering demands I respond.

Schopenhauer's sexism suggests he is not able to live up to the promise of his own theorizing. I'm not sure that that makes it any less powerful: if he can't, perhaps *we* can. Generosity arrives, not from pitying the other person, nor from using it to display our own financial resources to meet their need. Generosity is not experienced in a context where the other's failure becomes an opportunity for me to show my success. Rather, generosity is made possible when a common humanity is recognized. I realize the other person's suffering to be just as important as my own. Striving for this imaginative connection prepares the ground for the creation of good relationship. It makes possible an openness to the other, a willingness to engage with them, and to be changed by that engagement. Acknowledging loss becomes the thing which unites us, for all of us are subject to suffering, and just as we recognize we have need of the other person's care, so we must care for the other. Understandings of failure shift, too, when seen through this lens.

Like loss, to fail is a universal experience, a common condition of humanity.

Failure morphs from something that stands as an isolating judgement, into something that highlights the experience of all human beings. In the previous chapter we considered Marian Partington's attempts to forgive the Wests for their murderous cruelty. In part, her willingness to forgive stemmed from recognizing her own anger and callousness towards others. Rather than isolate her sister's murderers, she sought to make a connection. We may be appalled that she even attempts such a thing; but these words from the letter she sent to Rosemary West provide a sense of the kind of connection she seeks and that we might build upon in our relationships with others:

> I have made choices in my life that have hurt other people, especially when I was feeling deep confusion and pain about Lucy's inexplicable disappearance … I know that you have known a lot of fear. You said that you had always been looking over your shoulder, all your life. I feel fear in my belly. Sometimes I feel heavy and black … Our lives are connected and I am sending you the springing of the branch as a token of hope. May you be less burdened by fear. (Partington 2012: 168–9)

Few of us, I suspect, could show this level of generosity to people who had hurt us and those we love so much. But if we can shake off the feeling that this reaching out is extraordinary, we might be able to see in these words the possibility of a different way of thinking about failure: even when the failures being examined are the failures of relationship that should concern us most. Partington suggests that there is connection, if we look for it, between ourselves and others, even in contexts when that seems most unlikely to be the case.

Not that Partington's generosity of spirit met with a fitting response. She doesn't know whether Rosemary West reads her letter; all she knows is that West sends word through the prison authorities that she does not want any future letters from her. A dead end? Perhaps. But imagine a political realm where we attempted to shout less and listen more; where we attempted to hear others into speech. Making loss and failure central to our account of the human opens up possibilities for our engagements with other people. There is no certainty as to where this will lead, but it does suggest different possibilities for the social world where it is possible to fail, to suffer loss, and still hold to the fragile hope that we might be able to live well together.

Homo religiosus and relationship with the universe

A more obvious way of reading relationship accompanies the framing of human beings as *homo religiosus*. In religious practice, an attempt is made to connect with that which lies beyond the human. This can be rendered as 'God' or 'Allah' or 'Yahweh', or any of the other names for a divine presence or reality. This attempt can involve practices aimed at bringing the self to realization of the true nature of things, so that an escape from the endless cycle of craving might be effected. Religious traditions, beliefs and practices are diverse; yet something unites them. Through practice and ritual, the gaze is directed beyond the self's concern with itself, towards the other person, but also beyond the human itself. Attention is paid to placing the self, its longings and anxieties, in the wider context of the universe.[47]

The desire for relationship defining *homo religiosus* does not stop with the connections we make with other human beings. For me, the connection found in discovering politics was just the start. I actively started looking for places where community was being made: residents groups, local charities, neighbourhood groups. Eventually I realized that I needed something else too: I desired connection with that which lay beyond the human, and I returned to church practice after an absence of some twenty years. Here was another community of which I wanted to be a part, and here was a community that gathered together to seek a different kind of connection.

As we saw in Freud's tale of 'the Broken Venus', it is possible to find in the human need for relationship the longing for another kind of relationship: one which transcends – yet embraces – the desire to relate that shapes us as individuals. This desire is for connection with that which lies beyond the self, beyond the human world itself. To attain this kind of connection requires a de-centring of the self, and it is here that we find further impetus for moving beyond the concerns of the economic individual of neoliberalism. The obsession with achieving success and the fear of failure reflects an unhealthy form of attention to the self. Neurotic self-regard informs the kind of metric monitoring encountered in the previous chapter. Acknowledging the reality of the other person makes it possible to go someway to escaping this fretful self-centredness: but something more is needed to evade the anxiety that comes with acknowledging the fragility of our dependence on the processes of this world.

In a helpful intervention made in the late 1950s, Paul Tillich analyses the problems of a secularism that thinks all will be well if only we put aside religion. As human beings, we require something with the power to make sense of our lives. Faith, it transpires, is not an optional extra that can be given up as the claims of formal religion recede. All of us require something or someone in whom to place our trust. Faith is, if you like, the fundamental component for being human.[48] What is faith, if it is so important that it transcends formal religious attempts to cultivate it? Here's Tillich's definition:

Faith is a total and centred act of the personal self, the act of unconditional, infinite and ultimate concern. ([1957] 2009: 9–10)

His language might sound strange, 'the ultimate' suggesting the kind of religious beliefs that might make us uneasy. Tillich, however, challenges claims that the ultimate can only be read through the language of formal religion. Ask instead: what is the thing that you take most seriously? What it is it that gives your life meaning and focus? What do you trust? What do you value without reservation? It might be money, wealth, your job, another human being. Then he asks another question: this thing in which you place your faith; what happens if it is not the *ultimate* but something *penultimate*? Not something that is final, but something which is 'almost' final? When we place our faith in something, we endow it with a kind of *unconditional* concern. It becomes the lens through which we approach everything in life. It becomes the bedrock for how we live. It takes on the character of the divine:

> Everything which is a matter of unconditional concern is made into a god. ([1957] 2009: 50)

The language is unsettling, particularly for people who may well think that they have rejected belief in God or gods; and this is precisely what Tillich intends. But he is adamant: none of us can escape the need for faith. We are beings who have to place our faith in something. Problems arise when that faith is placed in something which 'claims to be ultimate but is only preliminary, transitory, finite' ([1957] 2009: 11).

Think of the neoliberal focus on the economic as the sole criteria for value. If we apply Tillich's assessment, the financialization of everything makes money a matter of unconditional concern. We live in a society where we are supposed to see economic arguments as the end point of any discussion. But what is money for? Itself? That can't be right. If it were, hoarding chests of gold, like some latter-day Scrooge, would be enough to make us happy. Presumably money is acquired in order to achieve some other end, valued for its use. Is it about ensuring or denoting success? If it is, the meaning of our life will always be precarious, based on securing and then maintaining the success we have worked so hard to achieve. This does not sound like a convincing account of what has ultimate significance and what might be worthy of our faith.

Tillich lived through the Second World War, and in his discussion we hear echoes of the disaster that accompanied the faith placed by his fellow Germans in one man, Adolf Hitler. When the penultimate – be that Hitler, money, numbers, another human being – is mistaken for the ultimate, we meet with 'the inescapable consequence [which] is "existential disappointment"' (Tillich [1957] 2009: 13). The penultimate cannot bear the weight of being made ultimate.

Let's unpack this claim. We are relational animals. We require connection with others in order to flourish. In religion, there is the suggestion that relationship extends beyond the human to that which lies beyond the human itself. It need not be only in the formal claims of religion that the truth of this statement can be found. Even if I refuse to be trapped in the materialism that accompanies the financialization of everything, the meaning of my life cannot be grounded entirely in the life of another human being, no matter how good that relationship is. If it is, I will be devastated if/when they die, or if they leave me. Now, as we have seen, we cannot avoid grief if we enter into relationship. But if we are to live well we require another kind of relationship that enables us to continue living even if that precious relationship is lost. We need a relationship that transcends, but that also embraces, the relationships that give our lives meaning as relational animals.

It would be an obvious move to identify this other relationship with 'God'. For some of us, this might be the conclusion we reach. Tillich is rather more subtle, emphasizing, instead, the *quality* of this other relationship. The ultimate cannot be confused with money, or success, or another human being, for it is 'the ground of all being' or 'being itself'.[49] It is that from which we originate as existent things and from which we derive our being. Here is the relationship that supports all relationships. To live well, we must connect with it once more. The kind of flourishing relationships considered in the last section provide the impetus to move towards acceptance of this relationship which embraces all relationships:

> Love is the power in the ground of everything that is, driving it beyond itself toward *reunion with the other one* and ultimately with *the ground itself* from which it is separated. (Tillich [1957] 2009: 132; my emphasis)[50]

But the desire for connection cannot stop with the relationship with that one special person, or with my friends or my family, or even with the people with whom I share my world. The importance of connection demands that I place my life in the context of the universe itself. Religious people, take note, do not have a monopoly on the cultivation of this relationship. They are just as capable of mistaking the penultimate for what is ultimate as anybody else; perhaps more so, as images of God can all-too-easily be mistaken for literal representations of Being Itself.[51] To live well requires committing ourselves to the practice of making good relationships with others; but it also requires re-orientating ourselves towards the universe that brought us into being.

In the final chapter I suggest some practices for locating our lives within this bigger, cosmic picture. As *homo religiosus*, we are shaped by our relationships with others, and grounded in the universe which gave rise to us. Something interesting happens to success and failure when our life is located against the backdrop of this wider world. The desire for success and the fear of its shadow, failure, seem rather paltry concerns when placed within the context of the cosmos.

The pressure to be a success, to avoid failure, dissipates as we direct our attention to connecting with the ultimate.

The self that emerges from this endeavour cannot be reduced to an isolated economic unit, bravely facing the world alone. We are beings who desire connection, with others and with the universe itself. Read through *homo religiosus*, loss emerges, less as a threat to the self, and more as an inevitable feature of life in this cosmos. What matters is accepting this fact, while committing ourselves to ways of living with the reality of being mutable beings in a changing world. What matters is finding ways not to resist, but to embrace failure and loss.

6

ACCEPTING FAILURE, EMBRACING LOSS

We have arrived, then, at a very different way of thinking about human beings than is offered under neoliberalism. Understood through the values of *homo religiosus*, we are social animals, connected to each other and to the world upon which we depend for our existence. In our perceptions of failure, and our experiences of loss, we are confronted with limits that define our humanity. In the experience of loss – be that of physical or mental capacity, of disease or of death – we are confronted with processes which transcend our individual hopes and expectations, which confound the arrogance that would place human desires at the centre of the world. In failure, these limits are felt in ourselves and in our relationships, in the roles we have assumed to be central to our life, in economic and social forces beyond our control. Confronted with limits, we might despair or become defensive; we might blame others, and we saw something of the effect of that strategy on women and their bodies in Chapter Two. We might succumb to self-pity, an obvious response, when considered in the light of illness, death and dying, investigated in Chapter Three. Or we might consider these experiences quite differently, seeing in them prompts to different ways of living.

In this chapter I explore ways of re-orientating our sense of what makes for a meaningful life. It is possible to experience loss, to feel its hurt and terror tighten the heart, and yet find ways of living with, rather excluding, that pain. Likewise, it is possible 'to be a failure' – to fail to achieve or to be successful according to the template offered by contemporary society – and still go on to live well. It may even be that success obscures the kind of perspective needed for a fulfilling life. Failure and loss emerge, if we allow the values of *homo religiosus* to shape our lives, not as features of life to be avoided, but as experiences providing space for engaging more deeply with the reality of being human. We can become more at ease with loss and failure: not just finding ways of facing them, but even embracing them.

The fly in the ointment: The problem of evil

All of which sounds just peachy, and, of course, it is not as simple as that. Life rarely is. 'Laugh and the world laughs with you; cry and you cry alone' would not be the hoary old adage it is if it did not sum up the rejection and alienation felt by those struggling through hard times. In suggesting that we might be able to embrace loss, we must begin with the recognition, expressed so clearly by Schopenhauer in the previous chapter, that no one is immune from it. Just as inevitably we will all, at some time or another, need the support and care of others, so we must also be prepared and willing to support those struggling with the weight of the world.

If all are vulnerable to suffering, it is important not to ignore an uncomfortable truth: suffering is not evenly distributed. Some have far deeper losses, far more wide-reaching failures, to contend with than others. Some groups suffer much more than others. Any discussion of the suffering accompanying loss must take seriously this disparity. When evil is defined, it is vital to acknowledge, not just individual moral failings but also the broader social and political structures that foster its social manifestations. To understand injustice, its enactment and continuation through political and social structures must be addressed. Structural evils, like racism, sexism and classism, mean that some suffer more than others.[1] There is, then, a political imperative for *homo religiosus*, not just to enact discrete forms of support for individuals, but to challenge the suffering which results from economic and social injustice and to use the power of collective action to overcome both.

There is also a personal imperative contained in the urgency with which political action is undertaken. With so much pain and suffering in the world, so much despair and unhappiness, the very least we must do is commit ourselves to acting in ways that do not add to the sum total of suffering. It is this concern that underpins Marion Partington's extraordinarily forgiving attitude to the Wests. Drawing attention to their lack of empathy, made manifest in the horrific violence they inflicted on their victims, she asks that we consider the effects of the abuse they had themselves suffered at the hands of others.[2] In seeking the conditions for good relationships, methods for breaking the cycle of violence are needed. Evil is 'the violation of relation in human life' (Carter Heyward 1982: 154), and cultivating good relationships requires paying attention to our personal attitudes, as well as the kind of public policies that would strive to make abusive relationships a thing of the past. Given the realities of human relationship, this sounds overly optimistic: but it should at least be possible to develop political interventions that enable the kind of spaces required for healing the hurts of broken relationship.

Emphasizing political action should not, however, blind us to a significant truth. Life *is* tragic; there are no easy ways through it. Some might come to believe that an experience of failure or loss has made them. Some, to the contrary, may be broken by such experiences,[3] for 'not all are equal in the face of the misfortunes of life' (Green 2011: 56). Much in life comes down to luck, contrary to the reassuring thought that shapes neoliberal accounts of the successful life and that would have us believe we are all responsible for our fates. One of Freud's last – and most beautiful – papers offers an example of the role luck plays in shaping a life. He tells the story of a woman who leaves his practice apparently cured of the neurotic condition from which she had been suffering. Out in the world, she encounters misfortune after misfortune, against which she stands up valiantly. All seems to be going well. Then she falls ill, requiring an operation. She falls, disastrously, in love with her surgeon. Tormented by this unrequited love, she succumbs to a fresh onslaught of her illness from which she does not recover. Were it not for meeting this man, Freud notes sadly, things might have turned out quite differently for her.[4] Hard work – be it in the workplace or on the self – does not always lead to a happy outcome, and nowhere is this more the case than when confronted by the losses and failures inherent in mutable human life.

Loss and the way to depth

If our losses are not to consume us, if our failures are not to lead to despair, we have to find ways of living with them: and, while there is solidarity to be found in sharing our pains with others, inevitably no one else can take on that task for another. The solutions to which we come, and the way in which we live with those things we would much rather had not happened will be as distinctive as each one of us. No wonder it is tempting to hide from a frank engagement with failure and loss! The way out of these experiences cannot be contained in a simple set of 'how to' rules provided for us by someone else: so I'm afraid if that is what you hoped for from this book, you will be sorely disappointed. Yet if we can bear to pay attention to these painful experiences we can find, I believe, in such unpromising ground the possibility for living in new, richer ways.

It's easy to say this, and there is always the danger that the pain of these experiences can be somehow neutered by the precision of words on paper. I've written throughout this book the stories of *my* losses, *my* failures. I fear that my words may have rendered these gut-wrenching, visceral stories all-too neat and tidied up. I've placed the loss of motherhood in paragraphs that coolly contain what it meant. I've placed it at the long end of a telescope, seen from the point where I am now, living a life that is, most of the time, fulfilling and varied. That loss is still there, however, like a scar that's just about visible under the layers of the past twenty years. I feel uneasy picking away at it, worried that if I do the blood trapped beneath its fragile layer of healing will flow so strongly I won't be able to stop it.

Glimpses of that time come back to me. The afternoon of the miscarriage. The trip to the bathroom. The trace of blood. The colleague who was kind enough to drive me the fifty-odd miles from work to Oxford. Laying in bed. Panicking. Saying over and over 'please stay, please stay', and wondering all the time if saying 'please stay' indicated my ambivalence, that I wasn't sure I wanted it/him/her to stay and so I had to keep saying it, over and over, to convince it/him/her, myself.

The hospital. Being mistaken for a 'real' doctor who would understand what was happening to her. The feeling between my legs as the little life inside me slipped out into the bed pan and was no more. (I never looked at it. Would it have been different if I had? If I had acknowledged then and there the loss of that child, of myself as a mother? If I hadn't bottled up the pain, the fear, the grief?) And then the blood that wouldn't stop, the pain as a doctor tried to stem the flow by scraping out my womb. The procedure, the bliss of anesthetized oblivion, the waking up to the joy of life. I didn't want to die, I wanted to be alive, to feel the sun on my skin. My husband, bereft as well, yet so relieved I wasn't dead, the loss of fatherhood blotted out by relief.

Home. The early spring sunshine. Trying to come to terms. Burying, burying deep. The temptation of cliché: how the life we have and love couldn't be if we had had that child. How hard to accept that something *was* lost, something that can never be recovered. Not just this tiny child, but years of watching him or her grow, the possibility of a family, of being someone's mother. Instead, there are two, not three or four.

Like so many others, I feel myself to be a wounded storyteller,[5] scarred by loss. The question posed by this book is a real one for me when I consider my failure to be a mother: can *I* be a failure and still live well? There is still that wound in myself, still a place that hurts when touched. There is, though, in that pain connection too – fragile, like pottery that has been carefully mended but easily broken again – with all who lose, all who fail to live up to the image of life held out in magazines and TV shows. Perhaps it is in this very pain that it is possible to glimpse the heart of a universe not easily conceived when life is going according to plan.

When we lose something precious, when we fail in something we wanted, when we feel the cold stone in the stomach descend, the sickness of heart that cannot be evaded, it can seem best to retreat, to seek a return to 'ordinary' life as quickly as possible. Trapped in pain, tortured by regret, broken-hearted, our losses and our failures appear as threats, outrages; even, perhaps, as demonic intrusions, and the idea that they could have anything to do with the well-lived life seems absurd. Their only value seems to lie in the future, when we might transform their memory into the fertilizer that was necessary for our future success, our future happiness. The temptation for me has always been to rush on to the next thing as a way of hiding from the pain of loss. Sometimes that has simply exacerbated the feelings of loss. It is only in the last few years that I have felt at ease with other people's children and have found pleasure in being the honorary auntie, godmother and neighbour; the woman who plays a different – and not unimportant – role in a child's life.

What happens if loss and failure are seen not as experiences to escape from, or as staging posts to a successful future, but as vital for enabling a deeper engagement with life? Karen Armstrong suggests something of what this might mean when she writes of the religious quest as not involving the discovery of 'the truth' or 'the meaning of life', 'but about living as intensely as possible here and now' (Armstrong 2004: 271).

Living intensely.

Seen in this way, failure and loss are no longer experiences to be hidden or discarded but are instead necessary aspects of a life, capable of being woven into a vivid fabric of the self.

Failure and loss have this in common: they disturb our equilibrium, they disrupt our routines, and out of that disruption comes the possibility for thinking again about the things we take for granted and the things that form the focus for our living.

Loss and failure unsettle us. They disrupt the ordinary flow of things, and as a result they open up the possibility of looking beyond the surface of our lives. In contrast to cultural celebrations of the superficial, failure and loss force us to confront the depths of existence. Here is the possibility that came out of my loss. I had to look beneath the surface of my presentation as a 'successful' academic; I had to find a deeper way of thinking about my life.

'Depth' is an interesting word, for it denotes two, apparently different, experiences.

It can refer to the depths of our loss or our unhappiness. This meaning is played out evocatively in the story of Jonah and the Whale. Jonah is the resistant prophet, told to go to Nineveh to proclaim God's judgement on a decadent culture. Not much fancying this task, he runs from God's grasp. There is no escape from this pursuing God, and Jonah is cast into the ocean depths, where he is swallowed by a mighty fish. He describes his plight in the language of the deep: 'Out of my distress I cried to the Lord … from the belly of Sheol I cried … You cast me into the abyss, into the heart of the sea … The seaweed was wrapped round my head at the roots of the mountains. I went down into the countries underneath the earth, to the peoples of the past.'[6] This spatial metaphor of descent is used again and again in the Judaeo-Christian scriptures to capture the experience of suffering and loss. 'Out of the depths I cry to thee' wails the Psalmist as he struggles to find God in the midst of his suffering.

Religious ideas of Hell draw upon that language of the depths through images of that which lies beneath our feet and which might swallow us up in an instant. In the Christian confession of faith, Christ 'descends into hell' in order to free those who languish there. For the Psalmist, God is found even in Hell; present even if the poet were to 'make his bed in Sheol', the world of the dead.[7] In Greek mythology, the Goddess Persephone is dragged down into the realm of the God of the Underworld, Hades, when she unwisely picks a flower poking out of a fissure in the earth. The analogy of falling, of being lost in the earth, is apposite when faced with the unhappiness accompanying loss and failure: remember Joan Didion's 'vortex', in danger of sweeping her up as she struggled to live with her memories after the deaths of her husband and daughter.

'Depth' also has another meaning. We use it to describe more mature, more satisfying engagements with the world. We fall more deeply in love; we become deeper friends with someone. We come to a deeper understanding of the things we learn and do when, with Matthew Crawford who we met in Chapter One fixing old motorbikes, we commit ourselves to becoming better versed in a subject or a practice.

Two meanings for 'depth', but we should not think they are unconnected. The experiences which confront us with the depths also open up the possibility of depth.

There is no depth without the way to depth.[8]

'The depths' and 'depth' are intimately connected. Eularia Clarke's painting 'Storm over the Lake' captures something of why this might be the case.[9] Here is another biblical story, this time of Christ stilling the storm. A ship is partly submerged, the waters teeming with the struggling figures of passengers and crew. Some are clinging to each other or to the parts of the boat still visible above the tempestuous waters. Others are covering their eyes with their hands, or crying out. Some have faces distorted by the fear of drowning. In the prow of the ship is an over-sized Christ, his hand held out in benediction. Some of the survivors have their eyes fixed on him; others are clustered behind him. Clarke's painting is replete with the horror of loss and the struggle for life, and we should note that just because some of the drowning have fixed their eyes on Christ, it does not mean that their anguish is diminished, or that they have somehow escaped the turbulent waters.

They haven't. They are still in the water, still terrified. But they are lifting their eyes above the waves, holding on to the fragile hope that they won't be destroyed by what is happening to them. Clarke's painting expresses a number of possible ways for engaging with loss and failure. We can sink, go under. We can be rendered numb, stuck in our pain. Or we can redirect our gaze, change our perspective, and, while not losing our fear, we can seek a fragile solace in the face of the torments of life.

It is no surprise to find religious stories offering accounts of that redirected gaze. For Christians, there is the New Testament story of Saul of Tarsus, heading for Damascus to continue his persecution of this new religious sect. Blinded, the traumatic loss of his vision enables him to come to 'see' things differently; a changed perspective that requires a new name, 'Paul'. This gain is caught up with loss. He loses his standing in his community, he loses the habitual framework for his life. This has to be so if he is to find a new way of flourishing. For Buddhists, there is the story of Siddhartha Gautama, the prince living a comfortable life, whose excursion outside the walls of his palace forces him to confront the many faces of suffering. As he meditates more deeply on the nature of things, he is transformed. Wealth and the craving for things have to be put aside if he is to find a way of living which responds appropriately to the reality of suffering. He is enlightened, and as the Buddha, he founds a new discipline whose practice looks beyond the world of chance and change. Forced out of the ordinary, confronted with a world that does not conform to their wishes or their assumptions about it, these stories show how new ways of living become possible when we are confronted with failure and loss. And if we look beneath the surface of narratives like these we see recognition of the limits of endeavour, the fragility of success.

Being successful turns out to not be particularly helpful for developing a deeper engagement with one's world. Herbert Hensley Henson, Bishop of Durham in the 1920s, pertinently comments on the limits of success for framing a life as he reflects on his career:

Then as to success in life, I think that all turns on the meaning attached to success. From one point of view, I do not doubt that my professional career may fairly be described as successful, but that is not the point of view which at any time has secured my acceptance.[10]

Grounding the meaning of your life in the glittering prizes you might – or might not – accumulate does not enable the kind of perspective necessary for negotiating the storms of life. Let us return to Eularia Clarke's shipwreck survivors. The things we accumulate, the status we achieve, tend to drag us down, distracting us from undertaking any deeper engagement with what it means to be a human being, living at this time, in this place. There was a reason why the Ancient Stoics were apprehensive about placing too much trust in the good fortune deemed necessary for worldly success. Fortune, personified by the Roman Goddess Fortuna, was a fickle mistress, and just as she could enable success, so she could send failure. Better not to trust her at all: not least because when you are 'the secret parts of Fortune',[11] the temptation is to believe that the universe revolves around the realization of your individual desires and hopes. This might well seem the case when all is going well, but it is a mistake to trust this egocentric vision of the world. If you do, you are likely to find yourself battered and bruised, outraged and angry, when things take a turn for the worse. Better by far to 'decentre' the self, and Stoic practice involved cultivating the kind of perspective that enabled its practitioners to align themselves correctly with the ebb and flow of the universe. Out of this exercise came a wisdom which limited the extent to which a person could ever feel disappointed with their life.[12]

Failure promises more than success if you want to engage more deeply with life.

This sounds counterintuitive. But if we think about the successes of life, they invariably make it possible to be content with the superficial aspects of our lives, allowing us to skate along the surface, trusting in the penultimate things of which Tillich exhorts us to be wary. I come to believe that things will always be this good; I come to believe in the security of the trappings of my success; I come to believe in the power of my wishes to shape my future. Yet such things are always passing away, incapable of permanence in a world of chance and change.

Theologian and backpacker Belden Lane sees failure as important, precisely because it allows the space for redirecting one's gaze:

> Failure points us back to the true measure of our worth, to something grounded in nothing that we do, but only in what we are. (Lane, 2015: 138)

That last part of his sentence is important. A proper sense of our worth is *grounded in nothing that we do, but only in what we are*. That which we use to aggrandize the self, to present an appealing, confident mask to the world, is removed by failure; by loss, too. Our superiority or sophistication, our status or privilege, cannot protect us from life's blows, and in these moments we are confronted as in a mirror by who we really are. Like King Lear, stripped of the trappings of his kingship, we are left naked to the blast, fragile beings in a world of chance and change. Faced with failure, confronted by loss, we become aware that we exist in a universe so much more immense than our desires to shape it. How small our concerns seem in the immensity of that universe! How differently we might come to value the things by which we live if we shifted our gaze, seeing our life from the perspective of the movements of the stars and the planets, the patterns of the seasons, the changing of the tides.

Loss and failure: Pivotal moments

How to shift our gaze? How to decentre the self? Loss and failure provide pivotal moments which disrupt the ordinary pattern of life. We are confronted by the limits of our control, and, if we make space to reflect upon these limits, we can find ways of living that allow the things that happen to us not to diminish, but rather to enrich, our experience of our world.

Failure and loss are experiences none of us actively seek. For this reason they thrust us into an alien landscape. Remember Joan Didion's refrain on the loss of her husband:

'Life changes fast. Life changes in an instant. You sit down to dinner and life as you know it ends.'

The ordinary markers of life, the things by which we define ourselves, are illuminated by these major upheavals. The way we see ourselves, the routines that shape us, the labels that neatly package our existence, may well lose their power to make sense of our experience. We are forced to think again about the things which give meaning to our lives.

To reshape experiences of loss and failure as pivotal moments requires being prepared to attend to them. This takes time. We cannot rush on from their disruptive power. We need to find ways of sitting with our losses and our failures, finding practices which enable us to bear the pain and discomfort that comes in their wake. This can be extremely hard, for we have entered a strange land.

Theologian Alan Lewis provides a useful image for this uncomfortable place for reflection in his account of Easter Saturday.[13] This aspect of the Easter story is often overlooked, and Lewis is at pains to show why it deserves attention, and not just by Christians. For our purposes, this day provides an imaginative place for attending to failure and loss. Easter Saturday stands between Good Friday and Easter Sunday. Traditionally, it denoted Christ's descent into hell in order to free the souls of the damned. Lewis notes the pivotal space of this Saturday between the suffering, horror and failure of the cross on Good Friday, and the joyful triumph of Christ's resurrection on Easter Sunday. Christians, he says, tend to ignore its ambivalent character, preferring to read it with the hindsight provided by Easter Sunday. In reality, it has a dual character. It looks back to Good Friday, as well as forward to Easter Sunday. The trick is to accept *both* readings at the same time, so that it becomes a place where joy and sorrow are held together.

Lewis's focus on Easter Saturday asks us to think about the space *we* occupy when we experience failure or loss. Good Friday is a day of activity and spectacle. It is the day which sees Christ mocked, tortured and executed in one of the most brutal ways possible as a criminal and enemy of the state. There is a horrible energy to this day that replicates the frenetic activity that often accompanies our own experiences of loss and failure: telling people what has happened, sobbing, feeling shocked, making plans for funerals, emptying desks, destroying old love letters. Easter Saturday – like every 'day after' – is dull, almost boring, by comparison. This is the day when the reality – and finality – of Friday's events hits home. For Christ's disciples, all hope is dashed; nothing remains, save a sense of the total failure of Christ's ministry. It is a day of disappointment, of the dull feeling that accompanies the recognition that something precious has been irreparably broken.

Yet this day is not only about mourning what is lost. It also offers a necessary pause.[14] Its dual perspective offers a place where the pain of the past is not absent; yet neither is the hope for better things. Instead, hope *and* hopelessness, joy *and* sorrow, triumph *and* defeat are held together in order to encourage a new way of engaging with life. By pausing, by attending to that dull pain and that glimmer of hope, it becomes possible to think again about what it means to be human; to think again about what it is to cultivate a way of living that acknowledges life in all its fullness.

'Pausing' can seem a rather neutral – even neutered – term for what this feels like in practice. It can feel more like you've run headlong into a brick wall: you've been left smashed and bleeding on the pavement and all you want to do is get up and carry on with life as normal.

But if we can allow for this pause in our lives, failure and loss might
emerge, not as experiences merely to be gotten through, but as
events that open up new – even vital – ways of thinking about life.

When we pause, we make space. We allow in the things we would
rather ignore. In pausing we might just be able to detach ourselves
from the relentless activity that is so useful for obscuring an honest
engagement with our self and with others. Christ's disciples spent that
bleak Saturday in hiding, trying to make sense of their loss; and so
might we take advantage of the disruption wrought by failure and loss
to take time out from the relentless normality of daily life to think again
about what really matters.

Therapist and Holocaust survivor, Viktor Frankl offers a similar
account of the possibilities inherent in failure and loss. A prisoner
in Theresienstadt and Auschwitz, Frankl's later work as a therapist
saw him rejecting Freud's claim that the primary motivation of human
beings is the pursuit of pleasure. For Frankl, it is meaning-making
that constitutes the central human activity. Loss and failure are crucial
to this process. *All* experiences, Frankl claims, are capable of being
made meaningful.

This is a staggering claim that might well be rejected out-of-hand
as unbelievably thoughtless, were it not voiced by someone who had
himself experienced the worst of humanity: while Frankl survived,
his wife was murdered in the Nazi death machine of Bergen-Belsen.
Frankl rejects the idea that the aim of life is to achieve happiness. Life
does not owe us this, and we are mistaken if we think its meaning
could be shaped by single-mindedly pursuing it. Happiness is, rather,
'the unintended side-effect' of dedication: to a cause greater than
one's self, or to another person.[15] What life offers us is the *possibility* of
finding or creating meaning. Crucial to this process are those moments
when we are 'questioned by life' (Frankl 2004: 85), challenged to make
meaning out of the upsetting, troubling, even devastating things that
happen to us. Everything might be taken from us (and Frankl really
does mean 'everything'), but we are always left with one thing: 'The

last of the human freedoms – to choose one's attitude in any given set of circumstances, to choose one's own way' (2004: 75). In moments of loss and despair we are called 'by life' to think again about how to live: to cultivate a perspective that enables us to cope with the things that happen.

The image of human freedom accompanying Frankl's approach might well trouble us. Aren't some more capable of responding to that question life asks than others? Don't some have better resources – mentally and materially – to deal with the slings and arrows of outrageous fortune? Aren't some experiences easier to make meaningful than others? Frankl does not disagree. But talk of 'the problem of evil' that concerned us at the beginning of this chapter only distances us from the reality of our situation. We cannot approach evil and suffering as we would an academic puzzle. This is fine for the scholar in their study, but it is pointless when we are grappling with life's ills.

Regardless of its unfairness, all will be questioned by life. What matters is how we respond.

Times of loss and failure open up new vistas for contemplating the meaning of our lives. They are vital, as much as they are painful. But it is not only when we are caught up in the pain of loss or the frustration of failure that such a perspective is open to us. We can develop ways of reflecting that are relevant at any time, and which hold out the possibility of not getting lost in the stresses of the things that happen to us. It is not so much that we should always anticipate loss or expect failure. This kind of neuroticism suggests an unhealthy self-centredness that cannot see beyond the self or its concerns. Rather, the reflective spaces I have in mind make it possible to accept the ever-present possibility of loss and failure, if we cultivate an appreciation of our place in the wider universe. Re-orientating our lives to the patterns of that universe opens up ways of living well which are not distorted by contemporary narratives of what it is to be a success or to be a failure. Shaken out of reliance on narratives that would make work and achievement markers for a well-lived life, we come, instead, to simpler ways of shaping the flourishing life.

Cultivating space for the pause

The shock of the strange experienced when life is off-kilter allows for the possibility of looking up from the concerns of the self. While the experiences of loss and failure open up space for this kind of pause, there are regular ways of practising this kind of detachment in order to cultivate a deeper engagement with life. In psychoanalytic practice, the space between therapist and patient allows the patient to step out of their life. Here, the patient's experiences can be viewed as objects, allowing for a kind of detached attention that means I need not get lost in painful emotions or destructive behaviours. I come to think differently about my life as I cultivate this kind of reflection. I become less caught up in myself, more able to place myself and my desires in the range of relationships that shape my life. Religious practice, similarly, offers a space for stepping out of the hurly-burly of life. The self is placed in a broader frame. The mundane world becomes a place where I can access the eternal through following the festive patterns of the religious year. The day-to-day exists alongside a playing out of these recurring cycles. In practices like prayer and meditation, I attempt to refocus my gaze. My hopes and fears, desires and anxieties are framed against reflection on the broader patterns of the universe. I come to see myself as dependent on a universe that is so much greater than me, and as a result my concerns lose some of their weight.

Religious practices and psychoanalytic therapies enable perspectives that challenge the centrality of our immediate desires. Taking time out of one's ordinary day, resisting the frenetic rush to fill up our time with activity, makes room for a different kind of reflection. This requires making space for silence: allowing in that which we might seek to control by filling our lives and thoughts with activity and clutter. Silence holds a problematic place in today's society.[16] It requires stillness, not easy to practice in a technological society that prioritizes speed. It requires an ability to be alone. Being alone can be translated as loneliness; silence as a sign that there is no one with whom we can talk. Unwanted loneliness is one of the social ills of the twenty-first century, and Olivia Laing's memoir of loneliness in an American city describes something of its desperation and isolation:

> I don't want to be alone. I want someone to want me. I'm lonely. I'm scared. I need to be loved, to be touched, to be held. (Laing 2016: 14)

The feelings she describes attest to the human need for companionship, and having argued that as *homo religiosus* we are social animals, I cannot disagree. But not every form silence takes should be equated with loneliness, or as an indicator that something is being evaded or covered up.[17] It is necessary to be at ease with silence if we are to enable the kind of reflection that helps raise our eyes above our desires and our hurts in order to establish more fulfilling ways of anchoring the meaning of our lives.

The poet R. S. Thomas was a master at describing the importance of silence for establishing new ways of living. Crotchety, pessimistic, a heterodox Anglican priest and Welsh nationalist, Thomas describes 'the silence in the mind' as the time 'when we live best, within/listening distance of the silence/we call God'. His God is not shaped by the kind of theistic language that models God as a human being, only greater. A radically different account of the divine emerges in his poetry, which mirrors the language encountered in Tillich's theology:

> This is the deep
>   calling to deep of the psalm-
>   writer, the bottomless ocean

The deep – the ground from which we come – is calling to the deep places in ourselves. And for Thomas there is no end point to the quiet reflection which engages with these depths. This is a never-ending process of orientating the self towards that which lies outside the self. 'We launch the armada of/our thoughts on, never arriving', he writes:

> It is a presence, then,
>> whose margins are our margins;
>> that calls us out over our
>> own fathoms. What to do
>> but draw a little nearer to
>> such ubiquity by remaining still.[18]

I direct my gaze to that which transcends the passing shortness of my life, to that which is eternal. In the pause of this silence and stillness, I move outside myself, reaching out to that which transcends the human world.

It is not easy to find the silent spaces for making this move. As I write, I am alone in my brother's apartment in Downtown San Diego. The apartment is 'quiet', but I can hear the monotonous drone of the cars on the freeway that runs some seven floors below where I sit. I hear the roar of the planes descending to land at the nearby airport. I hear the whirr of the fridge freezer, and the occasional slamming of nearby doors. I cannot but be reminded of the world beyond my desk where people are hurrying to work or to meetings, even as the computer pings with the sound of incoming emails. In a world that values busy-ness as much as business, that prefers sound and fury to quiet contemplation, it is difficult to find the spaces to experience the silence necessary for reaching out to that more fulfilling basis for a life indicated by R. S. Thomas's words. Thomas is a Christian poet, yet if we expect to find silence in religious spaces, we may well be disappointed. The success of evangelical and charismatic forms of religion might be explained by their willingness to embrace the world of distraction and noise, making a virtue of music and chatter. In doing so, they (unintentionally?) limit the possibility of that more profound conversation of 'deep calling to deep'. If failure and loss enact a break in the ordinary, so might we need to break out of our daily lives to find stillness and silence. We might need the shock of strange places to enter the spaces that allow for different perspectives on what it is to live well.

The shock of fierce landscapes

People seeking to escape the stresses and strains of the everyday world have often turned to the desert. In the Christian tradition, the Desert Fathers and Mothers found such inhospitable places provided suitable backdrops for the work of quiet contemplation.[19] The shock of inhabiting fierce places not amenable to human life forced the reorientation they deemed necessary for the well-lived life. For the Desert Fathers and Mothers, worldly success did not enable the space for this necessary reappraisal; success merely enshrined the sense of the rightness of the world's values. To fail was preferable for establishing the well-lived life, for it acted as a reminder of the lowly place of humans in the cosmos. Here is one story of failure, told from this monastic perspective:

> A brother questioned Abba Poeman saying, 'If I see my brother sinning, should I hide the fact?' The old man said, 'At the moment when we hide a brother's fault, God hides our own. At the moment when we reveal a brother's fault, God reveals our own.' (Williams 2003: 29–30)

Failure confronts us with the limits of our efforts, the extent to which we are not in control of our destinies. It also reminds us of a universal and shared fallibility and is therefore better than success at enabling spiritual growth.

We should not get fixated on the idea that to reorientate the self we, too, need to decamp to a literal desert. As Belden Lane says, 'the desert' can be any landscape whose indifference to the desires of the human heart forces a person to look beyond themselves. The 'wastelands' of industrial spaces like those found in Detroit, emptied of people as a result of the collapse of traditional industries, can be just as disturbing to the belief in human significance as deserts. Spaces devoid of human activity – literally, devoid of human industry – reveal the superficiality of the assumptions about how you 'should' live peddled by society or family. For those of us living in a culture struggling to move beyond neoliberal assumptions, these deserts, like their natural counterparts, provide potent places for disrupting stories of human success. In deserts – be they natural or manmade – easy assumptions of what makes for the good life come to look strange, based – rather aptly – on sand.

Geological deserts work better than the deserts created by human economics at enabling this move, I think: not least because these fierce landscapes confront us with things that are truly outside our power to control. The names given to such places reflect their refusal to accommodate human desires. The Spanish conquistadors, confronted with the Canyons for the first time, dismissed them as 'badlands', useless and rotten because they were incapable of supporting human settlements. The names of desert places suggest a similar outraged rejection: Devil Canyon in Nevada; Hell's Canyon in the Sonoran Desert; The Devil's Golf Course in Death Valley; a natural gas field in the Karakum Desert which locals refer to as The Door to Hell. 'Useless' for humans, they become demonic in their apparent desolation.

Yet these strange places have a powerful draw for those wanting to think again about what it means to be human. Asked why he loves the desert, author and environmentalist Ed Abbey tells the story of a solitary walk in Coconino County in Arizona. Seeking a new route home, he scrambles up a canyon wall and finds himself 'on top of the world'. He is certain that his are the first feet to have attempted this makeshift route. Then he notices something on the ground in front of him: a stone arrow, three feet long, 'pointing off into the north toward those same old purple vistas, so grand, so immense, and mysterious, of more canyons, more mesas and plateaus, more mountains, more cloud-dappled, sun-spangled leagues of desert sand and desert rock under the same old wide and aching sky' (Abbey 2005: 116). The arrow points north; but what *precisely* is it pointing at? It isn't clear, except that it points to *that* landscape and *that* sky. Realizing from the sheer amount of dust compacted around the arrow that it has been there for at least a hundred years, Abbey continues: 'There was nothing out there. Nothing at all. Nothing but the desert. Nothing but the silent world' (Abbey 2005: 117). We might run from that silence, that 'nothingness', finding it oppressive because it renders human concerns so small and insignificant. But for Abbey – and for his fellow traveller from so many years before – it is that very 'nothingness' that makes the desert a place that demands to be loved.

In Abbey's writing, and in that of other desert lovers, the desert is a place that helps you put your stuff in its rightful place. The desert landscape is not pretty; it is not easily definable or accessible; it is not something that can be reduced to a postcard or a fridge magnet. As a result it takes us into a place that challenges attempts to shape everything around the human. It punctures human pomposity, stripping away those things that we hide behind in order to show our importance. For Belden Lane, 'one initially enters the desert to be stripped of self, purged by its relentless deprivation of everything once considered important' (Lane 1998: 6). Abbey's 'nothingness' – that absence of human civilization – makes possible this scouring of self.

The silence encountered in the desert has a quality unlike anything else. During a walk in the Mojave Desert's Death Valley, we entered a rocky hollow. The narrow strip of road was behind us, no longer glimpsed behind high rocky walls. This place was so devoid of noise – of people, of traffic, of birds, of wind in vegetation – that it was deafening. It was a silence that left us feeling we had been 'unskinned',[20] forced back to basics, just as the desert (to the untrained eye, at least) seems stripped of everything but rock and sand.

In the desert it is impossible to avoid the world which exists beyond *and without* the human. Death Valley is awe-inspiring. We use words like 'awesome' unthinkingly:

'The Padres beat the Dodgers!' 'Awesome!"

'This pizza is awesome!'
'Class has been cancelled today!' 'Awesome!'

In Death Valley, 'awe' recovers its roots in religious terror. Covering an area of some three thousand square miles, it is bounded by the Amargosa Mountains to the east, the Panamint Mountains to the west, the Sylvania Mountains to the north and the Owlshead Mountains to the south. It includes Badwater Basin, the lowest point on the American continent, a salt pan lake of sheer white which crackles underfoot as you walk on it. It is one of the hottest places on earth, recording a record high temperature of 134 degrees fahrenheit. Temperatures regularly soar over 100 degrees fahrenheit in the summer months. It has less than two inches of rainfall a year. Ninety five per cent of this land is designated 'wilderness': yet mammals and reptiles manage to live here, thanks to the presence of isolated oases. The weirdness of a landscape so immense that it combines mountains, sand drifts and salt lakes makes it impossible not to recognize the insignificance of your concerns. As the novelist Barbara Kingsolver pertinently comments, 'It did not take me long in the desert to realise I was thinking like a person, and on that score was deeply outnumbered' (Kingsolver 2001: 19).

To be in such a place is disorientating. We'd stayed at the touristy oasis of Furnace Creek: a couple of restaurants, a convenience shop, rooms with running water and comfy beds. We'd drunk beer sitting round a fire pit, listening to locals shooting the breeze. We decided to exit the Valley by driving across the desert floor to Trona. Trona itself looks like the set for a schlock horror movie. Consisting largely of abandoned houses and factories, it seems almost completely emptied of people. If anything is a testament to the failure of neoliberal economics, it is Trona. Buying petrol and using the restroom at the town's only working gas station, we were treated to a cursory nod from the old timer sitting in the shade, who was clearly surprised to see anyone stopping in this godforsaken place.

He had a point. Our initial decision to take this route had been driven by the typical tourists' desire to 'see something different'. We had been lulled into a sense of security by our comfortable overnight stay. Shortly into the drive, the joys of twentieth century plumbing and American hospitality were forgotten as we realized the desert wasn't set up with our wishes in mind. The drive across the valley floor had started on a tarmac road. This ran out without warning to be replaced by shingle and sharp stones. The possibility of a puncture seemed immediately real. With it came the realization that if we got into trouble in this place, there would be little hope of being rescued, for during the hour-long drive we hadn't seen another car. It was probably a good thing that at that stage I hadn't read about the deaths which occur with disturbing regularity in Death Valley. It may be a National Park, but that doesn't make it any less dangerous, as ill-prepared tourists continue to find to their cost.[21]

I have never been so aware of my utter insignificance as I was during that drive. It forced me to accept the reality of a world quite disinterested in me, my hopes and my dreams. The desert had no interest in whether I returned home to finish this book; no interest in my lament about not being a mother; no interest in 'me', full stop. This wasn't because the desert was 'brutal' or somehow 'hostile' to me as an individual. My presence or absence just wasn't a factor at all. The abandoned Harmony Borax Mine revealed, if I needed further proof, the utter disregard of the desert for the desires of the people who had invested their hopes in making a fortune from this land. To see the stories of Death Valley played out on this landscape was a heady experience. The world shifted on its axis. I was left with a sense of how vulnerable humans are, how dependent on a world that does not have our hopes and dreams at its centre.

Recognizing the existence of spaces outside the comforting structures of the human world can be terrifying, and we may wonder why I want to make decentering the self necessary for the well-lived life. Sure, there is something terrifying in acknowledging the non-human world, but making this shift in perspective is liberating, too. These strange places illuminate the inadequacy of all attempts to reduce the meaning of a life to an assessment of whether a person has achieved success or avoided failure.

> *The desert throws us back on something else: something that defies the constraining dichotomy of success/failure, and which forces us to contemplate the fundamentals of our humanity captured in Chapter Five by homo religiosus.*

To be human is to be shaped by our relationships; but we are also shaped by and dependent on the universe which created us. To accept the weight of both claims opens up new priorities for living. How are we to develop good relationships with each other, *and* how are we to live in the light of the universe that surrounds us and that brought us into being?

Two stories about the desert illuminate the liberation that comes with adopting a perspective forged by these two questions. The first story comes from Ed Abbey. He was part of a team given the grim task of recovering the body of a tourist who had strayed from the path at Grandview Point on the South Rim of the Grand Canyon. Vultures had not, mercifully, started on this hapless man's body by the time the party found it, though crows were giving it their best shot. Later that evening, Abbey thinks back over his day, and adopts the vulture's eye view, seeing himself through 'those cruel eyes'. As he undertakes this imaginative exercise:

I feel myself sinking into the landscape, fixed in place like a stone, like a tree ... a human figure that becomes smaller, smaller in the receding landscape as the bird rises into the evening ... surrounded by a rolling wasteland of stone and dune and sandstone monuments, the wasteland surrounded by dark canyons and the course of rivers and mountain ranges on a vast plateau stretching across Colorado, Utah, New Mexico and Arizona ... and farther and farther yet, the darkened East, the gleaming Pacific, the curving margins of the great earth itself, and beyond the earth that ultimate world of sun and stars whose bounds we cannot discover. (Abbey 2005: 73)

This exercise punctures the vanity of the individual. It doesn't matter how successful you are, how loaded with treasure you are, how well-respected you are by others. Conversely, it doesn't matter if you have failed to achieve anything of note. The vulture's eye view makes clear that from the perspective of the wider universe none of that matters one iota.

In the second example, Belden Lane takes up this theme. Desert places make clear the limits of human striving. Yet for Lane – more so than Abbey – these spaces do not annihilate us, nor are they necessarily cruel. Rather, they offer a kind of comfort that makes it possible to hold more easily the pains and anxieties of our lives:

Imagine this exchange in the desert silence. You find yourself alone in a vast and empty terrain, sanding before a naked wall of red-hued rock rising hundreds of feet above the canyon floor … The stone never moves as you sit there facing it, but after a while it poses a question. How did the stone face of the canyon cliff change on the day of your divorce, the day your father or mother died, the day you came to admit your dependency on alcohol or drugs? (Lane 1998:167)

The answer comes back: it never changed at all.

With this knowledge comes the realization that you – your life, your joys, your sorrows – are not the centre of the world. For Lane, this is not a statement that extends the harshness of an unforgiving landscape to a judgement on the worth of the individual. Acknowledging our insignificance in the context of the rest of the natural world puts the things that trouble us in their rightful place.

Why worry about that failed job interview, that divorce, that lost child, that embarrassing moment? When viewed from the perspective of the desert, it really doesn't matter.

Its enduring resilience is not the only way of reading the desert. Read only like this, we might arrive at a view of ourselves as aliens in a strange land, and this will not help dislodge narratives which would consider everything from the perspective of the human. Instead, we might reflect on the eternal nature of the world in order to come to a new appreciation of our connection to all that is. Our lives are not lived in isolation: we are rooted in the earth's processes and materiality. For Lane, this perspective opens up a different view on the losses of life. However terrible they might be, the earth – which brought us into being and which embraces each and every one of us – has lost more than we can possibly imagine. The suffering *we* experience as individuals is but one part of the suffering of all beings that stems from the universe's creative processes. This knowledge should not crush us, but give us hope, for despite this, *the Earth survives*. In the desert, this hope is made manifest, for it provides a space for our pains and losses, our failures and disappointments, to be woven into that greater fabric of the universe. Lane puts this into the language of his own Christian faith:

> The landscape's silent immensity – and the God to whom it points – is able to absorb all the grief one can give it. (Lane 1998: 168)

Beneath his appeal to God is a sentiment echoed in the ideals of *homo religiosus*. We are made by relationship, but we are also shaped by our dependence on the world itself.

Failure, loss and embracing the everyday

So far, we've considered the shock of the strange as a way of enabling the reorientation of self from self-centredness towards a perspective that places our lives and concerns in the context of the universe. Failure and loss, I have suggested, enable the pause necessary for reconsidering what matters in life. In silence, in desert places, it becomes possible to think differently about the meaning of our lives. We come to value ways of being in the world that prioritize that perspective, finding in them liberation from the achievements that make up the neoliberal vision of the good life.

To stay with the shock of the strange is not enough if we are to live well with our failures and our losses. We may need to be jolted out of the ordinary to think again about what gives our life meaning; but is it possible to find in our everyday lives a place for a life liberated from the striving self which underpins our contemporary constructions of success and failure? Can we find space in our daily lives to embrace our failures and to live with our losses?

Stanley Spencer's paintings turn our attention to an everyday world seemingly immune from economic ideology. Born and raised in the Berkshire village of Cookham, this 'village in heaven' becomes for Spencer a canvas on which to paint eternal themes of joy and renewal, hope and desire. The glorious beauty of the natural world is present in the lush vegetation, the struggling swans, the fleshy figures of his paintings. Neighbours reach across wide, leafy hedges to pass each other vivid red flowers.[22] A corpulent Christ considers the lilies.[23] Religious themes play out against a homely backdrop of red brick houses and gossiping residents. But the everyday which Spencer paints is not an overly-romanticized vision of a village community. Suffering takes place in Cookham's streets, just as much as pleasure and laughter; loss is there as much as flourishing. Christ carries his cross past neat, well-kept houses.[24] He is crucified on Cookham High Street, the faces of the workmen nailing him to the cross distorted with loathing and disgust.[25] But always Spencer's paint captures something of the richness of life, all its experiences – the good and the bad, the joyous and the terrible – framed in glorious colours derived from everyday wonders.

Feminist theologian Heather Walton might well find Spencer's art to resonate with her concern that attending to the everyday should not domesticate our experiences of life. There is 'an ecstatic energy at the heart of things', she proclaims, and it is important that theologians do not attempt to tidy this up (2014: 12). Much in life *is* wonderful; but this does not mean forgetting that life is also tragic. Indeed, acknowledging the tragic is important, for this enables us to hold together disaster and liberation, and frees us from 'our allegiance to the pathetic comforts of the known world' (2014: 12).

There is something appealing about a vision of life that accepts loss and failure at the same time as celebrating the ordinary, fleshy facts of things. How might we share in the richness of the everyday world which Spencer paints, and of which Walton writes? For Crawford and Sennett, encountered in Chapter One, we live well when we focus our attention on cultivating practice, becoming better at what we do: and that might be the case in undertaking craft work, or in the making of good relationships. I have suggested, in similar vein, that we should work at cultivating flourishing relationships and communities. Alongside these practices, I want to suggest walking as a way of coming to terms with life: accepting its failures, embracing its losses.

Walking might seem a disappointing suggestion for living with life's inevitable losses. Yet in its very ordinariness is its strength. Having reorientated our perspective towards the universe, walking grounds us in a world that resists the pressures of neoliberal subjectivity. Walking is easy to do – at least for those capable of the mobility it requires – and, as we shall see, it is also possible to find ways of cultivating the space it opens up if we are not ourselves able to walk.

Therapeutic value has long been assigned to walking. For Augustine, all problems could be solved by it ('Solvitur Ambulando').[26] This is quite a claim, given that he writes at a time when the Roman Empire is teetering towards oblivion. Many of today's workplaces are now, in similar vein, offering 'wellbeing through walking groups'. 'Walking through grief' groups are becoming more common. Those suffering bereavement or struggling with the effects of terminal illnesses meet to walk and talk. New relationships are forged as these walkers share their pain, and come to terms with their losses.[27]

My advocacy of walking is rather different from these companionable schemes. Walking opens up a form of practice for aligning the self with the everyday world. In walking, we locate ourselves in one place. We are not racing along, paying no attention. We are developing a steady rhythm that makes us feel part of the world around us. Attentiveness accompanies this kind of walking. For Lane, 'I'm no longer simply observing. *I belong*' (Lane 2015: 158; my emphasis). This sense of belonging is the counterpoint to the feeling of being lost in the desert.

I am part of the world through which I walk.

For the novelist and essayist Will Self, walking around your neighbourhood holds out the possibility of engaging more deeply with the place that is called 'home'. Adopt the regular habit of walking, and you become aware of its ebb and flow, how it changes as the seasons reveal the passing of the year. There is a religious aspect to this changed perspective, in the sense that we explored in Chapter Five, and this is attested to in the language Self uses: 'Even staring at a rusting coal hopper next to a dank canal can seem a numinous experience.'[28] In this kind of attentive walking, a connection is made with the place where we live. This place is not something temporary or irrelevant, a series of streets through which we are merely passing. As we walk, it becomes part of us, just as we become part of it. This opens up a way of holding our losses and failures. These occurrences are not just about us and our lives but are encountered in the wider world of which we are a part. There is a therapeutic aspect to this activity. Walking relaxes the mind, allowing levels of contemplation and memory to emerge which disrupt the frenetic shaping of the self. The things that trouble us are unseated, a different engagement with life is allowed in.

These words have a particular relevance for me as I am writing this section slap bang in the middle of a very difficult time. My mother has been diagnosed with breast cancer, and we are awaiting anxiously the results of tests that will determine the kind of treatment she has: if she even has treatment. My head is awash with anxiety and fear. Sometimes I feel hopeful; sometimes not. I imagine what life would be like without her. In the midst of this turmoil, I go for a walk in my local park. It is a classically English summer's day: a few clouds, a light breeze. I hear the cry of the wood pigeon, a sound that takes me back to my grandparents' house – both of them now long dead – where I would play as a child. I am reminded of how they took interest in me, listened to me, and through that listening shaped me and my values. The smell of the grass reminds me of the summer of my first lost love: a poignant reflection on the passion of my early 20s. I thought I'd never love again, and now I find myself twenty-two years into a very satisfying marriage with someone else. I see the trees, so sturdy and strong, so full of the green life of early summer. Their leaves dance in the breeze, and I am reminded that these trees will be here long after I am no more. A place opens up for a broader perspective on my life. Rather than resent the world that will go on after my mother's death – that will go on after my own death – my mind becomes easier. I am part of this world; it embraces me. Not that I won't feel sad, or anxious, or unhappy, or distraught again: but I am reminded that it is possible to feel relief through paying attention to the world around me. I can develop a form of practice where my fears and my losses, my very self, is placed in the on-going dance of life.

I am not alone in claiming walking as a particularly potent way of shifting one's perspective. The poet Laurie Lee, back in the 1930s, stepped out of his home in the Cotswolds, and just started walking: towards London, towards the coast, eventually towards Spain.[29] On his journey, the scope of his world expanded, and he describes to fine effect the experience of entering strange places that challenge his perception of things. Nietzsche, likewise, makes walking vital for creative thought.[30] The idea of eternal recurrence comes upon him with the force of a revelation while walking at Sils-Maria in 1881: 'Six thousand feet beyond man and time', as he puts it in *Ecce Homo* ([1888] 2004: 69). This moment of elation provides the basis for Nietzsche's claim that we must say 'Yes' to life: in all its joy and suffering, hope and pain. It takes dramatic form. Imagine that you were confronted by a demon who tells you that you must live your life over again, with every tiny detail repeated in exactly the same way. Would you see this as a form of damnation or joyfully embrace it? Has there been one moment for which you would be prepared to live through everything else in order to experience it again? This becomes Nietzsche's test for how to live well, and his immersion in the astounding beauty of a mountain walk inspires it.

Walking is one way of locating oneself in the natural world. But we do not need the freedom to walk to do this. Stanley Spencer offers one way of engaging with our world through paint. We *see* it, we pay attention to it. Viktor Frankl offers examples drawn from a far more disturbing context than a Berkshire Village: his time in the concentration camp. They are examples which are not used to detract from the need for political action to end the cruelty that fuelled the Nazi regime and which made the Holocaust possible: far from it. They do, however, also suggest how some respite might be attained even in moments of the most appalling suffering. Frankl describes people in the midst of backbreaking and soul-destroying forced labour snatching a stolen moment to watch the beauty of a setting sun.[31] A bird's frank gaze is felt as a form of connection to the wife from whom Frankl has been so cruelly torn apart.[32] A woman points out to him the tree that is 'the only friend I have in my loneliness' (Frankl 2004: 78). These are terrible, dreadful circumstances, reminders of the ways in which human beings can fail so appallingly and so completely to treat others with respect and kindness. They urge us to act to stop such suffering. Yet even in these terrible places Frankl suggests some comfort can be found through placing one's suffering in the broader perspective of the natural world.

Dietrich Bonhoeffer, theologian and pastor, awaiting trial in a Nazi prison for his role in a plot to kill Hitler, finds similar solace through his glimpses of the natural world. He 'is grateful for little things', like the thrush that sings in the prison yard ([1953] 1971: 22). His imprisonment is at turns tedious, frustrating, terrifying; but in reminders of nature he finds a way of living with the things that are happening to him. 'Prison life', he writes, 'brings home to one how nature carries on uninterruptedly its quiet, open life, and it gives one quite a special … attitude towards animal and plant life' ([1953] 1971: 71). His Christian faith enables him to hope, but it is also in nature that he finds that which transcends his sense of loss and failure.

These examples are taken from extremely dark times. That such practices might be employed in such contexts holds out the possibility that they could be effective for us in our here and now. The experiences of Nietzsche, the walking philosopher, are probably closer to the kind of trials most of us face. Plagued by chronic illness that restricts him to his room for weeks on end, even these moments allow him space to reflect more broadly on his life: 'Sickness … gave me a right to a complete forgetting of my habits; it permitted, it commanded, forgetting; it bestowed on me the compulsion to lie still, to be idle, to wait and be patient … But to do that means to think! … My eyes alone put an end to all bookwormishness … I was redeemed from the book' ([1888] 2004: 92).

Illness draws Nietzsche's gaze inwards. For the playwright Dennis Potter, in the last stages of the cancer that will kill him, his gaze is directed to the fragile blossom that blooms outside his bedroom window. Its passing beauty calls him to participate in what he calls 'the nowness of everything'. He will not see the blossom bloom again – he knows this – but rather than feel despondent that this is so, this knowledge brings with it new wisdom: 'Things are both more trivial than they ever were, and more important than they ever were, and the difference between the trivial and the important doesn't seem to matter' (1994: 5). The fragile beauty of a constantly changing world that will be there long after he is gone puts everything in perspective: even the imminence of his own death.

We might see in Potter's appreciation of the blossom a very literal example of what it means to be 'brought to our senses'. What an often misread and misunderstood phrase this is. This is not about accepting a grim realism that forces the rejection of hopes or dreams.

Forget the claims that it is in money or status, the things we acquire and accumulate, that 'sense' is to be found. Forget the failures that haunt us. Forget the losses that pain us. In the vision of blossom, we are *brought to our senses*. We see what really matters, and it is the blossom's beauty, its gentle scent, the touch of its soft and fragile blooms, the sound of wind in the boughs from which it springs, the taste of the fruit which grows out of it. Here is life in all its fullness, offering us an intimation of our connection to a world that is so much more than we are. The senses tell us all this if only we pay attention to them.

In Anna Burns's novel *Milkman*, a similar idea is presented. Sunsets literally open up her nameless protagonist's horizons, holding out the prospect of a reality far more varied and colourful than is offered by the rigid sectarian ideologies shaping the violent conflict of 'the Troubles' in Northern Ireland during the last three decades of the twentieth century. Encouraged by her French teacher and 'maybe-boyfriend' to look – really look – at the sunsetting sky, she sees that, contrary to the claims of the two rival communities, the sky need not be perceived as just blue:

> As for this sky, it was now a mix of pink and lemon with a glow of mauve behind it … An emerging gold above the mauve was moving towards a slip of silver, with a different mauve in a corner drifting in from the side. Then there was further pinking. Then more lilac. Then a turquoise that pressed clouds – not white – out of its way. (Burns 2018: 73)

Attending to the sky – really seeing it – confronts her with a reality quite different from the constraining politics of her world: 'These colours were blending and mixing, sliding and extending, new colours arriving, all colours combining, colours going on forever, except one which was missing, which was blue' (Burns 2018: 77). The monochrome world is shattered for this moment, and 'the truth hit my senses' (Burns 2018: 76–7). There are other ways of living.

We can draw on examples such as these as we try to find our own methods for living well. Through placing our lives, our failures, our losses, in a larger context – be that through being outside, in the garden, in the street, in the park, through looking out the window, or hearing birdsong – we can all develop the kind of perspective that opens us up to the world of which we are a part. Here is the promise of *homo religiosus* that destabilizes and ultimately defeats the constraining structures of *homo economicus*.

The economic is not the only way of constructing a life.

Through cultivating a broader connection with the everyday, through connecting to the world around us, we can find ways of holding our losses and failures lightly. We need not be consumed by them, or destroyed by them, for they are not the only thing that defines us. We can look again at what matters in our lives: and here we can find a place for relationship and for connection to the universe itself.

We can be failures, we can experience loss, and we can come to a perspective that enables us to live well.

CONCLUSION: BEING A FAILURE AND LIVING WELL

We have come a long way in our investigation of failure. We have considered its shaping through neoliberal categories, and, specifically, the world of work. We have seen how it gets caught up with loss, located in the bodies of women and in our fears of dying. We have considered attempts to control loss and failure through numbers and metrification. And I have suggested the effect of replacing *homo economicus* with *homo religiosus* for our ability to live well.

Adopting the perspective I suggest enables us to locate our life in the broader swell of the universe described in Chapter Six. To do this is not, of course, to find ourselves suddenly immune to loss or impervious to failure. There is no escaping the universe we inhabit. It is defined by chance and change, ebb and flow, growth and decay. We are part of these self-same structures, whether we like it or not. Our lives inevitably include joy and sorrow, happiness and unhappiness, growth and decline, success and failure. Rather than striving to shape a life which accepts only the supposedly positive sides of those binaries and which judges the merit of a life accordingly, a better way, as I hope I have shown here, is to recognize just how intimately connected we are to all that is. Life consists of the good and the bad, the painful and the joyful. Shifting our focus away from the obsession with achievement, away from the desire to be a success, is to become better placed to embrace all that is included in the limits placed on being human. This is grounded in a helpful realism, for life is by its very nature unpredictable. By resisting the desire to evade loss, thinking we can somehow escape it, by rejecting the fantasy that the avoidance of failure will somehow make us invincible, we become capable of embracing the totality of experience. What happens *to* us is not the final word: what matters is *how* we have lived, the relationships we have cultivated with others and with the world.

The story of Kirsty Boden provides a fine example of the qualities that come from holding to such a view of life. Boden was a nurse caught up in the van and knife attack perpetrated by Islamist terrorists on London Bridge in 2017. Wanting to help those wounded, she ran towards, rather than away from, the horror. As a result she became one of those killed that day. Her family in their grief and bereavement focused on *how she had lived* not the manner of her death. She was a generous person who loved helping people. Her life was defined by her care for others not by its violent end. Commitments like these, lived out daily, make sense of one's life, regardless of the things that happen.

If we try to read Boden's actions through the categories of neoliberalism, they make no sense. The financialization of everything, the idea that we are atomistic subjects separate from each other, cannot explain why she acted the way she did that day. There are no monetary calculations that could explain why she put her life at risk for others. There was no advantage for herself that she sought to gain. Yet her life reveals something of the best that humanity can be, for it transcended the pettiness of self-centredness. To assess her life as a success or a failure would seem an inadequate and altogether peculiar way of describing what makes her inspiring. A better way is to see her as providing an example of how we might shape our lives in such a way that they reflect a similar love for others.

In the end, it is the quality of our relationships that are most likely to make up the meaning of our lives. Through the lens of *homo religiosus*, I have suggested that it is relationship in all its diverse forms that enables the well lived life. Such a life is grounded, not in restricting the extent of our relationships only to those we love, or to those who we happen to know. When we accept our place in the world as part of a much wider web of life, it becomes possible to extend the relational to include all aspects of the fragile world we inhabit, to include all those with whom we share this world.

I am not advocating that we embrace a privatized form of spirituality. Actively shaping the political realm is necessary to address the injustices that lend some to be dismissed as failures not worth bothering with, or which give all the good things in life to those deemed successes. But to highlight the importance of political action does not mean we should ignore cultivating the kind of reflection that enables us to decentre the self. Placing the self in relationship to the broader universe makes possible a new perspective where we take seriously the needs of the others with whom we share this fragile world. It also makes possible a different way of thinking about loss and failure. Accepted as part and parcel of life, they become experiences we must weave into the rich fabric of life. They become accepted parts of our stories, events that forge us, part of who we are. As Frankl puts it: 'What you have experienced, no power on earth can take away from you' (2004: 90). Lane goes further: 'We recognise the wounds we carry as gifts' (2015: 217). We don't just have to live with loss, we can embrace it. We are vulnerable, we are fallible, but rather than resist these realities, we can come to realize that we are all the better for that.

NOTES

Introduction

1 Audre Lorde, *Cancer Journals* (San Francisco, CA: Aunt Lute Books, [1980] 1997).

2 Michèle Le Doeuff, *Hipparchia's Choice: An Essay Concerning Women, Philosophy, Etc*. (New York: Columbia University Press, [1989] 2007).

3 Belden Lane, *The Solace of Fierce Landscapes: Exploring Desert and Mountain Spirituality* (Oxford: OUP, 1998).

4 Lawrence Hatab, *Nietzsche's Life Sentence* (London: Routledge, 2005).

5 Mark Oakley, *The Collage of God* (London: DLT, 2001).

6 A similar point is made by Martha Nussbaum in *The Fragility of Goodness* (Cambridge: Cambridge University Press, 1986).

7 Hannah Tillich, *From Time to Time* (New York: Stein and Day, 1973).

8 The language of soul is making something of a comeback: see Peter Tyler, *The Pursuit of the Soul: Psychoanalysis, Soul-Making and the Christian Tradition* (New York: Bloomsbury, 2016); Mark Edmundson, *Self and Soul: A Defense of Ideals* (Cambridge, MA: Harvard University Press, 2015).

9 See Allan V. Horwitz and Jerome C. Wakefield, *The Loss of Sadness* (Oxford: OUP, 2007) for an account of how psychiatry transformed sorrow into depressive disorder.

Chapter One

1 Josh Wilson, 'Work Related Stress Now Accounts for Over Half of Work Absences', *The Telegraph*, 1 November 2018 https://www.telegraph.

co.uk/news/2018/11/01/work-related-stress-mental-illness-now-accounts-half-work-absences/. Accessed 1 March 2019.

2 Health and Safety Executive, 'Work Related Stress Depression or Anxiety Statistics in Great Britain, 2018', published 31 October 2018 http://www.hse.gov.uk/statistics/causdis/stress.pdf. Accessed 1 March 2019.

3 Patricia Hill Collins's introduction to her *Black Feminist Thought* (London: Routledge, 1991) makes clear her intention to use theory, but always in a way which reflects the needs and concerns of black women's community out of which she writes.

4 See Marshall McLuhan (2005) for discussion of 'environment' and what it takes to be 'anti-environment'.

5 The French philosopher Michel Foucault is a master at rendering strange the world and the practices that we take for granted. See e.g. *Madness and Civilization* (1961) and *Discipline and Punish* (1975), where he refuses to assume the superiority of modern accounts of madness or punishment, and by engaging with historical practices makes us think again about the values shaping our accounts of each.

6 By focusing on Western societies, I appreciate the limits this places on the scope of this book. It is, however, vital for those living in the West to pay attention to the values that emanate from its dominant economic and social models: not least because the reality of globalization is that these models are being busily imposed upon other cultures and contexts, with little thought paid to whether such structures are good or bad for the flourishing of individuals and communities.

7 The so-called TINA doctrine, and a favourite slogan of Margaret Thatcher.

8 David Harvey's analysis of China shows something of this: see Harvey (2005), chapter 5 'Neoliberalism "with Chinese Characteristics"', pp. 120–51.

9 See Harvey (2005, chapter 1) for detail of the context out of which the neoliberal consensus emerged.

10 For an exciting account of this battle of ideas, see Philip Mirowski (2014, chapter 2).

11 See Harvey (2005: 3).

12 See Sennett (2006) for use of this descriptive term.

13 See Standing (2011: 43).

14 See Rose (1999: 102).

15 The term '*homo economicus*' is coined by Michel Foucault in his lectures on 'The Birth of Biopolitics' given in 1978–9. In these lectures he explores, presciently, the extent to which economics is coming to shape the human subject. The transcription of these lectures was first published in complete form in 2004 (edited by Michel Senellart; translated by Graham Burchell, London: Palgrave Macmillan, 2008).

16 See Wendy Brown (2015) for the phrase 'the financialization of everything', p. 28.

17 For reflections on the changing nature of work, see Keith Thomas's introduction to his collection on this theme (1999).

18 See Calum Brown, *The Death of Christian Britain* (London: Routledge, 2000) for details of the detrimental effect of secularization on participation in voluntary associations. While there is much to commend his analysis of the role secularization plays, in more recent years it has been the extension of 'the working world' to all areas of life that has, I would contend, compounded the problem.

19 See Standing (2011: 206–8).

20 Standing (2011: 76–81).

21 See Rose (1999: 56).

22 See Rose (1999: 113).

23 In November 2017, Uber lost their appeal to a UK judgement that rejected their claim that their drivers were self-employed. An important ruling, this meant they had to pay their drivers the national minimum wage and provide paid holidays.

24 See Harvey (2005: 65) for discussion of this point.

25 The continuing commitment to this strategy cannot be ignored: the slogan for the Conservative Party Conference in September 2018 was one word, 'Opportunity'.

26 For a critique of the implications of this way of thinking upon educational practice, see Ecclestone and Hayes (2008).

27 Cited in Commons debates, 1986, 2003-07-02, col. 407.

28 For powerful reflections on the shame of being poor, see Walker (2014).

29 See Bradley Allsop, 'The BBC's "Britain's Hardest Grafter" Show Should Be Britain's Greatest Shame', HuffPost, 3 June 2015, http://www.

huffingtonpost.co.uk/bradley-allsop/britains-hardest-grafter_b_7499800.
html.

30 See, e.g. Lawrence Mead, appointed as an advisor to the Coalition
Government in the UK in 2010, who wrote in 1986 that 'the government
must persuade [benefit claimants] to blame themselves' (quoted in
Standing 2011: 246). Such views are enshrined in government policy,
not just in the attitudes of some TV makers.

31 See Genesis 3.17.

32 See Marx ([1844] 1981).

33 According to an article published on the This Is Money website on 30
December 2015, the real value of wages in the UK had 'plummeted' by
14 per cent since the financial crash of 2008.

34 See Standing (2011: vii) for discussion of this point.

35 The rise of 'an anti-work movement' suggests both an awareness of
the mismatch about claims made concerning work and an openness to
exploring the possibilities of life beyond work. See Srnicek and Williams
(2016).

36 See Standing (2011: chapter 1).

37 Sennett (2006: 53).

38 See Standing (2011: 98).

39 See Liam Byrne's Social Market Foundation report on 'Robbins
Rebooted: How We Make Our Way in the Second Machine Age',
published in 2014.

40 Srnicek and Williams (2016) suggest embracing the possibilities of
automation, seeing in the extension of automation the possibility of
greater freedom. I am less convinced of this outcome, given the history
of technology under capitalism.

41 See Arendt ([1958] 1998: 105).

42 See Arendt ([1958] 1998: 100).

43 Arendt ([1958] 1998: 144).

44 See also Sennett (2006) for a discussion of uselessness in *The Culture
of the New Capitalism*, pp. 83–130.

45 In Chapter Five, we will return to the importance of community for
framing the good life.

46 See Arendt ([1958] 1998: 191).

47 See Arendt ([1958] 1998: 233).

48 The growing disparity between top and bottom incomes suggests something is not right with the assumption that work is good for us. In 2015, the Equality Trust reported the richest 10 per cent of UK households held 44 per cent of all wealth, while the poorest 50 per cent held just 9.5 per cent. In the United States, this figure is even more astounding, CNN reporting in August 2016 that 10 per cent of US households held 70 per cent of the nation's wealth.

49 As Guy Standing comments, 'By saying jobs should make us happy and that jobs define us and give us satisfaction, we are setting up a source of tension because the jobs most of us have to perform will fall short of these expectations' (2011: 243).

50 Dante Alighieri, *The Divine Comedy*, translated by Courtney Langdon (Cambridge: Harvard University Press, 1918), p. 3.

51 See Rose (1999: 230).

Chapter Two

1 As Judith Butler notes, 'Exclusions … haunt signification as its abject borders or as that which is strictly foreclosed: the unlivable, the nonnarrativizable, the traumatic' (1993: 188).

2 'The basic anxiety, the anxiety of a finite being about the threat of non-being, cannot be eliminated' (Tillich [1952] 1977: 48).

3 See McDowell and Court's trinity of feminine virtues: 'sociability, caring and, indeed, servicing' (cited by Adkins 2002: 60).

4 See Susan Faludi's powerful study of the effect of changes to the workplace on American men in her *Stiffed* (1999).

5 For an analysis of this factor, see Adkins (2002: 59).

6 See also Adkins (2002: 62).

7 See Butler (1990).

8 See Susan Hekman (2014) for an analysis of the influence of Beauvoir on later feminist theorists: and, specifically, the debt to her work in theories like those of Butler.

9 See Adkins (2002: 62).

10 See Adkins (2002: 76).

11 For Gillard's reflections on the sexism of Australian politics, see her
        autobiography, *My Story*, London: Bantam Press, 2014. For Bill
        Heffernan's description of her as 'deliberately barren' and the fruit bowl
        incident, see pp. 101–2.

12 May Bulman, 'Andrea Leadsom on Theresa May and Motherhood',
        9 July 2016 https://www.independent.co.uk/news/uk/politics/
        andrea-leadsom-interview-theresa-may-mother-tory-leadership-
        campaign-a7128331.html. Accessed 1 March 2019.

13 See for example Melanie Klein ([1946] 1997) and Anna Freud ([1937]
        1993) for two rather different psychoanalytic approaches that maintain
        the centrality of achievement of psychosexual development to
        psychoanalytic theory.

14 See Freud (1925).

15 While there is a move to downplay the significance of bodily sexual
        markers in light of the experience of people identifying as 'transgender',
        I am not sure that the significance of sexual identity, present at birth,
        can be so easily ignored, given the way in which such physical markers
        have been used in the process of socialization. If we wish to challenge
        such notions, we cannot ignore the history of ideas that have shaped
        understandings of male and female; hence my concern to consider
        success and failure as grounded in the experience and interpretation of
        the body.

16 See James Nelson (1994) for reflections on what this model of male
        identity means for understandings of spirituality.

17 See Luce Irigaray's critical reflections on Freud's theory of female sexual
        development, *Speculum of the Other Woman*, trans. Gillian Gill (Ithaca,
        NY: Cornell University Press, 1985).

18 See Freud's 'Female Sexuality' (1931) for the complex account of female
        sexual identity at which he finally arrives.

19 Freud (1920b) suggests that women who look beyond this identification
        are suffering from a pathological condition.

20 See Jean-Paul Sartre, *Sketch for a Theory of the Emotions*
        (London: Routledge, 1971), section II for Sartre's critique of
        psychoanalytic theory.

21 For this description, see Sartre ([1943] 1969: 608).

22 'The transcendent' is Sartre's term for the one who is able to 'ex-sist', to 'stand out' from the world. For discussion of the role Sartre assigns to the female body, see Clack (2002: 43–51).

23 For Beauvoir on motherhood, see *The Second Sex*. Recent feminist reappraisals of Beauvoir's work suggest a rather more complex account of motherhood in her writing than simple rejection: see Alison Stone, 'Beauvoir and the Ambiguities of Motherhood', in ed. Laura Hengehold and Nancy Bauer, *A Companion to Simone de Beauvoir* (Oxford: Wiley Blackwell, 2017, pp. 122–33). According to Stone, 'a more positive portrayal of embodied maternity – its pleasures, values and complexities – can also be found in *The Second Sex*, so that Beauvoir's attitude to motherhood goes beyond simple hostility' (p. 125).

24 For the range of theorists offering such views of women, see Clack (1999).

25 See Kant ([1764] 1960: 77).

26 Although as Kant points out, the whole point of being noble is not to hope to receive such a title, as much as to bestow it ([1764] 1960: 76).

27 For a feminist analysis of this hierarchical construction of moral frameworks, see Carol Gilligan's classic account (1982).

28 See Immanuel Kant, *Grounding for Metaphysics of Morals* (Indiana: Hackett, [1785] 1981), pp. 11–12.

29 We will return to this claim in order to contend, with Schopenhauer, that a morality located in feeling for others might actually provide a rather better basis for moral action than Kant suggests (see pp. 163–4).

30 Kant does suggest that as a woman ages and her 'charms diminish, the reading of books and the broadening of insight could refill unnoticed the vacant place of the Graces with the Muses, *and the husband should be the first instructor*' ([1764] 1960: 92; my emphasis). Female learning is placed carefully within the boundaries of male approval.

31 For Schopenhauer, women remain 'big children, their whole lives long' (Schopenhauer [1851] 1970: 81).

32 See Plato, *Symposium*, trans. Robin Waterfield (Oxford: OUP, 1994), 209a.

33 Val Plumwood's *Feminism and the Mastery of Nature* (London: Routledge, 1993) offers a compelling analysis of the detrimental impact Plato's dualism has on the appreciation and preservation of the physical world.

34   See *Symposium* 209c–211c.

35   See *On the Generation of Animals* 729b–730b.

36   See Aristotle, *On the Generation of Animals* 737a.

37   See *Summa Theologiae* Ia. 92, 1.

38   Aquinas, *Summa Theologiae* 1a. 93, 4.

39   A similar argument, and doubtless one that Aquinas draws upon, is made by Augustine in *De Trinitate* Book XII, chapter 7.

40   For a classic exploration of the 'Man' of Reason, see Lloyd (1984).

41   We might add something about the uses to which the biblical figure of Eve has been put over the centuries: sin and punishment came into the world through the actions of Eve, not through those of Adam. See Elaine Pagels, *Adam, Eve and the Serpent* (Harmondsworth: Penguin, 1988); Uta Ranke Heinemann, *Eunuchs for the Kingdom of Heaven* (Harmondsworth: Penguin, 1991) for two important accounts which trace this process at work.

42   For a ground-breaking feminist analysis of the cosmetics industry, see Naomi Wolf's *The Beauty Myth* (London: Virago, 1990).

43   The exposure of widespread sexual abuse in Hollywood in 2017 and the '#MeToo' campaign on Twitter revealed the continuing presence of sexism, misogyny and sexual harassment.

44   See Banyard (2010: 39).

45   According to the UK's Human Fertilisation and Embryology Authority in 2014, the success of IVF according to age was as follows: women under 35, 32.2 per cent; women between 35 and 37, 27.7 per cent; women between 38 and 39, 20.8 per cent; women between 40 and 42, 13.6 per cent; women between 43 and 44, 5 per cent; women 45 and over, 1.9 per cent.

46   See Yahoo7 Lifestyle, 22 October 2014.

47   For the 'full story', see *Daily Mail*, 23 August 2016, http://www.dailymail. co.uk/tvshowbiz/article-3753829/Maybe-stay-sun-Renee-Actress-looks-tired-wrinkled-promotes-new-Bridget-Jones-film-Australia. html#ixzz4Uyepxo00. Accessed 17 July 2019.

48   In contrast to the criticism directed at Zellweger, 'Peaches&Scream' (@ keli_juepner) posted: 'People talking about Renee Zellweger like they're surprised women look older when they age' (8 August 2016).

49 See Kristeva (1982: 3) for description of these elements as the abject.

50 The abject is found in death 'as it really is,' not in how it might be presented, aesthetically, to us. Thus, 'the corpse, seen without God and outside of science, is the utmost of abjection. It is death infecting life. Abject' (1982: 4).

51 Umberto Eco is a powerful advocate of this method (see Eco 2007: 8).

52 So Tertullian: 'Those women who torment their skin with make-up, or stain their cheeks red and extend the line of their eyes with soot sin against him. There can be no doubt that these women dislike what God has created' (in Eco 2007: 160); and Boccaccio 'You saw her tall and slim...just as you believed her face was real, not having seen those drooping jowls concealed by rouge and powder' (in Eco 2007: 164).

53 See Beauvoir ([1970] 1996: 169–71) on the treatment of elderly women in art and literature where she makes a similar point.

54 See Greer (1991: 4).

55 See Clack (1999), Lloyd (1984), Plumwood (1993) for discussion of this connection.

56 An article on the online magazine Caring.Com suggests the fear of becoming invisible is the number 1 fear women have about ageing. https://www.caring.com/articles/5-things-women-fear-about-aging.

57 The perceptive title of Beauvoir's (1970) work on this theme.

58 See Zita (1993).

59 'The loss of health, of life, of love, never leaves us unaltered' (Anderson 2017: 16).

60 I am wary of the kind of philosophy of sexual difference that shapes Luce Irigaray's writing and that was developed by Grace Jantzen in her *Becoming Divine* (1998).

61 See Beauvoir ([1970] 1996).

62 See Beauvoir (1970: 377), but also Heidegger, *Being and Time*, for a discussion of the role of death.

63 Sartre makes a not dissimilar distinction between 'being-for-others' whereby a person over-identifies with the values and judgements of others, and 'being-with-others' whereby a secure subjectivity enables authentic action with others. See Cooper (1990, pp. 101–6) for discussion of this distinction.

Chapter Three

1   See Philippe Ariès account of attitudes to death in his *Western Attitudes toward Death from the Middle Ages to the Present* (London: Marion Boyars, 1976).

2   My wording of Lucretius' famous 'symmetry argument', made in his *On the Nature of Things*, Book 3, lines 972–7. For discussion of this argument, see Stephen Rosenbaum's 'How to Be Dead and Not Care: A Defence of Epicurus', in John Martin Fischer, ed., *The Metaphysics of Death* (Stanford: Stanford University Press, 1993), pp. 119–34.

3   Dekkers (2000: 83–7; 171–3).

4   See Hick (1985); also Zaki Badawi in Neuberger and White (1991: 141–51).

5   See Peter Harvey in Neuberger and White (1991: 105–21).

6   See Pagels (1988, chapter 6) for details of this debate.

7   For details of Augustine's argument, see Pagels (1988: 128).

8   From Augustine's *Opus Imperfectum* quoted in Pagels (1988: 133).

9   See Heidegger (1962: 264), also Cooper (1990: 136–9) for discussion of the broader application of this concept.

10 Cederström and Spicer (2015: 4).

11 'Welfare to Work' programmes have been in place in the UK since the 1990s. Initially constructed to get the long-term unemployed back into work, their remit increasingly covers getting the long-term sick or those with disabilities into work. The extent to which such schemes are helping people has been criticized by a number of charities. In 2015 the mental health charity Mind called on the UK government to 'radically overhaul the benefits system, to one with less focus on pressurising people and greater investment in tailored, personalised support'.

12 See Cederström and Spicer (2015: 4).

13 See Cederström and Spicer (2015: 51); also Lisa Isherwood, *The Fat Jesus: Christianity and Body Image* (New York: Seabury Books, 2007), where this image of Christ emerges a part of a liberation perspective that challenges the last taboo.

14 Bauman (1992: 138).

15 See Sharon Kaufman's study of the end of life in American hospitals (2005, especially p. 82).

16 For details of these pressures, see Kaufman (2005: 37).

17 For a description of one of these facilities, see O'Connell (2017: 22–41). It would be tempting to write off the practices that take place in facilities like the Alcor Life Extension Foundation as irrelevant to the wider world, were it not for the creeping extension of interest in these attempts to overcome death. Indeed, in 2016 cryonics entered the public consciousness with a UK court case where the judgement found in favour of a 14-year-old girl's desire – she was suffering from cancer – to be cryonically frozen after her death.

18 BBC website, 13 October 2016.

19 See O'Connell (2017: 171).

20 A legal case played a key role in shaping the notion that the individual has the right to a good death. In the mid-1970s – note, again, the significance of that time for establishing the primacy of neoliberal ideals – the publicity surrounding the case of Karen Quinlan opened up the discussion of what it meant to have one's own death. Quinlan had been in a coma for months, and her parents sought to have the machines supporting her switched off. Her doctors opposed this: mainly because they feared criminal prosecution. Her parents won their action, and Quinlan died some nine years later, having lived on in an unresponsive state. Quinlan's case opened up questions of what to do with those kept alive by medical procedures previously undreamt of. More significantly, it suggested that death was now a matter of *deciding* when a person should die, and when a person was considered dead (Kaufman 2005: 64–5). Death was not something over which the individual had no control; although we should note the fact that what was at stake was not *not* dying, but having the possibility of deciding *when* to die. (In Quinlan's case, this was a decision taken by her parents, a fact that explains something of the disquiet of some critics of assisted dying that it is not the needs of the dying that are reflected in such decisions, but of those surrounding them.) Choice is what matters, and even in dying, the neoliberal subject is to be defined by the choices they make.

21 See Kaufman (2005: 154) for discussion of this pressure.

22 Alastair Campbell said of his boss and his administration, 'We don't do God.'

23 Gould (2012: 56).

24 The idea of pausing as a method for structuring the well-lived life will be addressed in Chapter Six.

25 For a criticism of this kind of faith see Dietrich Bonhoeffer ([1953] 1971: 361).

26 Gould (2012: 201).

27 A number of governmental strategies from the New Labour period suggest aspiration as something to be promoted in all areas of life. For a critique of this approach, see Konstanze Spohrer, 'Deconstructing "Aspiration": UK Policy Debates and European Policy Trends', *European Educational Research Journal*, vol. 10, no. 1 (2011): pp. 53–63.

28 Frances Ryan, 'Death Has Become a Part of Britain's Benefit System', *The Guardian*, 27 April 2015. For a dramatic rendition of such real-life scenarios, see Ken Loach's film from 2016, *I, Daniel Blake*.

29 See his *Confession* (1882).

30 She identifies C.S. Lewis's *A Grief Observed* as one the few sustained pieces on this phenomenon.

31 See Joan Didion, *The Year of Magical Thinking* (London: Harper Perennial, 2006), p. 16.

32 I was first introduced to these poems by Pamela Sue Anderson some years before her own struggle with and death from oesophageal cancer. Reading them now, they take on my grief at Pam's death, and my continued mourning of her loss.

33 It is, as Mark O'Connell says, a law that says that 'the universe was in a state of ongoing and nonnegotiable decline' (2017: 209).

34 See Frank ([1991] 2002: 116).

Chapter Four

1 See Freud (1927: 15).

2 For full discussion of how Freud does this, see Freud 1930; also Brian R Clack's interesting discussion in *Love, Drugs, Art, Religion: The Pains and Consolations of Existence* (Farnham: Ashgate, 2014).

3 Watching a game played by his grandson, Freud notes how the child throws out a cotton reel, saying 'fort' ('go') as he does so, and then, as he draws the reel back, saying 'da' ('there'). In the 'fort/da' game, Freud recognizes the child's attempt to command through play the comings and goings of the mother. The absence of the mother is experienced as something frightening; in the game the child feels able to control her.

4 The phrase the 'good enough' mother comes from Donald Winnicott's work, and suggests not that the mother need be perfect, just that she needs to be good enough in her responses to the child to cultivate a sense of security in relation to the external world. See D. W. Winnicott, 'Transitional Objects and Transitional Phenomena', *International Journal of Psychoanalysis*, vol. 34 (1953): 89–97.

5 See Freud (1911), 'Formulations on the Two Principles of Mental Functioning' in Standard Edition Volume 12, pp. 213–26.

6 See Freud (1927, p. 50). At one point he is even fascinated by claims that death need not be considered something natural (see Freud 1920a, pp. 44–61).

7 See Max Weber, *The Theory of Social and Economic Organisation* (New York: Simon & Schuster [1947] 1964).

8 See Perry Hinton (2000) for a fascinating discussion of the limitations of rational decision-making. As he points out, it is not so much that we do not use reason in order to come to our decisions, but that we more often use surrounding cultural forms in order to make shortcuts in the process of decision-making: shortcuts that are not always welcome.

9 See Beecham (1996) for discussion of Weber and the nature of bureaucracies.

10 See Arendt ([1948] 1968: 143). For Arendt, the solutions offered by totalitarian ideologies to human problems are merely extreme versions of a more generalized belief in science as something, citing Eric Vogelin, 'that will magically cure the evils of existence and transform the nature of man' (1968: 346).

11 In 1937, the Nazis held an exhibition of degenerate art in Munich. Modern, abstract and non-representational art was included as not conforming to an appropriately Aryan aesthetic.

12 See Arendt (1964: 65).

13 See Heather Morris, *The Tattooist of Auschwitz* (London: Zaffre, 2018).

14 'Father of Two Deported to Mexico after 30 Years in the US', *New York Post*, 17 January 2018, https://nypost.com/2018/01/17/father-of-two-deported-to-mexico-after-30-years-in-us/. Accessed 15 May 2019.

15 His lectures on 'The Birth of Biopolitics' were given in 1978–9 and the transcription published in complete form, edited by Michel Senellart, in 2004 (English translation by Graham Burchell, London: Palgrave Macmillan, 2008).

16 See Gane's definition: 'An architecture of power that works through the correction and normalisation of the body and the soul or even life' (2012: 614).

17 For a criticism of Foucault's account of power in the neoliberal age, see Mirowski (2014: 93–106).

18 Whether Deleuze's development is an extension of Foucault's discussion of disciplinary and control societies or a completely new development is debatable: see Jeremy Gilbert and Andrew Goffey's introduction to 'Control Societies' in *New Formations* (2015): pp. 5–20.

19 See Ecclestone and Hayes (2008) for details of these practices.

20 See Gilles Deleuze, 'Postscript on the Societies of Control', October, vol. 59 (1992): pp. 3–17.

21 Nikolas Rose describes what this means rather well: 'Control is better understood as operating through conditional access to circuits of consumption and civility: constant scrutiny of the right of individuals to access certain kinds of flows of consumption goods; recurrent switch points to be passed in order to access the benefits of liberty' (Rose 2000: 326).

22 See Steven Shaviro blog 'The "Bitter Necessity" of Debt', 1 May 2010.

23 See Richard Thaler and Cass Sunstein's *Nudge: Improving Decisions about Health, Wealth and Happiness* (New Haven, CT: Yale University Press, 2008). Their methods were influential with American and British governments, and were used by David Cameron in the UK and Barack Obama in the United States.

24 The scope of these attempts to influence political behaviour is still being uncovered at the time of writing. See for example report in *The Guardian*, 5 April 2018, of the use of data in Nigerian elections in 2015. https://guardian.ng/news/jonathan-unaware-of-cambridge-analytica-campaign-role/.

25 See Hacking (1990), Scott (1998).

26 See Scott (1998: 13).

27 A popular business studies textbook on metrics and marketing offers a useful definition of a metric which suggests something of its scope: 'A

metric is a measuring system that quantifies a trend, dynamic or characteristic. In virtually all disciplines, practitioners use metrics to explain phenomena, diagnose causes, share findings and project the results of future events. Throughout the worlds of science, business and government, metrics encourage rigour and objectivity. They make it possible to compare observations across regions and periods. They facilitate understanding and collaboration' (Farris et al. 2009: 1).

28 A comment from the nineteenth-century mathematical physicist and engineer Lord Kelvin drives this point home: 'When you can measure what you are speaking about, and express it in numbers, you know something about it; but when you cannot measure it, when you cannot express it in numbers, your knowledge is of a meagre and unsatisfactory kind' (in Farris et al. 2009: 1).

29 Even the church has not been immune from the language of business theory and specifically the practices of managerialism: see Lyndon Shakespeare's study, *Being the Body of Christ in the Age of Management* (Eugene, OR: Cascade Books, 2016) for detail and critique of this approach.

30 For a potted history of the development of this practice, see Stefan Collini, *What Are Universities For?* (London: Penguin, 2012).

31 See Roger Burrows (2012) for an account of this extension.

32 For those interested in this debate, see HEFCE's report, published on 9 July 2015, 'The Metric Tide'. Note that while highlighting the concerns of academics about the extension of metrics into non-science subjects, the conclusion was to continue developing 'responsible metrics' for assessing research excellence.

33 Ian Hacking, *The Taming of Chance* (Cambridge University Press, 1990).

34 Hacking (1990: 194).

35 Hacking (1990: 194).

36 Katherine O'Flynn's novel *What Was Lost* (2007) goes some way to challenge the claim that to ask this question is to fall prey to nostalgia. She suggests something of the pain of individual loss alongside a social commentary on the effect the 1980s move from shops on a high street to the out-of-town mall has on neighbourhoods, including the loss of community accompanying this shift.

37 Blogger Susan Crozier makes powerful use of this question in her reflections on failure as something to actively cultivate: see Crozier,

'Towards a Manifesto: On the Love of Failure', in Beverley Clack and Michele Paule, *Interrogating the Neoliberal Lifecycle: The Limits of Success* (Cham, Switzerland: Palgrave Macmillan, 2019), pp. 169–88.

38 See Bettina Stangneth, *Eichmann before Jerusalem: The Unexamined Life of a Mass Murderer* (New York: Vintage, 2015).

39 Arendt (1963: 89).

40 See Alex Grobman, Daniel Landes and Sybil Milton, eds, *Genocide: Critical Issues of the Holocaust* (Dallas: Rossel Books, 1983), p. 223 on the training of the SS.

41 In Chapter 5 we will consider Schopenhauer's ethics as part of my alternative model of the human. In the personal is located the ethical, as we shall see.

42 See Arendt ([1958] 1998: 243–7).

43 Note that Arendt shapes her reflections on 'the promise' through Nietzsche who 'saw in the faculty of promises (the "memory of the will", as he called it) the very distinction which marks off human from animal life' (([1958] 1998: 245).

44 See Arendt ([1958] 1998: 237).

45 See Partington (2012: 167–9).

46 Partington (2012: 169).

47 George Matheson (1842–1906), *Hymns and Psalms*, Number 685 (London: Methodist, 1983).

48 See Scott (1998: 12–13).

49 See Scott (1998: 20).

Chapter Five

1 See Davies (2014) for a discussion of the scope and limitations of the neoliberal model of competition.

2 Grace Jantzen's feminist philosophy of religion provides the questions that shape the concerns of this chapter: how do we develop trustworthy community (1998: 204–26)? How do we enshrine the practices that enable us to live well (1998: 227–53)?

3 The term *homo religiosus* appears and reappears in the history and philosophy of religion in a variety of ways: for discussion, see Bellah (1964), Hamilton (1965), Miller (1966). Sometimes it is used positively to denote the human desire for the sacred (Eliade 1959), emphasizing the necessity of aligning one's self to the deepest aspects of one's being in order to live well (Tillich 1965). At other times it is used negatively to denote false or superstitious ways of thinking. So Karl Barth argues that, in order for the revealed truth of the Christian God to be realized, claims that God can be found in nature are to be resisted (Barth 1934). Barth's criticisms are in part directed at the easy adoption of religious forms (based in land and race) by the Nazis against whom he was battling. Likewise, Dietrich Bonhoeffer, hero of the German resistance to Hitler, argued against grounding Christian belief in religious attitudes, advocating, instead, a 'religionless' form of Christianity which embraces human maturity and accepts the secular world (Bonhoeffer [1953] 1971: 327).

4 A similar alliance is to be found between the Far Right politician Jair Bolsonaro, elected Brazilian president in October 2018 and evangelical Christian groups.

5 The subtitle of Nietzsche's *Twilight of the Idols* ([1888] 1990) is 'How to Philosophise with a Hammer'.

6 Here I am borrowing the title of Paul Tillich's collection of sermons ([1949] 1962). For Tillich, deepening our engagement with life requires this kind of deliberate upheaval.

7 For discussion of this destructive anthropocentrism, see Goodchild (2002), Plumwood (1993).

8 Those versed in the philosophy of religion or the study of religions will be aware of the torturous, and not entirely successful, attempts of scholars to define what, precisely, 'religion' means. See Clack and Clack (2008, chapter 1) for discussion of the range of theories offered.

9 In defining the human animal as *homo religiosus*, I am drawing upon an account of the religious that I have developed in previous publications (see Clack 2008 (with Brian R. Clack), 2012, 2013).

10 See Augustine, *Confessions*, Book 1.

11 The introduction to Brian R. Clack and Tyler Hower's edited collection, *Philosophy and the Human Condition* (Oxford: OUP, 2018), makes plain the centrality of reflection to philosophical accounts of the human.

12 See Freud (1907; 1919).

13 They are linked to the kind of magical thinking identified in the actions of the child who believes their wishes control their mother (see discussion in pp. 110–11).

14 For interesting reflections on this and Freud's other superstitious behaviours, see Palmer (1997: 10–11).

15 For discussion of the various ways in which Freud uses fate, see Clack (2013, chapter 5).

16 See Aristotle, *Politics*, Book 1.

17 See for the most detailed account of this structure Freud (1923).

18 Freud's controversial account of the psychic life of the child, shaped by the desire to possess the parent of the opposite sex, while being rid of the parent of the same sex. See Freud (1916–17: 332–8; 1933).

19 See Klein (1945); also Britton (1989) for discussion of the relationships involved in the child's psychic development.

20 For a useful way into Lacan's work on language, see Joel Dor, *Introduction to the Reading of Lacan* (New York: Other Press, 2004).

21 It is worth noting that Kristeva has written an extensive study on Klein as part of her 'Female Genius' series (Kristeva 2001).

22 See introduction to 'Stabat Mater' by Morny Joy, Kathleen O'Grady and Judith Poxon in their *French Feminists on Religion: A Reader* (London: Routledge), pp. 112–14 where they suggest ways of reading this complex text.

23 These words, engraved on the floor, sparked protest, as they seemed to suggest that all Germans were victims, and for some they glossed over the actions of German Nazis in creating the horrors of the Second World War and the genocide of the regime.

24 For discussion of the memorial, the work and the controversy see https://theculturetrip.com/europe/germany/articles/k-the-kollwitz-and-berlin-s-neue-wache/ which includes these words from Kollwitz.

25 Andre Green's work on the 'dead mother' explores some of the problems that can surround this break. He focuses on the child's experience of the depressed mother as psychically dead to the child, and notes the impact this can have on the child's subsequent experience of others and the world. See Gregorio Kohon, ed., *The Dead Mother* (London: Karnac, 1999); Andre Green, 'The Dead Mother', *Life*

Narcissism, Death Narcissism (London: Free Association Books, 2001), pp. 170–200.

26 French psychoanalyst André Green suggests something of the on-going nature of this work when he considers the 'ensemble of binding and unbindings of the psychical apparatus' (2011: 19).

27 See Freud (1920a: 21).

28 For discussion of Butler's approach to loss, see Pamela Sue Anderson's 'Life, Death and (Inter)Subjectivity', *International Journal of Philosophy of Religion*, December 2005.

29 When Hannah Arendt offers her account of the kind of political realm that would enable human flourishing, she makes these qualities that establish friendship central to it (see Jon Nixon 2015: 128).

30 When Arendt promotes plurality as vital for the political sphere, she sees the professional political party as something problematic precisely because it subsumes the individual in the collective will. For a discussion of an Arendtian politics, see Nixon 2015, chapter 9.

31 Maev Kennedy, 'Grayson Perry to unveil Brexit vases in Channel 4 show Divided Britain', *The Guardian*, Tuesday 30 May 2017, https://www.theguardian.com/artanddesign/2017/may/30/grayson-perry-to-unveil-brexit-vases-channel-4-show-divided-britain. Accessed 18 July 2019.

32 See Nixon (2015: 180) for Arendt's reflections on this kind of politics.

33 See Charles Taylor on how conversation creates a form of political engagement that allows for difference while creating a sense of united action: 'A conversation is not the coordination of actions of different individuals, but a common action in this strong, irreducible sense: it is our action' (Taylor 1995: 189).

34 Arendt identifies political structures that would allow for this kind of communal practice, emphasizing civic associations, democratic participation, local organizations, and community-led education (Nixon 2015: 180).

35 See Evans (2006: 158).

36 This term for black feminism is coined by Alice Walker in her *In Search of Our Mothers' Gardens*, 1983.

37 See Alice Walker's *The Color Purple* (1982), where Celie does not simply experience oppression at the hands of whites, but also from members of the black community.

38 See Patricia Hill Collins, *Black Feminist Thought* (London: Routledge, 1990), for a complex account of work, family and community.

39 See Linsey McGoey's recent critique of 'the new golden age of philanthropy' for development of this theme (McGoey 2015).

40 Despite giving away so much of his wealth, Bill Gates has also been a vociferous opponent of those calling for a wealth tax. In a widely reported conversation with Thomas Piketty, Gates is said to have commented, 'I love everything that's in your book, but I don't want to pay more tax' (McGoey 2015: 24). We might wonder at the idea that philanthropy can deliver a better world when its causes will always be discrete and will not have the strategic overview that informs state intervention, for example, through the use of direct taxation.

41 Arendt offers a similar critique: 'Without the presence of misfortune, pity could not exist, and it therefore has just as much vested interest in the existence of the unhappy as thirst for power has a vested interest in the existence of the weak ... Pity, taken as the spring of virtue, has proved to possess a greater capacity for cruelty than cruelty itself' (*On Revolution* (London: Penguin), pp. 79–80; quoted in Nixon (2015: 172)).

42 Schopenhauer extends this argument to animals, arguing that this compassionate feeling for a fellow being in pain should affect their treatment (Schopenhauer 1995: 179). David Cartwright dismisses Nietzsche's criticism, arguing that Nietzsche's pity and Schopenhauer's compassion are not the same. Cartwright draws attention to the relationship Nietzsche identifies between pity and contempt: there is no parity of esteem in pity.

43 See Solomon (2003: 98) who accepts Nietzsche's claim that Schopenhauer's *mitleid* does not convey the parity of esteem between sufferer and subject, represented by his own use of *mitgefühl* as a basic virtue.

44 Defined as '*mitleid*' or 'fellow-feeling'.

45 In making this identification, 'the barrier between the ego and the non-ego is for the moment abolished' (Schopenhauer 1995: 166).

46 For a similar, and perhaps better known, reflection on the ethical imperative called forth by the face, see Levinas, *Of God Who Comes to Mind* (Stanford University Press, 1998), pp. 137–51. Also Jantzen (1998) for her discussion of his ethics.

47 For an attempt to acknowledge together diversity and unity in religion, see John Hick, *An Interpretation of Religion* (London: Macmillan, 1989).

48 See Tillich ([1957] 2009: 123).

49 'That which is infinite is being itself … everything participates in being itself' (Paul Tillich, *Systematic Theology*, vol. 1 (Chicago, IL: University of Chicago Press, 1951), p. 239).

50 A similar dynamic is found in Plato's account of *eros* in *the Symposium*. There, erotic love acts as that which propels the individual towards the Good.

51 See Tillich's perceptive comments on the dangers of theism as he advocates 'the God above the God of theism' ([1952] 1977: 180). Philosophers of religion, take note!

Chapter Six

1 For a detailed discussion of structural evils, see Claudia Card, *Confronting Evils: Terrorism, Torture, Genocide* (Cambridge, Cambridge University Press, 2010).

2 See Partington (2012: 116, 138).

3 There is a rich literature on this theme in the philosophy of religion, most notably explored by John Hick. See his *Evil and the God of Love* (London: Palgrave Macmillan, [1966] 2010), pp. 333–6 for discussion of how suffering can both make character and break a person.

4 See Freud (1937: 222–3).

5 On the back cover of Arthur Frank's *The Wounded Storyteller* (1995), Larry Dossey's endorsement captures this sentiment perfectly: 'We are all wounded, and our process of healing is aided by telling our story.'

6 See Jonah 2.3-7.

7 Psalm 139.8.

8 See Tillich ([1949] 1962: 61); also p. 12 of introduction to this book.

9 Eularia Clarke, 'Storm over the Lake' (1963), Methodist Modern Art Collection, http://www.methodist.org.uk/our-faith/reflecting-on-faith/the-methodist-modern-art-collection/index-of-works/storm-over-the-lake-eularia-clarke/. Accessed 19 July 2019.

10 See this quote from his 'Retrospect on an Unimportant Life',
Oxford: Oxford University Press, 1950, used as an epigram by Susan
Howatch in *Glittering Prizes* (London: HarperCollins, 1994), p. 337, one
of her series of novels about the Church of England.

11 Hamlet, Act 2, Scene 2.

12 For discussion of Stoic remedies for the ills of life, see Martha
Nussbaum, *The Therapy of Desire* (Princeton, NJ: Princeton University
Press, 1994), chapters 9, 10, 11 and 12; also Beverley Clack, *Sex and
Death* (Cambridge: Polity Press, 2002), chapter 5.

13 See Alan Lewis, *Between Cross and Resurrection: A Theology of Holy
Saturday* (Grand Rapids, MI: Wm. B. Eerdmans, 2001).

14 I am indebted to Cathryn McKinney for conversations on the idea of
pause and its significance for coming to terms with loss.

15 See Frankl (2004: 12).

16 This point is made in Sara Maitland's *A Book of Silence*
(London: Granta, 2010). For the varieties of silence, see Diarmaid
MacCulloch's *Silence: A Christian History* (London: Penguin, 2013).

17 A trawl of the academic catalogue suggests numerous academic
articles on silence, mainly locating it as something problematic. See
examples from a number of disciplines: Enrique Gracia, 'Unreported
Cases of Domestic Violence Against Women: Towards an Epidemiology
of Social Silence, Tolerance, and Inhibition', *Journal of Epidemiology
Community Health*, vol. 58 (2004): 536–7; David Schwappach and
Katrin Gehring, 'Trade-Offs between Voice and Silence: A Qualitative
Exploration of Oncology Staff's Decisions to Speak Up about Safety
Concerns', BMC Health Services Research, vol. 14 (2014): 303; Louise
Westmarland, 'Police Ethics and Integrity: Breaking the Blue Code of
Silence', *Policing and Society*, vol. 15, no. 2 (2005): 145–65.

18 R. S. Thomas, *Counterpoint* (Newcastle upon Tyne: Bloodaxe Books,
1990), p. 50.

19 For a short but compelling account of some of these hermits, see
Rowan Williams, *Silence and Honey Cakes: The Wisdom of the Desert*
(Oxford: Lion Hudson, 2003).

20 See Maitland (2010: 54).

21 In 2009 a mother and son went into the Valley on a camping expedition.
Relying on GPS, they ended up in a remote part of the park where they
were not found for five days. The mother survived; her son died.

22 'Neighbours', 1936. https://artuk.org/discover/artworks/neighbours-27349. Accessed 19 July 2019.

23 'Christ in the Wilderness' (1939–54): 'Consider the Lilies'. https://www.wikiart.org/en/stanley-spencer/christ-in-the-wilderness-consider-the-lilies. Accessed 19 July 2019.

24 'Christ Carrying the Cross' (1920). https://www.tate.org.uk/art/artworks/spencer-christ-carrying-the-cross-n04117. Accessed 19 July 2019.

25 'The Crucifixion' (1958). https://www.wikiart.org/en/stanley-spencer/the-crucifixion-1958. Accessed 19 July 2019.

26 Thanks to my colleague Nick Swarbrick for reminding me of Augustine's words.

27 For an item on this approach to grief, listen to BBC Radio 4's Woman's Hour, 11 June 2018.

28 Will Self, 'Take to the Streets for a Walking Adventure', *The Guardian*, 1 February 2015.

29 Laurie Lee, *When I Stepped Out One Midsummer Morning* (Harmondsworth: Penguin, 1969).

30 'Only ideas won by walking have any value' (Nietzsche [1888] 1990: 36).

31 See Frankl (2004: 51).

32 See Frankl (2004: 52).

BIBLIOGRAPHY

Abbey, Edward ([1984] 2005), *The Best of Edward Abbey*, San Francisco, CA Sierra Club Books.

Adkins, Lisa (2002), *Revisions: Gender and Sexuality in Late Modernity*, Buckingham: Open University Press.

Alighieri, Dante (1918), *The Divine Comedy*, translated by Courtney Langdon, Cambridge: Harvard University Press.

Allen, Ansgar (2015), 'The Cynical Educator', *Other Education: The Journal of Educational Alternatives*, vol. 4, no. 1, pp. 4–15.

Anderson, Pamela Sue (2006), 'Life, Death and (Inter)Subjectivity: Realism and Recognition in Continental Feminism', *International Journal of Philosophy of Religion*, vol. 60, pp. 41–59.

Anderson, Pamela Sue (2009), ' "A Thoughtful Love of Life": A Spiritual Turn in Philosophy of Religion", *Svensk Teologisk Kvartalskrift*, vol. 85, pp. 119–29.

Anderson, Pamela Sue (2017), 'Silencing and Speaker Vulnerability: Undoing an Oppressive Form of (Wilful) Ignorance', unpublished paper given at 'Vulnerability and the Politics of Care' Conference, British Academy, 9–10 February 2017.

Arendt, Hannah ([1948] 1968),*The Origins of Totalitarianism*, New York: Harcourt.

Arendt, Hannah ([1958] 1998), *The Human Condition*, Chicago, IL: University of Chicago Press.

Arendt, Hannah ([1963] 1977), *Eichmann in Jerusalem: A Report on the Banality of Evil*, Harmondsworth: Penguin.

Ariès, Philippe (1976), *Western Attitudes toward Death from the Middle Ages to the Present*, London: Marion Boyars.

Armstrong, Karen (2004), *The Spiral Staircase: My Climb Out of Darkness*, New York: Anchor.

Axford, Barrie (2013), *Theories of Globalisation*, Cambridge: Polity Press.

Baker, Jeff (July 2010). 'Q&A: Bret Easton Ellis Talks about Writing Novels, Making Movies', *California Chronicle*.

Banyard, Kat (2010), *The Equality Illusion*, London: Faber & Faber.

Barth, Karl (1934), 'No! Answer to Emil Brunner', in *Natural Theology*, edited by Emil Brunner and Karl Barth and translated by Peter Fraenkel, Oregon: Wipf and Stock, 2002.

Bauman, Zygmunt (1992), *Mortality, Immortality, and Other Life Strategies*, Cambridge: Polity Press.

Bauman, Zygmunt (1996), 'From Pilgrim to Tourist: Or a Short History of Identity', in *Questions of Cultural Identity*, edited by Stuart Hall and Paul du Gay, London: Sage, pp. 18–36.

Bauman, Zygmunt (2000), *Liquid Modernity*, Cambridge: Polity Press.

Beauvoir, Simone de ([1949] 1972), *The Second Sex*, London: Penguin.

Beauvoir, Simone de ([1970] 1996), *The Coming of Age*, New York: W. W. Norton.

Beecham, David (1996), *Bureaucracy*, 2nd edition, Buckingham: Open University.

Bellah, Robert (1964), 'Religious Evolution' in *American Sociological Review*, vol. 29, no. 3, pp. 358–74.

Bonhoeffer, Dietrich ([1953] 1971), *Letters and Papers from Prison*, London: SCM.

Bourdieu, P. et al. (1999), *The Weight of the World: Social Suffering in Contemporary Society*, Cambridge: Polity Press.

Britton, Ronald (1989), 'The Missing Link: Parental Sexuality in the Oedipus Complex', in *The Oedipus Complex Today*, edited by John Steiner, London: Karnac, pp. 83–101.

Brown, Peter (1988), *The Body and Society: Men, Women and Sexual Renunciation in Early Christianity*, New York: Columbia.

Brown, Wendy (2015), *Undoing the Demos: Neoliberalism's Stealth Revolution*, New York: Zone Books.

Bulman, May (2016), 'Andrea Leadsom on Theresa May and Motherhood', 9 July, https://www.independent.co.uk/news/uk/politics/andrea-leadsom-interview-theresa-may-mother-tory-leadership-campaign-a7128331.html. Accessed 1 March 2019.

Burns, Anna (2018), *Milkman*, London: Faber & Faber.

Burrows, Roger (2012), 'Living with the H-Index? Metric Assemblages in the Contemporary Academy', *Sociological Review*, vol. 60, no. 2, pp. 355–72.

Butler, Judith (1990), *Gender Trouble*, London: Routledge.

Butler, Judith (1993), *Bodies That Matter*, London: Routledge.

Butler, Judith (2004a), *Undoing Gender*, London: Routledge.

Butler, Judith (2004b), *Precarious Life: The Powers of Mourning and Violence*, London: Verso.

Card, Claudia (2010), *Confronting Evils: Terrorism, Torture, Genocide*, Cambridge, Cambridge University Press.

Carter Heyward, Isabel (1982), *The Redemption of God: A Theology of Mutual Relation*, New York: University Press of America.

Carter Heyward, Isabel (1995), *When Boundaries Betray Us*, San Francisco, CA: HarperSanFrancisco.

Cartwright, David (1988), 'Schopenhauer's Compassion and Nietzsche's Pity', *Schopenhauer Jahrbuch*, vol. 69, pp. 557–67.

Cederström, Carl, and André Spicer (2015), *The Wellness Syndrome*, Cambridge: Polity Press.

Clack, Beverley (1999), *Misogyny in the Western Philosophical Tradition: A Reader*, Basingstoke: Macmillan Press.

Clack, Beverley (2002), *Sex and Death: A Reappraisal of Human Mortality*, Cambridge: Polity Press.

Clack, Beverley (2012), 'Being Human: Religion and Superstition in a Psychoanalytic Philosophy of Religion', *Royal Institute of Philosophy Supplement*, edited by Constantine Sandis and M. J. Cain, Volume 70, Cambridge: Cambridge University Press, pp. 255–79.

Clack, Beverley (2013), *Freud on the Couch: A Critical Introduction to the Father of Psychoanalysis*, London: One World Publishers.

Clack, Beverley, and Brian R. Clack ([1998] 2008), *The Philosophy of Religion: A Critical Introduction*, 2nd edition, Cambridge: Polity Press.

Clack, Beverley, and Michele Paule, eds (2019), *Interrogating the Neoliberal Lifecycle: The Limits of Success*, Cham, Switzerland: Palgrave Macmillan.

Clack, Brian R. (2014), *Love, Drugs, Art, Religion: The Pains and Consolations of Existence*, Farnham: Ashgate.

Clack Brian R., and Tyler Hower, eds (2018), *Philosophy and the Human Condition*, Oxford: OUP.

Collini, Stefan (2012), *What Are Universities For?*, London: Penguin.

Collins, M. L., and C. Pierce (1980), 'Holes and Slime: Sexism in Sartre's Psychoanalysis', in *Women and Philosophy*, edited by C. C. Gould and M. W. Wartofsky, New York: Pedigree, pp. 112–27.

Collins, Patricia Hill (1991), *Black Feminist Thought*, London: Routledge.

Cooper, David (1990), *Existentialism: A Reconstruction*, Oxford: Blackwell.

Crawford, Matthew (2010) *Shop Class as Soulcraft: An Inquiry into the Value of Work*, Harmondsworth: Penguin.

Crozier, Susan (2019), 'Towards a Manifesto: On the Love of Failure', in Beverley Clack and Michele Paule, *Interrogating the Neoliberal Lifecycle: The Limits of Success* (Cham, Switzerland: Palgrave Macmillan, 2019), pp. 169–88.

Davies, William (2014), *The Limits of Neoliberalism: Authority, Sovereignty and the Logic of Competition*, London: Sage.

Davies, William (2015), 'The Chronic Social: Relations of Control Within and without Neoliberalism', *New Formations*, vol. 18, no. 84/85, pp. 40–57.

Day, Keri (2016), *Religious Resistance to Neoliberalism: Womanist and Black Feminist Perspectives*, London: Palgrave Macmillan.

Dekkers, Midas (2000), *The Way of All Flesh*, London: Harvill Press.

Deleuze, Gilles (1992), 'Postscript on the Societies of Control', October, vol. 59, pp. 3–7.

Didion, Joan (2006), *The Year of Magical Thinking*, London: Harper Perennial.

Didion, Joan (2011), *Blue Nights*, London: Fourth Estate.

Dor, Joel (2004), *Introduction to the Reading of Lacan*, New York: Other Press.

Ecclestone, Kathryn, and Dennis Hayes (2008), *The Dangerous Rise of Therapeutic Education*, London: Routledge.

Eco, Umberto (2007), *On Ugliness*, London: Harvill Secker.

Eliade, Mircea (1959), *The Sacred and the Profane: The Nature of Religion*, New York: Harcourt Brace.

Ellis, Bret Easton (1991), *American Psycho*, London: Picador.

Euripides (1963), *Medea and Other Plays*, translated by Philip Vellacott, Harmondsworth: Penguin.

Evans, Gillian (2006), *Educational Failure and Working Class White Children in Britain*, London: Palgrave.

Faludi, Susan (1999), *Stiffed: The Betrayal of the Modern Man*, London: Chatto & Windus.

Farris, Paul, Neil Bendle, Philip Pfeifer and Daniel Reibstein (2009), *Key Marketing Metrics*, Edinburgh: Pearson Education.

Foucault, Michel (2008), *The Birth of Biopolitics*, London: Palgrave Macmillan.

Frank, Arthur ([1991] 2002), *At the Will of the Body: Reflections on Illness*, Boston, MA: Houghton Mifflin Harcourt

Frank, Arthur (1995), *The Wounded Storyteller*, Chicago, IL: University of Chicago Press.

Frank, Arthur (2004), *The Renewal of Generosity: Illness, Medicine and How to Live*, Chicago, IL: University of Chicago Press.

Frankl, Viktor (2004), *Man's Search for Meaning*, London: Rider.

Freud, Anna ([1937] 1993), *The Ego and the Mechanisms of Defence*, London: Karnac.

Freud, Anna (1967), 'About Losing and Being Lost', *The Psychoanalytic Study of the Child*, vol. 22, pp. 9–19.

Freud, Sigmund (1901 [1907]), *The Psychopathology of Everyday Life*, Standard Edition of the Complete Works of Sigmund Freud (hereafter SE), Volume 6, translated and edited by J. Strachey, London: Hogarth Press/ Virago.

Freud, Sigmund (1907), 'Obsessional Practices and Religious Rituals', SE 9, pp. 115–27.

Freud, Sigmund (1916–17), *Introductory Lectures on Psychoanalysis*, SE 15 and 16.

Freud, Sigmund (1919), 'The Uncanny', SE17, pp. 217–56.

Freud, Sigmund (1920a), 'Beyond the Pleasure Principle', SE18, pp. 1–64.

Freud, Sigmund (1920b), 'The Psychogenesis of a Case of Homosexuality in a Woman', SE18, pp. 145–72.

Freud, Sigmund (1923), 'The Ego and the Id', SE 19, pp. 3–66.

Freud, Sigmund (1925), 'Some Psychical Consequences of the Anatomical Distinction between the Sexes', SE 19, pp. 243–58.

Freud, Sigmund (1927), *The Future of an Illusion*, SE 21, pp. 1–56.

Freud, Sigmund (1930) *Civilisation and Its Discontents*, SE 21, pp. 57-145.

Freud, Sigmund (1931), 'Female Sexuality', SE 21, pp. 223–43.

Freud, Sigmund (1937), 'Analysis Terminable and Interminable', SE 23, pp. 209–53.

Gane, Nicholas (2012), 'The Governmentalities of Neoliberalism: Panopticism, Post-Panopticism and Beyond', *Sociological Review*, vol. 60, pp. 611–34.

Gawande, Atul (2014), *Being Mortal: Illness, Medicine, and What Matters in the End*, London: Profile Books.

Giddens, Anthony (1991), *Modernity and Self-Identity: Self and Society in the Late Modern Age*, Cambridge: Polity Press.

Gillard, Julia (2014), *My Story*, London: Bantam Press.

Gilligan, Carol (1982), *In a Different Voice*, Cambridge, MA: Harvard University Press.

Goodchild, Philip (2002), *Capitalism and Religion: The Price of Piety*, London: Routledge.

Gould, Philip (2012), *When I Die: Lessons from the Death Zone*, London: Little, Brown.

Gracia, Enrique (2004), 'Unreported Cases of Domestic Violence against Women: Towards an Epidemiology of Social Silence, Tolerance, and Inhibition', *Journal of Epidemiology and Community Health*, vol. 58, pp. 536–7.

Gray, John (2011), *The Immortalisation Commission: Science and the Strange Quest to Cheat Death*, New York: Farrar, Straus and Giroux.

Green, Andre (2001), 'The Dead Mother', in *Life Narcissism, Death Narcissism*, London: Free Association Books, pp. 170–200.

Green, Andre (2011), *Illusions and Disillusions of Psychoanalytic Work*, London: Karnac.

Greer, Germaine (1991), *The Change: Women, Aging and the Menopause*, New York: Ballentine Books.

Greer, Germaine (1999), *The Whole Woman*, London: Doubleday.

Gross, Kate (2015), *Late Fragments: Everything I Want to Tell You (About This Magnificent Life)*, London: William Collins.

Grosz, Stephen (2013), *The Examined Life: How We Lose and Find Ourselves*, London: Chatto & Windus.

Hacking, Ian (1990), *The Taming of Chance*, Cambridge, MA: Cambridge University Press.

Hall, Donald (1998), *Without*, Boston: Houghton Mifflin.

Hamilton, Kenneth (1965), 'Homo Religiosus and Historical Faith', *Journal of American Academy of Religion*, vol. 33, no. 3, pp. 213–22.

Hardy, Thomas ([1891] 1981), *Tess of the D'Urbervilles*, London: Pan.

Harvey, David (2005), *A Brief History of Neoliberalism*, Oxford: OUP.

Hatab, Lawrence (2005), *Nietzsche's Life Sentence*, London: Routledge.

Hayek, Friedrich (1944), *The Road to Serfdom*, London: Routledge.

Heidegger, Martin ([1947]1983), 'Letter on Humanism', in *Basic Writings*, London: Routledge, pp. 213-265.

Heidegger, Martin (1962), *Being and Time*, Oxford: Blackwell.

Hekman, Susan (2014), *The Feminine Subject*, Cambridge: Polity Press.

Hick, John ([1966] 2010), *Evil and the God of Love*, London: Palgrave Macmillan.

Hick, John (1985), *Death and Eternal Life*, London: Macmillan.

Hick, John (1989), *An Interpretation of Religion*, London: Macmillan.

Hinton, Perry (2000), *Stereotypes, Cognition and Culture*, London: Routledge.

Howatch, Susan (1994), *Glittering Prizes*, London: HarperCollins.

Irigaray, Luce (1985), *Speculum of the Other Woman*, translated by Gillian Gill, Ithaca, NY: Cornell University Press.

Isherwood Lisa (2007), *The Fat Jesus: Christianity and Body Image*, New York: Seabury Books.

Jantzen, Grace (1998), *Becoming Divine: Towards a Feminist Philosophy of Religion*, Manchester: Manchester University Press.

Jones, Richard G. and Ivor H. Jones, eds (1983), *Hymns and Psalms*, London: Methodist Publishing House.

Kant, Immanuel ([1764] 1960), *Observations on the Feeling of the Beautiful and Sublime*, Los Angeles: University of California Press.

Kaufman, Sharon (2005), *...And a Time to Die: How American Hospitals Shape the End of Life*, Chicago, IL: University of Chicago Press.

Kennedy, Maev (2017), 'Grayson Perry to unveil Brexit vases in Channel 4 show Divided Britain', *The Guardian*, Tuesday 30 May, https://www.theguardian.com/artanddesign/2017/may/30/grayson-perry-to-unveil-brexit-vases-channel-4-show-divided-britain. Accessed 18 July 2019.

Kenyon, Jane (1996), *Otherwise*, Saint Paul, MN: Graywolf Press.

Kingsolver, Barbara (2001), 'Making Peace', in *Traveller's Tales, American South West*, edited by Sean O'Reilly and James O'Reilly, San Francisco, CA: Travellers Tale Guides, pp. 12–21.

Klein, Melanie (1945), 'The Oedipus Complex in the Light of Early Anxieties', in *The Writings of Melanie Klein*, Volume 1, London: Vintage, 1988, pp. 370–419.

Klein, Melanie ([1946] 1997), 'Notes on Some Schizoid Mechanisms', in *Envy and Gratitude and Other Works 1946–1963*, London: Vintage, pp. 1–24.

Kohon, Gregorio, ed. (1999), *The Dead Mother*, London: Karnac.

Kostova, Elizabeth (2006), *The Historian*, London: Time Warner.

Kristeva, Julia ([1977] 2002), 'Stabat Mater', in *French Feminists on Religion: A Reader*, edited by Morny Joy, Kathleen O'Grady and Judith Poxon, London: Routledge, pp. 113–38.

Kristeva, Julia (1982), *Powers of Horror: An Essay on Abjection*, New York: Columbia University Press.

Kristeva, Julia (1989), *Black Sun: Depression and Melancholia*, New York: Columbia University Press.

Kristeva, Julia (2001), *Melanie Klein*, New York: Columbia University Press.

Laing, Olivia (2016), *The Lonely City: Adventures in the Art of Being Alone*, New York: Picador.

Lane, Belden (1998), *The Solace of Fierce Landscapes: Exploring Desert and Mountain Spirituality*, Oxford: OUP.

Lane, Belden (2015), *Backpacking with the Saints: Wilderness Hiking as Spiritual Practice*, Oxford: OUP.

Lee, Laurie (1969), *As I Walked Out One Midsummer Morning*, London: Andre Deutsch.

Le Doeuff, Michèle ([1980] 1989), *The Philosophical Imaginary*, London: Athlone Press.

Le Doeuff, Michèle ([1989] 2007), *Hipparchia's Choice: An Essay Concerning Women, Philosophy, Etc.*, New York: Columbia University Press.

Lemke, Thomas (2001), '"The Birth of Bio-Politics": Michel Foucault's lecture
    at the Collège de France on neo-liberal governmentality', *Economy and
    Society*, vol. 30, no. 2, pp. 190–207.
Levinas, Emmanuel (1996), *Basic Philosophical Writings*, edited by Adriaan
    Peperzak, Simon Critchley and Robert Bernasconi, Bloomington: Indiana
    University Press.
Lewis, Alan (2001), *Between Cross and Resurrection: A Theology of Holy
    Saturday*, Grand Rapids, MI: Wm. B. Eerdmans.
Lloyd, Genevieve (1984), *The Man of Reason: 'Male' and 'Female' in Western
    Philosophy*, London: Methuen.
Lock, G., and H. Martins (2011), 'Quantified Control and the Mass
    Production of 'Psychotic Citizens', *EspacesTemps.net*. http://
    espacestemps.net/document8555.html.
Lorde, Audre ([1980] 1997), *Cancer Journals*, San Francisco, CA: Aunt
    Lute Books.
MacCulloch, Diarmaid (2013), *Silence: A Christian History*, London: Penguin.
Maitland, Sara (2010), *A Book of Silence*, London: Granta, Kindle Edition.
Mannion, Gerard (2003), *Schopenhauer, Religion and Morality*,
    Farnham: Ashgate.
Marx, Karl ([1844] 1981), *Economic and Philosophic Manuscripts of 1844*,
    Moscow: Lawrence and Wishart.
McGoey, Linsey (2015), *No Such Thing as a Free Gift: The Gates Foundation
    and the Price of Philanthropy*, London: Verso.
McLuhan, Marshall (2005), *The Relation of Environment to Anti-Environment*,
    Berkeley, CA: Gingko Press.
Merton, Thomas (1968) *Conjectures of a Guilty Bystander*, New York:
    Image Books.
Miller, David L. (1966), '"Homo Religiosus" and the Death of God', *Journal of
    Bible and Religion*, vol. 34, no. 4, pp. 305–15.
Minnich, Elizabeth (2017), *The Evil of Banality*, Lanham, MD: Rowman and
    Littlefield.
Mirowski, Philip (2014), *Never Let a Serious Crisis Go To Waste: How
    Neoliberalism Survived the Financial Meltdown*, London: Verso.
Morris, Heather (2018), *The Tattooist of Auschwitz*, London: Zaffre.
Nelson, James (1994), 'Embracing Masculinity', in *Sexuality and the Sacred*,
    edited by James Nelson and Sandra P Longfellow, London: Westminster
    Press, pp. 195–215.
Neuberger, Julia, and John A White, eds (1991), *A Necessary End: Attitudes
    to Death*, London: Papermac.

Nietzsche, Friedrich [1882] 2001), *The Gay Science*, Cambridge: Cambridge University Press.

Nietzsche, Friedrich ([1888] 1990), *Twilight of the Idols/Anti-Christ*, Harmondsworth: Penguin.

Nietzsche, Friedrich ([1888] 2004), *Ecce Homo*, London: Penguin.

Nietzsche, Friedrich ([1878–80] 1996), *Human, All Too Human*, Cambridge: CUP.

Nixon, Jon (2015), *Hannah Arendt and the Politics of Friendship*, London: Bloomsbury.

Nussbaum, Martha (1986), *The Fragility of Goodness*, Cambridge: Cambridge University Press.

Nussbaum, Martha (1994), *The Therapy of Desire*, Princeton, NJ: Princeton University Press.

Nussbaum, Martha (2004), *Hiding from Humanity: Disgust, Shame and the Law*, Princeton, NJ: Princeton University Press.

Oakley, Mark (2001), *The Collage of God*, London: DLT.

O'Connell, Mark (2017), *To Be a Machine: Adventures Among Cyborgs, Utopians, Hackers, and the Futurists Solving the Modest Problem of Death*, London: Granta.

Pagels, Elaine (1988), *Adam, Eve and the Serpent*, Harmondsworth: Penguin.

Palahniuk, Chuck (2003), *Lullaby*, London: Vintage.

Palmer, Michael (1997), *Freud and Jung on Religion*, London: Routledge.

Partington, Marian (2012), *If You Sit Very Still*, Bristol: Vala Publishing Co-operative.

Peck, Jamie (2010), *Constructions of Neoliberal Reason*, Oxford: OUP.

Plato (1941), *The Republic*, translated by Francis MacDonald Cornford, Oxford: OUP.

Plato (1994), *Symposium*, translated by Robin Waterfield, Oxford: OUP.

Plumwood, Val (1993), *Feminism and the Mastery of Nature*, London: Routledge.

Potter, Dennis (1994), *Seeing The Blossom*, London: Faber & Faber.

Radnor, Abigail (2012), 'Are We the Lost Generation?', *Times Magazine*, 11 August, pp. 34–39.

Rohr, Richard (2011), *Falling Upwards*, San Francisco, CA: Jossey-Bass.

Rose, Nikolas (1999), *Governing the Soul: The Shaping of the Private Self*, London: Free Association.

Rose, Nikolas (2000), 'Government and Control', *British Journal of Criminology*, vol. 40, pp. 321–39.

Rosenbaum, Stephen (1993), 'How to Be Dead and Not Care: A Defence of
    Epicurus', in *The Metaphysics of Death*, edited by John Martin Fischer,
    Stanford: Stanford University Press.
Ryan, Frances (2015), 'Death Has Become a Part of Britain's Benefit
    System', *The Guardian*, 27 April.
Sarton, May ([1978] 1981), *A Reckoning*, New York: W. W. Norton.
Sartre, Jean-Paul ([1943] 1969), *Being and Nothingness*, translated by H. E.
    Barnes, London: Methuen.
Sartre, Jean-Paul (1971), *Sketch for a Theory of the Emotions*,
    London: Routledge,
Schopenhauer, Arthur ([1839] 1995), *The Basis of Morality*,
    Indianapolis: Hackett.
Schopenhauer, Arthur ([1851] 1970), *Essays and Aphorisms*,
    Harmondsworth: Penguin.
Schopenhauer, Arthur ([1862] 1974), *Parerga and Paralipomena*, Volume 2,
    Oxford: OUP.
Schupmann, Benjamin (2014), 'Thoughtlessness and
    Resentment: Determinism and Moral Responsibility in the Case of Adolf
    Eichmann', *Philosophy and Social Criticism*, vol. 40, no. 2, pp. 127–44.
Schwappach, David, and Katrin Gehring (2014), 'Trade-Offs between Voice
    and Silence: A Qualitative Exploration of Oncology Staff's Decisions to
    Speak Up about Safety Concerns', BMC Health Services Research, vol.
    14, p. 303.
Scott, James (1998), *Seeing Like a State*, New Haven, CT: Yale
    University Press.
Self, Will (2015), 'Take to the Streets for a Walking Adventure', *The Guardian*,
    1 February.
Seneca (1969), *Letters from a Stoic*, translated by Robin Campbell,
    Harmondsworth: Penguin.
Sennett, Richard (2006), *The Culture of the New Capitalism*, New Haven,
    CT: Yale University Press.
Shakespeare, Lyndon (2016), *Being the Body of Christ in the Age of
    Management*, Eugene, OR: Cascade Books.
Solomon, Robert (2003), *Living with Nietzsche*, Oxford: Oxford
    University Press.
Spohrer Konstanze (2011), 'Deconstructing "Aspiration": UK Policy Debates
    and European Policy Trends', *European Educational Research Journal*,
    vol. 10, no. 1, pp. 53–63.
Srnicek, Nick, and Alex Williams (2016), *Inventing the Future: Postcapitalism
    and a World without Work*, London: Verso.

Standing, Guy (2011), *The Precariat: The New Dangerous Class*, London: Bloomsbury.

Stangneth, Bettina (2014), *Eichmann before Jerusalem: The Unexamined Life of a Mass Murderer*, New York: Vintage.

Stoddard, Karen (1983), *Saints and Shrews: Women and Ageing in American Popular Film*, Westport, CT: Greenwood Press.

Stone, Alison (2017), 'Beauvoir and the Ambiguities of Motherhood', in *A Companion to Simone de Beauvoir*, edited by Laura Hengehold and Nancy Bauer, Oxford: Wiley Blackwell.

Taylor, Charles (1995), *Philosophical Arguments*, Cambridge MA: Harvard University Press.

Thaler, Richard, and Cass Sunstein (2008), *Nudge: Improving Decisions about Health, Wealth and Happiness*, New Haven, CT: Yale University Press.

Thomas, Keith, ed. (1999), *Oxford Book of Work*, Oxford: OUP.

Thomas, R. S. (1990), *Counterpoint*, Newcastle upon Tyne: Bloodaxe Books.

Tillich, Hannah (1973), *From Time to Time*, New York: Stein and Day.

Tillich, Paul ([1949] 1962), *The Shaking of the Foundations*, Harmondsworth: Penguin.

Tillich, Paul (1951), *Systematic Theology*, Volume 1, Chicago, IL: University of Chicago Press.

Tillich, Paul ([1952] 1977), *The Courage to Be*, Glasgow: Fount.

Tillich, Paul ([1957] 2009), *Dynamics of Faith*, New York: HarperCollins.

Tillich, Paul (1965), *Theology of Culture*, Oxford: OUP.

Tóibín, Colm (2013), *The Testament of Mary*, London: Penguin.

Tolstoy, Ivan ([1880] 1981), *The Death of Ivan Ilyich*, New York: Bantam Books.

Tyler, Peter (2016), *The Pursuit of the Soul: Psychoanalysis, Soul-Making and the Christian Tradition*, New York: Bloomsbury.

Tylor, E. B. (1891), *Primitive Culture*, London: John Murray.

Verbitsky, Horacio (2005), *Confessions of an Argentine Dirty Warrior*, New York: New Press.

Villa, Dana (1996), 'The Banality of Philosophy: Arendt on Heidegger and Eichmann', in *Hannah Arendt: Twenty Years Later*, edited by L. May and J. Kohn, Cambridge: MA: MIT Press, pp. 179–96.

Walker, Barbara (1985), *The Crone: Woman of Age, Wisdom, and Power*, San Francisco, CA: HarperCollins.

Walker, Robert (2014), *The Shame of Poverty*, Oxford: OUP.

Walton, Heather (2014), 'Seeking Wisdom in Practical Theology', *Practical Theology*, vol. 7, no. 1 pp. 5–18.

Weber, Max ([1947] 1964), *The Theory of Social and Economic Organisation*, New York: Simon & Schuster.

Westlake, Martin (2001), *Kinnock: The Biography*, London: Little, Brown.

Westmarland, Louise (2005), 'Police Ethics and Integrity: Breaking the Blue Code of Silence', *Policing and Society*, vol. 15, no. 2, pp. 145–65.

Wieland, Karin (2015), *Dietrich and Riefenstahl: Hollywood, Berlin, and a Century in Two Lives*, New York: W. W. Norton.

Williams, Rowan (2003), *Silence and Honey Cakes: The Wisdom of the Desert*, Oxford: Lion Hudson.

Williams, Tennessee ([1947] 1962), *A Streetcar Named Desire and Other Plays*, London: Penguin.

Winnicott, Donald ([1971] 2005), *Playing and Reality*, London: Routledge.

Wolf, Naomi (1990), *The Beauty Myth*, London: Vintage.

Young-Bruehl, Elisabeth (1996), 'Hannah Arendt among Feminists', in *Hannah Arendt: Twenty Years Later*, edited by L. May and J. Kohn, Cambridge: MA: MIT Press, pp. 307–24.

Zita, Jacqueline (1993), 'Heresy in the Female Body: The Rhetorics of Menopause', in *The Other Within*, edited by Marilyn Pearsall, Boulder, CO: Westview Press, 1997, pp. 95–112.

Zola, Emile ([1880] 1982), *Nana*, Harmondsworth: Penguin.

INDEX